The Complete Idiot's Re

monism   View shared by many pre-Socratic philosophers (ca. 600 B.C.) that all reality is made up of one substance.

epicureanism   Hellenistic school of philosophy that emphasizes happiness.

teleology   Study of the purpose of things and the belief that all things have special purposes.

stoicism   Hellenistic belief that nothing really matters, including pleasure and pain.

skepticism   Hellenistic view that we can't be sure of anything.

mysticism   Belief that human beings can be directly conscious of God.

neoplatonism   Ancient and medieval view that reality emanates from an ideal world of perfect forms.

scholasticism   Medieval universal philosophy combining Aristotle's logic with the belief in God.

Confucianism   Chinese philosophy emphasizing respect for others.

Taoism   Chinese mystic philosophy based on a harmony between humanity and nature.

Hinduism   Cluster of Indian philosophical traditions emphasizing detachment from pain and desire.

Buddhism   Offshoot of Hinduism that says to renounce the self.

monotheism   Belief in just one god.

humanism   Renaissance movement that saw human activity as a reflection of divinity.

empiricism   Scientific view that knowledge comes from observation.

rationalism   Scientific view that knowledge is possible without having to experience things.

vitalism   Belief that all material things are alive and capable of sense and thought.

dualism   View that the world and the mind are made up of two aspects: matter and spirit.

continues

tear here

alpha
books

Thirty Philosophies Worth Knowing
(continued)

deism   Belief that God exists but has not interfered with the world since creating it.

idealism   View that a transcendent mind is at work behind reality in general and human history in particular.

dialectics   Method of reasoning that moves back and forth between opposites.

Marxism   Economic philosophy emphasizing the plight of the modern worker.

structuralism   Linguistics-based philosophy that sees meaningful ideas as relative to one another.

phenomenology   Both a philosophy and a psychology based on the idea that we bring our own attitudes with us whenever we perceive things.

existentialism   View that each individual must come up with his or her own meaning for life.

logical positivism   View that logic applied to meaning can yield certainty.

analytic philosophy   Philosophy based on the application of mathematical logic to language.

deconstruction   View that meaning is unstable, exceeding intention and lacking self-coherence.

feminism   Philosophy and political orientation committed to describing and undoing the oppression of women.

new age   Belief that a new era of global human consciousness is at hand in which people will make unprecedented use of their mental powers.

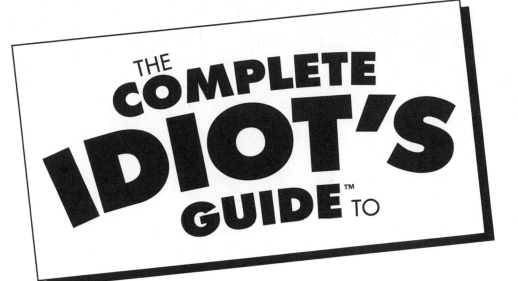

Philosophy

by Jay Stevenson

alpha
books

A Division of Macmillan Reference USA
A Simon and Schuster Macmillan Company
1633 Broadway New York, NY 10019-6785

Macmillan Publishing books may be purchased for business or sales promotional use. For information please write: Special Markets Department, Macmillan Publishing USA, 1633 Broadway, New York, NY 10019-6785.

International Standard Book Number: 0-02-861981-1
Library of Congress Catalog Card Number: 97-073180

02 01 00   12 11 10 9 8

Interpretation of the printing code: The rightmost number of the first series of numbers is the year of the book's printing; the rightmost number of the second series of numbers is the number of the book's printing. For example, a printing code of 98-1 shows that the first printing occurred in 1998.

Printed in the United States of America

This publication contains the opinions and ideas of its author. It is intended to provide helpful and informative material on the subject matter covered. It is sold with the understanding that the author and publisher are not engaged in rendering professional services in the book. If the reader requires personal assistance or advice, a competent professional should be consulted.

Contents at a Glance

Part 1: The Nuts and Bolts of Philosophy   **1**

1 The Big Picture   3
An overview of philosophy that shows what it's for and what it's about.

2 Being There   9
How ontology and metaphysics relate to the idea of God.

3 What There Is to Know About Knowing   15
Epistemology, including empiricism, rationalism, and idealism.

4 How to Act   25
Ethics and the significance of individualism vs. collectivism.

Part 2: Ancient and Medieval Philosophy   **33**

5 Golden Oldies   35
The pre-Socratics, the sophists, and Socrates get the ball rolling.

6 The Philosopher King   45
Plato's ideas about truth and knowledge set the tone for years to come.

7 A Sense of Purpose   55
Aristotle's logic and teleology provide an influential method of thought.

8 Ancient Hardheads   65
Hellenistic philosophy: stoicism, skepticism, epicureanism.

9 God and Knowledge   75
Neo-Platonism and scholasticism during the Middle Ages.

Part 3: Eastern Philosophy   **87**

10 Far Eastern Philosophy   89
Confucius and taoism in ancient China.

11 Indian Philosophy   97
From Hinduism and Buddhism to Gandhi.

12 Middle Eastern Religious Philosophy   105
Monotheism, including Judaism, Christianity, and Islam.

Part 4: Making Progress   **113**

13 People People   115
Renaissance humanists rethink the classics.

14 Science Rises from the Mud 125
Bacon, Hobbes, Descartes, and Newton separate matter from metaphysics.

15 Men and Women of Substance 135
Spinoza, Leibniz, and Cavendish say why matter can think.

16 Learning by Observing 145
British empiricism leads to new ideas about human nature.

17 Light on the Subject 155
The French Enlightenment brings about big changes in the name of reason.

18 Wheeling and Idealing 161
German idealism reconciles the mind and reality.

19 Ideas of Freedom 171
Mill, Marx, Kierkegaard, and Nietzsche talk about freedom and determinism.

Part 5: Modern Philosophy **181**

20 New Fields of Thought: Psych, Sosh, and Anthro 183
Freud, Jung, Weber, and Durkheim found the new social sciences.

21 The New Logic 191
The analytic philosophy of Frege, Russell, and Wittgenstein blends logic, language, and math.

22 To Be or Not To Be 199
Phenomenology and existentialism rethink human consciousness.

23 Structuring New Ideas 207
Structuralism looks at the systems behind language, culture, and the unconscious.

Part 6: Knowledge Now **217**

24 Pomo Sapience 219
Post-modernism finds too much and not enough meaning.

25 Women Get Wise 227
Feminism puts women in the picture.

26 The Shift Is On 235
New age looks ahead to higher global consciousness.

Appendix A   Words for the Wise 243

Appendix B   Further Reading: More Food for Thought 253

Index 255

Contents

Part 1: The Nuts and Bolts of Philosophy   **1**

1 The Big Picture   **3**

Why Ask Why? 4

You Are What You Think 4

A Slice of Life 5

Is You Ism or Is You Ain't My Philosophy? 5

How the Parts Fit Together 6

The Least You Need to Know 7

2 Being There   **9**

The Myth-Math of Existence.............................. 9

To Order Is to Understand............................... 10

Enter Metaphysics 11

Is There a God? 11

Perfection Is Truth 12

Being Leads to Knowing 13

Being and Thinking 13

Dualism vs. Materialism 13

Ways to Be 14

The Least You Need to Know 14

3 What There Is to Know About Knowing   **15**

A Time of Crisis 16

Descartes' Reason 16

Look Ma, No Senses! 16

Getting Testy 17

Can We Get There from Here? 17

Going Down: Deduction 18

Going Up: Induction 19

Double-Checking Your Hypothesis 19

The Ping-Pong Ball Called Dialectic 20

Pro or Con? 20

Both Sides Now 21

Can He or Kant He? Combining Reason and
Experience 22

Can History Think? 22

Marx on the Mind 23

The Least You Need to Know 23

4 How to Act   25

Me vs. Us 26
   Good Harmony 26
   The "We" Culture 26
Me First 27
Why I'm So Important 28
Religion's Part in Individualism 28
   Truth and Me 29
   Science and Me 30
   Capitalism and Me 30
   Philosopher See, Philosopher Do 30
The Least You Need to Know 31

Part 2: Ancient and Medieval Philosophy   33

5 Golden Oldies   35

It's Not About Us 36
   Earth, Wind, and Fire 36
   The Math and Music Man 37
   Who's a Monkey's Uncle? 38
   Out of His Senses 38
Virtue's in the Eye of the Beholder 38
   It's All Relative 39
   Double Standard 39
   What's Fair is Fair—or Is It? 40
   Politics as Usual 41
"Knowledge Is Virtue" 42
   Socrates, a Pain in the Protagoras 43
   Rebuilding Knowledge 43
The Least You Need to Know 44

6 The Philosopher King   45

Politics' Loss Was Philosophy's Gain 46
   Philosophy Through Dialogue 47
What's the Big Idea? 47
   Finding the Ideal 48
Understanding the Ideal World 48
   It's Logical 48
   I Think, Therefore It Is... 49

The Light at the End of the Tunnel 49
Remembering Truth 51
Immortal Souls 51
The True Sciences 51
Living Up to Perfection 52
The Republic—Plato's Paradise 52
Rulers, Soldiers, and Tradespeople 52
Better Than Democracy or Tyranny 53
The Least You Need to Know 53

7 A Sense of Purpose   55

Bad Form 56
Change Has Purpose 57
Changing Beliefs About Change 57
Aristotle vs. Darwin 58
Born to Think 58
Natural Soul 59
For a Good Cause 60
Why It Happened 60
Aristotle's Mental Breakdown 61
Aristotle's Categories 61
The Golden Mean 62
A Legacy Up for Grabs 63
The Least You Need to Know 64

8 Ancient Hardheads   65

Who Cares? 66
It's All in the Mind 66
People Are Scum 67
A Twist on Fate 67
Don't Worry, Be Happy 68
Why Suffer? 68
The Gods Make Us Crazy 69
It's All in the Atoms 69
Born Free 70
Not Their Scene 70
Alma Maters 71
Who Knows? 72
Are You Hallucinating? 72
Curb Your Dogma 72
The Seeds of Doubt 73
The Least You Need to Know 74

9 God and Knowledge   **75**

    Faith Meets Reason 76
        God Thinks of Everything 76
        Words Get in the Way 77
        The Hebrew Bible Goes Greek 77
    Getting a Read on Things 77
        If It's Written Down, It Must Be Important 78
        Time Warp 78
    It All Adds Up to One 79
        A Private Line to God 79
        You Can't Blame God 80
        The Reason for Evil 81
        Getting with It, or Get in the Way 81
    Philosophy Goes to School 82
        Aristotle Goes Islamic 82
        Proving God Exists 83
    Logic Chopping 83
        A Real Controversy 84
        Sidling Up to the Big Questions 85
        Shaving Explanations 85
        The Least You Need to Know 85

Part 3: Eastern Philosophy   **87**

10 Far Eastern Philosophy   **89**

    A Gentleman and a Scholar 90
        We're All in This Together 90
        Leading by Example 91
    Governing Wise-Li 91
        Just a Little Respect 92
        Working with Tradition 92
    A Good Mind-Set 92
        Respecting What You Do 92
        Confucius vs. Confusion 93
    Philosophy for the Well En-Tao'd 94
        Going with the Flow 94
        Worry Less, Live Longer 95
        The More Things Change, the More They Stay
            the Same 95
        Philosophy or Fortune Telling? 96
    The Least You Need to Know 96

11 Indian Philosophy   **97**

Above the Suffering 98
    Karma Chameleons 98
    Hindu Castes 99
Practice Makes Perfect 99
    Hindu Duty 99
    Is Karma a Good Idea? 100
The Awakened One 100
    Freeing the Self from Itself 101
    The Eightfold Path 102
    Budding Buddhism 102
Fighting with Peace 103
    You've Got to Admire His Moksa 103
The Least You Need to Know 103

12 Middle Eastern Religious Philosophy   **105**

One God 105
    Who's Got the Power? 106
    Somebody Up There Likes Me 106
    By the Book 106
    Sharing the Wrath 107
    Evil Ways 107
    Explaining Evil Under a Just God................................... 108
    The End Is Near 109
History Is Us 109
    You Always Hurt the Ones You Love 109
Brand X: Newer, Bigger, Brighter 110
    Come Again? 110
    Feeling Their Pain 111
The Latest Word 111
    The Five Pillars of Islam 111
    One God, Many Points of View 112
    The Least You Need to Know 112

Part 4: Making Progress   **113**

13 Renaissance Humanism   **115**

Philosophy Reborn 116
"Learned Ignorance" 116
    Will the Circle Be Unbroken?.. 117

We Are the World 118
    Change Across the Board 118
    Believing in Belief 119
Skepticism 120
    Gimme That Old-Time Religion 120
    Everybody Plays the Fool 120
Politics Is Torture 121
    Prince Not Charming 121
    Doubting Fairplay 121
Try, Try Again 122
The Least You Need to Know 123

14 Science Rises from the Mud   **125**

Bringing Home the Bacon 126
    A Man with a Plan 126
    Idolizing Error 126
    Don't Believe Everything You Read 127
Science and Spirit 128
    It's All in the Mind 128
    A Divided Mind 128
    A Passionate Affair 129
    Keeping Government in Mind 129
A Whale of a World View 130
    Not in the Spirit 130
    Thinking Machines 131
    Weak Minds, Strong Ruler 131
    Gentlemen Don't Fight 132
Eye of Newton 132
    Formulas for Everything 132
    Shedding New Light on Color 133
The Least You Need to Know 133

15 Men and Women of Substance   **135**

Being in the Know 135
God and Nature Are Us 136
    Spinoza à la Mode 137
    Where There's a Will, There's a Way 137
    The Truth Will Set You Free 138
A Man of Many Monads 138
    Many Views, One Picture 139
    What Happens to You Is Part of You 139

The World Is a Math Problem 139
A Man of Principles 140
It's Only Logical 140
Taking a Chance on Substance................................ 141
Pushing the Limits 141
The Matter with Cavendish 142
It's All Mental 142
Knowledge in Conflict... 143
Imagining Philosophy 143
The Least You Need to Know 144

16 Learning by Observing   **145**

The Sun Never Sets on British Empiricism...................... 146
Observant Brits 146
A Locke on Understanding 146
Your Mind Was a Blank 147
Is Knowledge Accidental? 147
Taking God out of Government 148
Divine Right Bites the Dust 148
Back to Nature 149
My Work, My Stuff 149
Society's Dotted Line 150
A Better Idea 150
If a Tree Falls in the Forest… 151
Soul Exceptions 151
Hume-an Nature 152
Blinded with Science 152
Ideas Associated 152
Hume's Fork 152
Inner Virtue 153
Is, Isn't, Ought 154
The Least You Need to Know 154

17 Light on the Subject   **155**

French Lights 156
Enlightened Luminaries 156
A New Look at Laws 156
Building from the Bottom Up 157
Taking Power Apart 157

The New God of Reason 157
    Keeping Freedom and Belief 157
    It's Still Ticking! 158
The Enlightenment Speaks Volumes 158
A Feel for Philosophy 159
    Civilized People Are Apple Polishers 159
    Inventing Virtue and Vice 160
    Learning to Be Natural 160
The Least You Need to Know 160

18 Wheeling and Idealing   **161**

Big Idealists 162
    Ideal-List 162
    A Falling Out Over Unity 162
Not Too Soft, Not Too Crunchy 163
    Judging Reality by Its Cover 163
    The Way the Cookie Crumbles 163
    Concepts Before Experience 164
    A New Copernicus 164
    We're All in This Together 165
Hegel Can Do What Immanuel Kant 165
    Philosophy Goes Down in History 166
    Alien Life Forms 167
    Slaves to Recognition 167
    Different Slants on Hegel 168
Will Is the Way 168
    A Will to Know 169
    Not a Pretty Picture 169
The Least You Need to Know 170

19 Ideas of Freedom   **171**

Determine One, Get One Free 172
Freedom Goes Through the Mill 172
    It All Comes Down to Happiness 173
    Poetry vs. Pushpin 173
    Freedom for Women 174
Determined to Be Free 174
    The Rat Race 175
    We Can't Go on Like This 175
    Factory-Sealed Thinking 175

Freedom Is in Meaning 176
  Trapped in Time 176
  Just Do It 177
It's a Poet! It's a Philosopher! No, It's Superman! 177
  Me and My Error 178
  You Ain't Herd Nothing Yet 178
  Deja Vu All Over Again 179
The Least You Need to Know 180

Part 5: Modern Philosophy   181

20 New Fields of Thought: Psych, Sosh, and Anthro   183

Socializing Science 184
A New Way of Thinking 184
  Secret Desires 185
  Rain on the Parade 185
  Tragic Beginnings 186
  Your Problem Is Obvious 186
Jung at Heart 187
Why We All Work Too Hard 187
  Mind over Money 188
  God and Money 188
It's All Culture 189
  Society's Big Mind 189
  Patterns and Purposes 189
The Least You Need to Know 190

21 The New Logic   191

Philosophy Chooses Up Sides 192
  It's All in How You Say It 192
  You Can't Reason Your Way Out of This 193
Eminently Logical 193
  Math's Deeper Meaning 193
  Math Spoken Here 194
  A Proposition You Can't Refuse 195
Where Does Reality Fit In? 195
  Logic Gets Real 196
  Logic Spaces Out 196
  We Make the Rules 196
  Meaning Is Everybody's Business 197

Philosophy Gets Practical 197
The Least You Need to Know 198

22 To Be or Not To Be 199

A Phenomenal Philosophy 200
Reality Meets Awareness 200
Intent on Thinking 200
The Intentions of Science 201
Bring on the Brackets 201
Painting with Your Brain 201
An Anti-Social Philosophy? 202
Let It Be 202
Time Traveling 203
Knowing What's What 203
The Real McCoy 204
Being Absurd 204
Too Free for Our Own Good 205
Heroic Existers 205
You Are What You Do 205
The Least You Need to Know 206

23 Structuring New Ideas 207

You Can't Beat the System 208
"Cat" Might as Well Be "Phthaloogazop" 208
History Is Now 209
Language on Parole 210
Them's Fightin' Words 210
Culture Is All Talk 210
Meaning Gets Organized 211
Kin to Language 211
There's a Mind in Here Somewhere 212
Modern Views of Meaning 212
Psyching Yourself Out 212
Your Ego Is Your Enemy 213
Mirror, Mirror 214
Rattling the Chains 214
A Formula for Excess Meaning 215
The Least You Need to Know 215

Part 6: Knowledge Now   **217**

24 Pomo Sapience   **219**

Philosophy Eats Itself 220
  Someone Who Dug Philosophy 220
  What You Know Can Hurt You................................. 220
  Power + Knowledge = Padded Cell 221
  Tell Me an Other.. 221
  Great Minds Think Alike 222
  Practicing What You Preach 222
  Breaking Up the Structure 222
Nowhere Man 223
  Meaning Turns Up Missing 223
  Self-Centered Language 223
  Vive la Differance 224
  Beware of Philosophy 224
Post-Modernism Lightens Up...................................... 224
  The Side-Show 225
  Does Society Need Philosophy? 225
  Same Concepts, Different Conclusions 225
  Smug or Sensible? 226
The Least You Need to Know 226

25 Women Get Wise   **227**

Woman Kinds.. 228
  Forms of Feminism 228
  Imported from France 229
Simone Says, "Take a Big Step Forward" 229
  Nature vs. Nurture 230
  A Lonely Leader 230
Different, but the Same 230
  Off the Mommy Track 231
  Labor of Love 231
Writing the Wrongs 231
Class Acts 232
  Politics Makes Strange Bedfellows 232
  God Gets a Sex Change 233
  Hooks into Race and Sex 233
  Butler Did It 234
The Least You Need to Know 234

26 The Shift Is On   **235**

Shifty Characters 236
  How the Other Half Thinks 236
  Make Yourself a Better World 237
A One-derful World 237
  Einstein-Fu 238
  The Metaphysical Kitchen Sink 238
  All Fads Lead to Oneness 239
Got Change for a One? 239
  Keep the Spirit Clean 240
  Bandwagon Earth 240
Cash Consciousness 241
  Lifting Your Spiritual Bootstraps 241
  No Business Like Know Business 241
What's Ahead? 242
The Least You Need to Know 242

A Words for the Wise   **243**

B Further Reading: More Food for Thought   **253**

Index   **255**

Foreword

In his *Poetics*, Aristotle wrote that to be learning something is the greatest of pleasures, not only to the philosopher but also to the rest of mankind, however small their capacity for it. This means that even an idiot, whose capacity to learn, according to my dictionary, falls in the lowest measurable range, loves to learn as much as any philosopher. Why not, then, learn about *philosophy*, (which means love of wisdom) and double our pleasure?

The Complete Idiot's Guide to Philosophy contains *everything* you have ever wanted to know about philosophy (and not a jot or a tittle more). Between the covers of Jay Stevenson's learned, informative, and (at appropriate moments) pleasantly silly book, you will find answers to such questions as: What was so great about the ancient Greeks, anyway? Did the Germans really have to write like that? Did Nietzsche start out crazy, or did he get that way by accident? And who died and left science in charge of the truth business?

I, for one, am extremely grateful to Jay. He has summarized, organized, de-bugged, and de-fogged all the navel-gazing, mind-tripping, logic-chopping, and deconstructing truth-tellers and nay-sayers in the history of philosophy. Now I don't actually have to read all those books I've been telling myself I'd get to some day—unless I happen to feel like it! And yet, I no longer have to go around thinking to myself, "Everyone else but me at this party knows what logical positivism is. I must go home immediately and curl up with some nice cozy Wittgenstein."

Jay has uncurled it all for us, the cozy and the not-so-cozy. He has divided the world's philosophies into ideas about being, knowing, and doing, and presents them here for us with astonishing clarity, and with many cute accessories like Philoso-Facts and Reality Checks. He even makes sense for us of the *po-mo*—those pesky post-modern ideas about truth and meaning that seem to tell us there is no such thing as truth and meaning. Hey— what would Plato think about all this po-mo stuff? And what about Darwin—I wonder whether he would have considered the Internet an evolutionary step in the right direction?

One thing is for sure: Folks on the Internet harbor strong opinions on these matters. For the past few weeks, for example, members of two different online discussion groups I've joined have been arguing about different theories of evolution and their philosophical as well as cultural implications. And these are no ivory tower folks. One group is devoted to body-building, the other to heavy metal music. What this indicates to me is, first, as The Firesign Theatre once put it, "we are all bozos on this bus"; and second, as my grandmother used to say, "Everybody is a phil-louse-opher." Welcome to *The Idiot's Guide to Philosophy*.

—Marcia Ian
Associate Professor of Modern British and American Literature,
Rutgers University

Introduction: Software for Your Brain

To me, philosophy is not only the most interesting field to think about, it is also something that's great to think *with*. Once you've got a good philosophical concept in your head, you can start to see ways of using it all over the place, and you begin to see how it ties in with other concepts with which you're already familiar.

Learning philosophy, in other words, is something like installing new software in your brain. This software can give you new ways of thinking—whole new ideas about what thinking is—as well as new things to think about. But all "software," like any other technology, changes and develops over time. *The Complete Idiot's Guide to Philosophy* outlines the most famous developments, right up to the present—the ones most people interested in philosophy find most intriguing and important.

Part 1, "The Nuts and Bolts of Philosophy," gives you a general sense of what philosophy is, breaking the subject down into the three main areas: being, knowing, and acting.

Part 2, "Ancient and Medieval Philosophy," describes the origins of philosophy in ancient Greece and outlines its development in the thinking of the pre-Socratics, Socrates, Plato, Aristotle, the Hellenistic philosophers, and the Christian philosophers of Europe during the ancient and medieval periods.

Part 3, "Eastern Philosophy," explains the major aspects of Eastern philosophy: from China, Confucius and Taoism; from India, Hinduism and Buddhism; and from the Middle East, the monotheistic religious philosophies of Judaism, Christianity, and Islam.

Part 4, "Making Progress," covers the major developments in western philosophy from the Renaissance to the 19th century, including rationalism, empiricism, the Enlightenment, idealism, utilitarianism, and Marxism.

Part 5, "Modern Philosophy," explores the period known as modern philosophy, including the rise of modern psychology, sociology, anthropology, analytic philosophy, phenomenology, existentialism, and structuralism.

Part 6, "Knowledge Now," looks at what's going on in philosophy now, including post-structuralism, feminism, and new age philosophy.

Extras

To make browsing through this book easier, you'll find boxes of interesting and helpful information throughout. These include definitions, things to watch out for, facts about the history of philosophy and of philosophers, and suggestions for applying philosophical ideas and viewpoints to your own life. Here's what these boxes look like:

Lexicon
These define special terms and concepts related to philosophy.

Philoso-Fact
You guessed it—these boxes have tidbits of information about a philosophy or a philosopher.

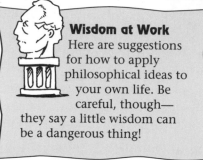

Wisdom at Work
Here are suggestions for how to apply philosophical ideas to your own life. Be careful, though—they say a little wisdom can be a dangerous thing!

Reality Check
Here you'll find an interpretation of a particular philosophy or viewpoint.

Acknowledgments

I'd like to thank my technical editor, Dave Nelson, for his penetrating suggestions and assiduous attention. I'd also like to thank Debra, Chris, Stephanie G., and Daveena for their moral support; the reading group: Bob, Scott, Kathy, and Michael, for their patience and good humor; and the poker crowd: Ann Dean, Nardo, Matt, Cora, Vic, Stephanie, Jenn, Kevil, Cathy, Kelly, and Yoly, for many invaluable lessons in ethics and prudence.

Special Thanks from the Publisher to the Technical Reviewer

The Complete Idiot's Guide to Philosophy was reviewed by an expert who checked the accuracy of what you'll be reading and also provided valuable insights and suggestions to ensure that this book gives you as complete and balanced a picture of philosophy as any book can. Our special thanks to David E. Nelson.

David Nelson received undergraduate degrees mathematics and philosophy from Grinnell College, in Iowa. He is completing his Ph.D. at Rutgers, the State University of New Jersey, where he has taught courses in symbolic logic, critical thinking, philosophy of science, and philosophy of religion. His specialties within philosophy are epistemology and the philosophy of science.

Part 1
The Nuts and Bolts of Philosophy

Since you picked up this book, you must be at least a little curious about philosophy. As life gets more complicated, it gets more confusing. Every day, more thorny problems—politics, the environment, religion, education, technology, family, the community—clamber for attention. Learning some philosophy can help you deal with life's difficulties by taking you away from them for a while, and by leading you back into them with new ideas about what it's all about.

Philosophy doesn't have to be hard to understand. It does help if you have some basic questions and ideas in mind as you look into a new philosophy. How do the new ideas compare with the ones you already think about? What problems do the new ideas have that the old ones don't? What problems does the new thinking manage to avoid?

The first part of this book thinks about philosophy in terms of three basic issues: being, knowing, and acting. Philosophy continually asks questions about these issues: What exists? Is existence organized? What counts as knowledge? How do we know things? How should we act? Do we act according to a human nature? Keeping these questions in mind makes it easier to make sense of particular philosophical ideas and of philosophy in general.

Chapter 1

The Big Picture

In This Chapter

➤ Why philosophers philosophize

➤ What philosophy is

➤ Why there are so many "isms"

➤ What the main branches of philosophy are and how they relate to one another

Philosophers think about everything. And they tend to take a broader view of everything than most other people. They look at things as if from farther away, to see how they all fit together. This book, in talking about philosophy as a whole, paints a big picture of lots of big pictures.

To some, philosophy may seem like a silly or irrelevant waste of time, a distraction from the obvious, important (though often boring) things that everybody has to deal with—work, school, relationships, bills. There is plenty of traditional support for this view. Legend has it that the ancient Greek philosopher, Thales, was out walking one night and was so intent on contemplating the stars that he didn't see where he was going and fell into a well. Focusing on far-away, irrelevant things, philosophers can sometimes lose sight of the here and now.

Why Ask Why?

Let's face it: Philosophy doesn't always give us anything we can take to the bank. Could it be that philosophy is basically useless?

The fact is, philosophy is unavoidable. Even if you think you don't already have a philosophy, you actually do. Like everybody else, you live your life according to ideas and assumptions about what the world is like that you picked up along the way.

If you're not as satisfied with the way things are as you think you should be—and who is?—you might want to rethink your ideas about what reality is all about. This rethinking is precisely what philosophers have been doing over the centuries.

For example, people used to think that, whenever anything bad happened, the gods were angry. They thought their gods wanted them to show their loyalty and obedience by making big sacrifices, even of their own children! Gradually, people with a philosophical turn of mind began questioning this assumption. Maybe the gods would be just as happy if we let our children live? This required a whole rethinking of what life, God, and human nature are all about—just the kind of rethinking philosophers do. Today, of course, the incidence of human sacrifice has been greatly reduced. Thank a philosopher.

You Are What You Think

People have a lot of great ideas, and stupid ideas, about reality. If you can sort out these ideas and make sense of them, it can help you understand your own reality. This book is intended to help you do just that. It will help you recognize and understand philosophical ideas when you come across them, and see which ones make sense for you and which ones belong on the scrap heap of history.

Wisdom at Work

Plato, the ancient Greek philosopher, offers the sound advice, "Know yourself." This idea, though, can be taken to mean different things: know what you want; know your limits and weaknesses; know how other people see you. These are only a few of the meanings possible in this maxim. The idea reinforces a famous statement made by Plato's teacher, Socrates: "The unexamined life is not worth living."

As you read this book, you'll learn that you think a lot of things already. Lots of the thinking that important philosophers have done is stuff that may have already occurred to you. Seeing where your ideas come from and how others have used them may help you make better sense of who you are and what your life is about.

Even though there is a lot philosophy can't do, such as give you big muscles like Auguste Rodin's statue, *The Thinker*, it can do some pretty important things. In particular, it can help you think about thinking. Everybody does it, and it's especially nice to be able to do it well, both for its own sake and for the practical benefits thinking can yield. To clarify your thinking about thinking, this book shows how philosophers throughout history have tried to shed light on the big, deep questions, and suggests ways you can apply some of their answers to your life.

Are you an idealist? A pragmatist? An existentialist? Do you think about things rationally? Empirically? Intuitively? Is your behavior directed by will? By other people? Is there more to reality than what we can see and measure? Reading this book will help you understand what these questions mean and why they are important.

A Slice of Life

People engage in philosophy when they think about life and everything in it. The word *philosophy*, meaning "love of wisdom," comes from ancient Greece, where people who liked thinking about life started calling themselves *philosophers*. Of course, "life" doesn't narrow things down very much. In ancient times and for centuries afterward, philosophy had an extremely wide scope, encompassing subjects we have since separated from philosophy, such as science, math, theology, psychology, sociology, and economics.

The ancient Greeks did not distinguish these fields from philosophy. As philosophers, they practiced them all—not, of course, in the same ways that a modern scientist studies science or a modern economist studies economics. These fields have changed and developed out of philosophy.

Philosophy still applies, however, to all of these fields. It is possible to study philosophy of science, or philosophy of religion, for example. Questions and problems that we call philosophical lie at the heart of all these subjects. Yet even after all of these fields have branched off from philosophy, there are still central issues and ways of thinking that are of particular interest to philosophers. To be more specific, philosophy tends to be concerned with broad, fundamental ideas about knowledge, cosmic reality, human nature, and society. And it is also, for better or worse, concerned with words.

Wisdom at Work
We can think of philosophy as occupying the spaces left in knowledge after science, sociology, psychology, economics, and religion (as we understand them today) tell us what they can about the world.

Is You Ism or Is You Ain't My Philosophy?

Philosophers can be hard to understand. That's because they often use words that sound like total gobbledygook to people who aren't philosophers. They have, in other words, a highly developed *lexicon*. A lexicon is a body of special words (jargon) used by a particular group of people—in this case, philosophers.

The philosophical lexicon is big because philosophy has dozens of different subdivisions and categories, and every category has a gazillion different movements, or *isms*. An ism is a system of belief, or a way of thinking that sees certain ideas as true or important while, inevitably, leaving other ideas out.

Lexicon
A **lexicon** is a specialized vocabulary; a group of words used by a particular group of people and not shared by most everyone else.

5

Grammatically speaking, isms are formed by turning a noun or adjective into a verb, then turning that verb back into a noun. For example, if you see knowledge as structural, and go on to structural*ize* knowledge, that means you subscribe to *structuralism*. If you believe Mickey Mouse holds the answer to life's deepest questions, and you Mickey*ize* your understanding of life, you believe in *Mickeyism*.

Lexicon

Ontology is the study of being or existence. Ontologists want to know what we mean when we say something exists. **Epistemology** is the study of knowing. Epistemologists want to know what we mean when we say we know something. **Ethics** is the study of moral and social behavior. Ethical philosophers want to know what it means to be a person and how people can and should act.

Some popular isms within philosophy include sophism, skepticism, stoicism, scholasticism, mysticism, taoism, empiricism, rationalism, idealism, naturalism, materialism, pragmatism, existentialism, and antidisestablishmentarianism, to name a few. And that doesn't include all the isms named after people (like Freudianism) and periods of time (like early post-modernism). They have to invent a new ism for every point of view—and there are *lots* of points of view.

What's more, philosophers have developed subdivisions within philosophy to deal with the deep questions they like to ask. The main subdivisions have to do with being, knowing, and acting. Philosophers call these subdivisions *ontology* (the study of being, or existence), *epistemology* (the study of knowing), and *ethics* (the study of how to act as a person). The next three chapters will look at each of these subdivisions in turn. The chapters after that explore specific philosophies—the isms and the people who invented them.

How the Parts Fit Together

Even though you can think about these three different subjects separately, they all work together to make philosophy what it is. Different philosophies place different emphases on these subjects. Most philosophers do their work by expanding on what they already think they know. Different philosophers identify different places to start—different foundational ideas on which to build their thinking. For example, Plato's epistemology and ethics are derived from his ontology. This simply means that his ideas about knowing and about how we should act are based on his ideas about existence.

This makes Plato different from a rationalist philosopher like Rene Descartes, who bases his ideas about being and acting on his ideas about knowing. Similarly, both Plato and Descartes are different from a post-structuralist philosopher like Michel Foucault, who believes that being and knowing depend on how people act.

These three branches of philosophy tend to work together. In fact, it has taken some philosophical thinking to see them as separate. For example, one of the main things that distinguished the earliest philosophy in ancient Greece from the myths the Greeks used to explain reality was the philosophical awareness that ontology, or existence, is not simply a cosmic reflection of ethics, or how people act. Whereas the myths presented reality as completely involved in, and centered around, human behavior, the first philosophers saw ontology, or existence, independently from human action.

This insight has led to new questions and answers about how people fit in with the rest of reality, and how human knowledge affects this relationship. The next three chapters talk about some of these questions, and say more about the three main branches of philosophy—being, knowing, and acting—and how they relate to one another.

The Least You Need to Know

➤ Whether you know it or not, you've got a philosophy. This is because you can't help but define reality for yourself.

➤ This book will help you sort out your ideas and those of others, to help you decide which of them have meaning for you.

➤ Philosophy consists of all kinds of thinking, including the social sciences, natural science, math, and religious thinking.

➤ Three main branches of philosophy are ontology (being), epistemology (knowing), and ethics (acting).

Chapter 2

Being There

In This Chapter

➤ How philosophers think about being

➤ Physical and metaphysical reality

➤ Is there a God?

➤ How being relates to knowing

What is there, and what do we mean by "there" anyway? This, in a nutshell, is what philosophy has focused on for centuries, and this is what you'll get to think more about here.

Philosophers think about ontology (being or existence) by using theories about what the world is made of, what this stuff is capable of doing, and whether reality is ordered in any particular way.

Throughout history, one of the really big ideas about existence has been God. This chapter, in talking about existence, focuses on how philosophers have dealt with God. (You can read more about God and philosophy in Chapter 9 on Medieval philosophy, and Chapter 12 on Middle Eastern religious philosophy.)

The Myth-Math of Existence

Even before philosophy got started, people were inventing myths to help explain reality. These myths usually portrayed natural forces as people or gods. By thinking about natural forces in human terms, people made sense of the strange and mysterious things going on around them: rain, thunder, sunshine, the seasons, birth, growth, death.

However, these myths did not attempt to explain what reality is physically made of; they were more concerned with explaining how reality affects human activities and relationships. Myths personified nature—it was one big, not-so-happy family. Earth is our mother, the sun or sky is Dad, the sea is a weird uncle, and the hill to the north is a distant cousin. Storms may be fights; a nice day may mean that the sky-daddy has found a new girlfriend; winter comes when Earth-mama finds out about it and gives everyone the cold treatment.

The first philosophers differed from the mythmakers by explaining reality in more general, less familiar terms. The ancient Greek philosopher, Thales, sometimes considered the first philosopher, said that all things were made out of water—everything that exists is really water in a more or less complicated form. Other early philosophers believed that everything was made of four "elements": earth, air, fire, and water. Still others thought the world was made of a single substance that could be broken down into tiny, indivisible particles called atoms.

These early theories about reality are not "scientific" as the word is used today—that is, they do not result from experimental tests or controlled observation. But they are impersonal and suggest rules for the stuff of reality and how it is organized. These early philosophers wanted to know not only what reality is, but how it is shaped and how it works. They came up with *theories*, rather than stories, to answer their questions.

Reality Check

Although it is useful to distinguish the ways myth and philosophy explain reality, the two ways of explaining are not totally separate. In fact, some consider philosophy itself a kind of mythmaking. The French philosopher, Jacques Derrida, describes philosophy as "white mythology"— mythology that has had all the familiar images bleached out of it.

To Order Is to Understand

Technological developments helped philosophers learn to think about reality in terms of impersonal rules of order. Practical arts like geometry, navigation, and medicine, for example, were developing in ancient Greece at about the time of the first philosophers. In fact, one of them, Pythagoras, is also known as an important mathematician. A number of other early philosophers were also extremely interested in math.

Math and other technological arts helped people stop thinking about reality as a big family of bickering gods, and start seeing the world as being made of things you can use to make more things, arranged according to mathematical rules. Craftsmen and artisans started it all by inventing technical terms for their work. Philosophers went even further, creating terms for talking about reality. Many of these terms refer to physical reality, like atoms and the elements.

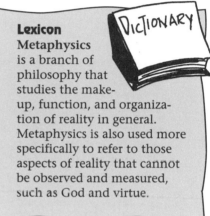

Philoso-Fact
Mathematics was so important to Plato that he had written over the entrance to his Academy "Let no one enter who has not studied mathematics."

Enter Metaphysics

Philosophers also came up with *metaphysical* terms, which refer not to what reality is physically made of, but to how it is organized and how it works. Some of the more famous metaphysical terms are *forms*, *substance*, *essence*, *categories*, *spirit*, *monads*, and *noumena*. God, too, is a metaphysical concept.

Philosophers, of course, have come up with all kinds of theories about reality. Each new philosophical system needs another set of metaphysical terms to describe its version of reality. Some of these metaphysical terms are pretty far-out—in more ways than one! In order to understand the philosophy of being and metaphysics, let me give you an overview of how metaphysical ideas have been used and have changed through history. This will help you see why metaphysical ideas are significant.

Lexicon
Metaphysics is a branch of philosophy that studies the make-up, function, and organization of reality in general. Metaphysics is also used more specifically to refer to those aspects of reality that cannot be observed and measured, such as God and virtue.

Is There a God?

Throughout the Middle Ages in Europe and the Middle East, a philosophical battle was waged between religious authorities on one side who felt that religious doctrine should be accepted on faith alone and religious philosophers on the other, who were interested in combining religious ideas with the teaching of the Greek philosophers, especially Plato and Aristotle.

In some cases, like that of the German monk and philosopher Meister Eckhart, the attempt to square philosophy and religion resulted in charges of heresy (the crime of having religious beliefs that contradict those of established religion). Eckhart made claims that sounded like he thought God was nothing more than nature itself and that this God/nature created itself. These ideas made the German bishops nervous, and Eckhart was punished.

Many philosophers, though, found success in bringing philosophical ideas based on reason and nature together with accepted religious beliefs. This was true of Christian, Jewish, and Islamic philosophers as well.

REALITY ✓

Reality Check

You might think that philosophers of the Middle Ages used philosophical ideas to prove God's existence because they wanted to encourage people to believe in God. Actually, though, God was so widely accepted that there was little point in trying to convince people—practically everyone already believed in God. A more likely reason for using philosophy in this way was to show that philosophy was not sacrilegious. Although philosophers seemed to be using philosophy to defend God, they were, in effect, using God to defend philosophy!

As a result, philosophy as practiced by the Greeks became acceptable to the new religions Christianity and Islam. In the West, many of the most important medieval philosophers practiced one of these religions. They studied existence both as philosophers and as theologians, trying to figure out how reality works for its own sake and trying to figure out what reality reveals about God.

Perfection Is Truth

These philosophers used philosophical ideas about being to prove the existence of God. For example, one argument goes that because the world exists, it must have a cause, namely, God. Might the whole thing have been an accident? No, reasoned the medieval philosophers, because reality seems so well organized and able to support life that God must have planned it.

Philoso-Fact
Many Christian philosophers believed that we can learn about God from two "books." The first book is the Bible and the second "book" is the world itself, which, if "read" in the right way, can yield divine knowledge.

But maybe what seems planned was still just accidental, and maybe the organization that seems to indicate the existence of God is really due to the way people think. What then? Maybe order is just an idea in people's minds.

To this objection the medieval philosophers offered their most imaginative idea of all: they reasoned that the idea of God is the most perfect idea possible. They also argued that one characteristic of perfection is existence. God *must* therefore exist.

Being Leads to Knowing

This argument, known as the "ontological proof" of God's existence, shows that when you push hard enough on the idea of *being*, the question of *knowing* comes up. To put it another way, whether or not you accept any one explanation of reality depends partly on the question of how you know things, and how the ability to know things fits in with the question of being.

But I'm getting ahead of myself. You'll have to wait until Chapter 3 to see how the study of knowing figures into philosophy in general. For now, the point is that the way we think about knowledge influences how we think about God.

Being and Thinking

Many philosophers in the West have associated God with knowledge. Some said that human knowledge is not capable of understanding God, so we have to take his existence on faith. Others said that knowledge reveals God's nature.

One of the more astonishing examples of this second view was put forward by the Portuguese-Dutch philosopher Baruch Spinoza, who believed that matter itself could think! He believed that things like rocks and water and trees and tile grout—all of reality—are alive and capable of knowing—a view called *vitalism*.

Not only can reality think, said Spinoza, but reality itself *is* God. God and nature, for Spinoza, are two sides of the same coin.

Wisdom at Work
Use **vitalism** to explain why things keep getting lost or broken. Say that your mother's antique vase was so filled with despair that it no longer wanted to exist; it jumped off the table and shattered as you were walking past.

Dualism vs. Materialism

As you might imagine, Spinoza's ideas attracted a lot of attention—and criticism—from other philosophers, and theologians too. A more popular and influential belief about the relationship between being and knowing is *dualism*, the idea that the world is made up of material and spiritual aspects. The spiritual aspects of reality are those capable of thinking, while the material aspects cannot think. Spiritual reality includes the human mind and—you guessed it—God.

The most famous dualist of the 17th century was the French philosopher Rene Descartes who believed that a spiritual portion of the mind allows us to understand perceptions that are conveyed to us physically by our senses. Descartes believed that the spiritual portion of reality was confined to God

Lexicon
A **vitalist** believes that everything that makes up reality is alive and capable of thinking. A **dualist** believes that reality can be separated into two components: material and spiritual. The spiritual part of reality makes thinking and knowledge possible.

and the human mind alone; the rest of reality was simply physical. Descartes' dualism was widely accepted by other philosophers and eventually by theologians as well.

Ways to Be

Here's some of the more important ideas philosophers have come up with to understand being and how it works:

➤ **Plato**   Perfect, unchanging, ideal forms lend order and understanding to physical reality.

➤ **Aristotle**   Each identifiable thing has an essence that supplies it with a purpose culminating in the prime mover.

➤ **Thomas Aquinas**   Reality was created by God according to His plan (confirmed by the "ontological proof").

➤ **Spinoza**   Reality is all one substance, including God and nature; everything that exists is a part of this one substance, which is capable of thought (*vitalism*).

➤ **Descartes**   Physical reality works according to mechanical principles. In addition, there is spiritual reality, including God and the mind, that can think (*dualism*).

Descartes' dualism made a neat separation between physical and metaphysical reality. An important result of this separation was that it allowed philosophers and scientists to study the natural world without having to worry about supernatural questions. In fact, since Descartes' time, many philosophers have argued that we should stop asking metaphysical questions—questions about God and anything else that can't be verified through observation.

Even so, other philosophers continued to see knowledge itself as metaphysical, much as Descartes did. Starting in Descartes' time—the 17th century—philosophers began arguing for and against two distinct ways in which being was related to knowing. These ways are known as *rationalism* and *empiricism*. Rationalism sees knowledge as metaphysical, existing independently of physical reality. Empiricism, on the other hand, sees knowledge as based on observable, physical reality. We'll learn more about rationalism and empiricism in Chapter 3, which covers epistemology, or knowing.

The Least You Need to Know

➤ The first ancient Greek philosophers made a distinction between physical reality and human social reality.

➤ Metaphysics is the branch of philosophy that studies how reality functions. The term is also used to refer to whatever cannot be verified through observation, including God.

➤ Ideas about God often depend on ideas about knowing.

➤ Descartes theorized a clear separation of physical and metaphysical reality in the 17th century.

Chapter 3

What There Is to Know About Knowing

In This Chapter

➤ Thinking without experiencing (rationalism)

➤ Basing thought on experience (empiricism)

➤ Thinking up and down and back and forth (dialectic)

➤ Reconciling reason and experience

➤ Thinking and history

As noted in Chapter 2, the French philosopher Rene Descartes proposed a dualistic philosophy—a way of thinking about reality that suggests that there is a physical, material reality outside of our minds, and a spiritual, living reality in our minds. Descartes was attempting, at one level, to answer the questions surrounding the connection between being and knowing. Descartes and his contemporaries came to see that if philosophers were going to continue to question being, or existence, they would also have to deal with the question of how they knew about existence.

Epistemology is the study of knowledge—what knowledge is, what we can know, and how we know it. Epistemology has been a major concern of philosophers ever since Descartes called attention to its importance in the 17th century.

A Time of Crisis

In Descartes' day, people's beliefs were changing drastically. The printing press had been around long enough so that books were widely available—more people than ever before could read and write. Since people were more informed, they could more easily challenge old ideas, especially religious ideas. In addition, science told people the shocking news: Earth is *not* the center of the universe! But not everyone accepted this idea. Faced with the old belief that the sun rotates around the Earth, and with the new idea of the Earth spinning around the sun, no one knew exactly where they stood!

To make things even more confusing, not everyone knew they had to go to work for a living like we do today. Some people (the nobility) believed that the work should be left to other people (the commoners). The nobility saw it as their job to spend the money the commoners made. But this idea was being challenged. In the words of historian Christopher Hill, the world was being turned upside down! Things got so out of hand that people weren't even sure they could trust their own senses.

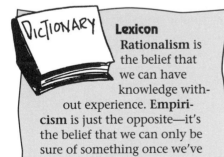

Philoso-Fact
Some philosophers, even after recognizing that their mathematical calculations made better sense from the point of view of the Earth circling the sun, continued to believe that the sun circled the Earth. The idea that humanity is the center of the universe made better sense to them emotionally.

Descartes' Reason

Then along came Descartes, who wanted a solution for this problem of not knowing what to believe. In order to do this, he attempted to figure out what we can know for certain without relying on tradition, on outside authority, or even on what our senses tell us.

Descartes said that, even though we can't believe everything we read, and even if we can't even believe our own senses, we can trust our reason if we settle down quietly and block out the world and all its craziness. Reason, for Descartes, could be relied upon to tell us what is true and what isn't. He reasoned that the very fact that he could think told him for certain that he existed. In his own famous words, "Cogito ergo sum," *I think therefore I am.*

Lexicon
Rationalism is the belief that we can have knowledge without experience. **Empiricism** is just the opposite—it's the belief that we can only be sure of something once we've tested it—once we've experienced it, so to speak.

Look Ma, No Senses!

Descartes' certainty that he existed led him to feel certain about other things too, such as the existence of God. Once he became certain that God exists, he felt he could be certain of other, more ordinary things, like the fact that the sky is blue and ants have six legs, and so forth.

Descartes' solution to the epistemological problem of what we can know is called *rationalism*. It's the belief that the mind is capable of knowing things even without experience.

Getting Testy

While Descartes was philosophizing about rationalism in France, philosophers in England were thinking up a different solution to what we can know. This alternative solution is known as *empiricism*. It's the belief that the best way to be certain of something is to test it with your senses—through actual experience. Empiricism became a major aspect of what we now call science—figuring things out by running tests and experiments.

During the Middle Ages, empiricism was not the obvious, common sense idea that it has become today. People tended to confuse how things worked and what things actually *did* with what things *meant* and how people *felt* about them. Gold, for example was not just a mineral you could make jewelry out of. People gave gold special meanings and thought it had special power—spiritual properties. Their feelings about gold actually kept them from studying gold empirically, through actual experience. In fact, before the empiricists came along, people tended to think the whole world and everything in it worked more or less by magic.

During and after the 17th century, empiricists like Francis Bacon and John Locke were rejecting the old, magical ideas and arguing that physical (empirical) reality works according to mechanical principles. By studying things empirically, these philosophers believed that they could figure out what these principles were.

To a degree, they were right. And science has been a thriving enterprise ever since. Still, empiricism alone can't tell us everything we want to know about reality and is far from the last word in philosophy.

Rationalism and empiricism, though, provide alternative solutions to epistemological problems. And as different as they are, they both rely heavily on an important, centuries-old tool used by philosophers in dealing with epistemological problems: *logic*.

> **Philoso-Fact**
> Bacon criticized old, magical ideas by calling them "idols of the mind," suggesting people worshipped them as part of a false religion.

Can We Get There from Here?

Both reason and experience, rationalism and empiricism, rely on logic to get from one idea to the next. Logic is a tool for figuring out everything that can truthfully be said based on what is already known to be true.

As you may have discovered if you've ever tried to have a logical discussion with someone who thinks differently than you, logic can be very slippery. It works great when applied to math, but when you substitute ideas for numbers, all kinds of funny things can happen.

Part of the problem is that words can have more than one meaning. If a word gets used in more than one way without your realizing it, your logic can get thrown out of whack. Another problem with logic is that you usually have to start with assumptions. This means that even if your logic is good, your assumptions may be mistaken and can lead to false conclusions. Finally, people's personalities come into play. Some people like to fool other people, either for the fun of it or to take advantage of them. Thus, someone may use slippery words and mistaken assumptions for the sole purpose of deceiving someone else. This is also why logic works best when people are left out of it and it is applied only to mathematics.

REALITY ✓ **Reality Check**

Logic rarely works in real arguments outside of academic disputes, and it *never* works in a personal relationship. Don't even bother pretending to use logic in order to win a fight with someone who's close to you. If you say, "Let's talk about this logically," you may get the response, "Okay, I deduce logically that you are a total jerk!"

Still, there are a number of ways we can use logic when dealing with ideas. Among the most important of these to philosophers are induction and deduction.

Going Down: Deduction

Deduction is the process of figuring things out that are necessarily true, provided that the assumptions we start with, called the premises, are true. Geometry is based on deductive thinking. So are all those word problems you had to do in math class.

Aristotle provided a famous example of a kind of deduction that he called a syllogism. It consists of three statements: two premises and a conclusion.

Here is Aristotle's syllogism about Socrates:

> All men are mortal.
>
> Socrates is a man.
>
> Socrates is mortal.

From the two premises, we can deduce the conclusion for certain.

As Aristotle himself noticed, the conclusion is only certain if the premises are in fact true. If all men aren't mortal, or if Socrates is not a man, then the conclusion that Socrates is mortal may be false.

As you'll see later in Chapter 7, Aristotle developed a whole philosophical system—including epistemology, metaphysics, and ethics—largely with the help of syllogisms that assured him that his ideas were logically consistent. And, for the most part, his ideas *are* logically consistent. Unfortunately, this does not make them all true. Many of Aristotle's premises can be shown to be false.

Even so, Aristotle's thinking has been extremely influential, partly because he has helped other philosophers focus on the logical consistency of their ideas. Deduction is the best way to expand what we already know. If we can be sure of our premises and the meaning of the words we use, it leads to reliable information.

Lexicon
Deduction is the process of determining what is true based on what is already known to be true. A **premise** is an assertion that leads deductively to a conclusion. A **syllogism** is a logical statement that presents a conclusion deduced from two related premises.

Going Up: Induction

Another important logical process is *induction*—a way of making generalizations about things. Induction, like deduction, moves from premises to conclusions. But unlike deduction, induction leads to conclusions that may *not* be true even if the premises are true. Inductive conclusions are only probable, not certain.

For example, if we want to know what color crows can be and we go out and find a good number of crows and all of them are black, it's a pretty good bet that all crows are black. But can we be sure? Even seeing a million black crows doesn't mean for certain that there isn't a crow out there somewhere that is lime green. The best we can do is say that all crows are *probably* black.

Induction is, in some ways, less certain than deduction, but induction can do a lot that deduction can't. Induction, for example, can help generate hypotheses. A *hypothesis* is a generalization that we think *might* be true, but that might not *actually* be true.

Lexicon
Induction is drawing conclusions from particular evidence; if certain things are true, we can induce that other things of the same kind will probably be true. A **hypothesis** is a theoretical statement that explains things but that may be disproved or confirmed by new evidence.

Double-Checking Your Hypothesis

Hypotheses are useful things to have in mind while trying to figure out new things. One way philosophers and scientists learn is by constantly testing their hypotheses with new ideas and information. If new information supports the hypothesis, it is just that much more likely that it's true. But what if the new information proves the hypothesis wrong?

That depends on how you feel about your hypothesis. These days, scientists and philosophers are often thrilled if they find a piece of evidence that refutes the leading hypotheses. It means they'll be famous and can start work on developing a whole new hypothesis capable of explaining the new evidence.

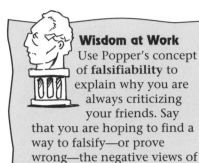

An example is the discovery of x-rays. X-rays didn't make sense at first, since current ideas about how molecules worked were not capable of explaining them. To explain x-rays, they had to throw out the old ideas about molecules and come up with new ones able to explain the new evidence. As a result, people developed all kinds of new knowledge about radioactivity that their old hypotheses prevented them from finding.

The idea that we learn the most when we discover how much we *don't* know is a key idea in modern science, where people are looking for ways to challenge each other's hypotheses about how reality works. It is associated with the work of the Austrian philosopher Karl Popper, who argued that science depends on the principle of *falsifiability*. We can't *ever* prove that general statements are always true, but we may be able to prove they are false. We can't *ever* prove that all crows are black, since there may be a green crow hiding somewhere out there. But if someday we do find a green crow, then we have falsified the general claim that all crows are black.

The Ping-Pong Ball Called Dialectic

The ancient Greek philosopher, Socrates, became famous for his ability to poke holes in other people's philosophies. He believed that learning how little we know for certain was the best way to gain knowledge. Socrates asked people questions in order to get them to think about the limits of their knowledge. Eventually, he led them to conclusions that showed them how they were mistaken.

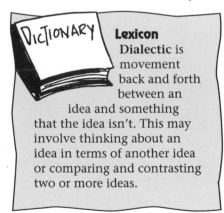

This procedure of teaching by asking questions is called the Socratic method—after Socrates. As you'll see in Chapter 5, the Socratic method involves the logical testing of propositions, or premises. In some ways, Socrates thought like a modern scientist, except that he didn't ask questions about x-rays or astronomy—rather, he focused on virtuous behavior.

Socrates tested ideas logically by seeing if they held up next to other ideas. Moving back and forth between ideas helped him to see how accurate they were. This back-and-forth movement, called *dialectic*, has become important to philosophers ever since.

Pro or Con?

Dialectic is the Greek word meaning *discussion*. This kind of discussion may take the somewhat rambling form of the Socratic method, or it can be more rigidly structured as in Aristotle's *Topics* in which he considers the pros and cons of a number of stated subjects.

A version of Aristotle's pro and con approach to dialectic is still used today in formal debates in which the debaters argue opposed positions on a given topic. After the debate, the audience, theoretically, is better able to understand the problem being debated and to decide where they stand.

Both Sides Now

Dialectic can be useful not only in deciding specific questions like whether or not abortion should be legal or if we all have a moral responsibility to take care of the poor; dialectic can also help clarify and bring together entire ways of understanding things.

The idea is that it can be easier to understand something when you are able to see it in relation to what it isn't. Can you really understand chocolate ice cream if you've never tried vanilla? Of course not.

Dialectic not only helps us understand opposing ideas, it can also lead to a new way of combining opposed ideas into a new unity. Let's go back to the examples of rationalism and empiricism again. These ways of studying knowledge were in conflict for over a century. Both of them had different strengths and weaknesses. Rationalism could do things empiricism could not and vice versa.

Wisdom at Work
Use **dialectic** to sort out disagreements after an argument has blown over. Try to see each point of view from the other side. You may be able to come up with a new, broader position that is more acceptable than either previous position.

The rationalists said that empiricism doesn't tell us anything about things that have been of major importance to philosophers, like whether God exists or whether human nature is basically good or evil.

The empiricists, on the other hand, complained that the rationalists had no hard evidence for their theories. Rationalist philosophy was an extremely speculative enterprise. The rationalists may have been just fooling themselves into believing that their minds are capable of obtaining metaphysical knowledge.

Although you could say that one approach makes up for the weaknesses of the other, you can't just combine the two into a bigger, stronger philosophy, because they're in conflict. The work of one perspective undoes the work of the other.

But, if you think dialectically, hitting the ping-pong ball of your mind back and forth between empiricism and rationalism, you may be able to see each perspective as a part of the other.

Can He or Kant He? Combining Reason and Experience

This is just what the German philosopher, Immanuel Kant did. He brought rationalism and empiricism together in two ways. First, he looked at rationalist ideals as empirical conditions of the mind. In other words, he reasoned that the fact that philosophers seem to want to believe in God (a rational ideal) shows us what the mind is like (an empirical fact). Rationalist thought, that is, is an empirical fact of the mind.

Lexicon
Idealism is the belief that reality is largely dependent on the mind.

Next, he looked at empirical things and reasoned that we can only know them with our minds. As a result, there is a lot about "the world as it is" that depends on how our minds work. This view is called *idealism*.

I'll go into Kant in Chapter 18. For now, the point is that dialectic is not only good for little things like deciding whether to have cake or pie for dessert, but for deep, trippy stuff like seeing the relationship between the mind and reality. It can be a whole way of knowing and of seeing what knowledge is.

But wait! If you think Kant is over the edge with his use of dialectic, hold on to your head! One of Kant's followers, the German philosopher Georg Wilhelm Friedreich Hegel, went even further in using dialectic to think about knowledge.

Can History Think?

For Hegel, dialectic is not just something the mind does in order to think about reality; it is something reality does to the mind. Hegel believed that human consciousness develops and changes through history, and that this historical process is dialectical.

Philoso-Fact
Hegel viewed ideas both as ways of understanding reality and as giving shape to reality as it changes through history.

We can use the dialectical relationship between empiricism and rationalism as an example. Hegel would say not that Kant worked out this dialectical relationship, but that it worked itself out within human consciousness. For Hegel, individuals are less important than what *everybody* thinks. What everybody thinks is influenced by the conflict of opposing ideas that take shape in history.

Hegel's use of dialectic puts a whole new spin on the study of knowledge by suggesting that what we know and how we know it depends on where we stand in history. The *reason* that figures things out is not the individual's reason, as it was for Descartes, but the shared human consciousness at work in history. Hegel believed that everyone's knowledge is part of a bigger knowledge.

In place of "I think, therefore I am," Hegel might say, "History works the same way thinking does, therefore a shared human consciousness exists."

Now let's look at just one more philosophical perspective on the study of knowledge, one that borrows from Hegel's use of dialectic. The German philosopher and political economist, Karl Marx, made new use of some of Hegel's ideas while changing them in some important ways.

Marx on the Mind

Marx argued that the dialectic of history was not evidence of a universal human consciousness as Hegel described it. Instead, dialectical movement in history involved changes in the ways society takes care of people's material needs.

Lexicon
Ideology is a system of beliefs or ideas that reinforce the values of a particular class or group of people.

This meant that Marx was less interested in the dialectical, or contrasting, relationship between rationalism and empiricism than in the dialectical relationship between industrialism and farming. Marx believed that history was structured by changes in economic relationships. These economic relationships, he argued, influence the way people think.

Like Hegel, Marx thought that the mind of the individual was only part of the larger picture, a larger picture that influenced how people think. For Hegel, that larger picture was the universal human consciousness. For Marx, the larger picture was the economic forces that determined people's social relationships.

Since, for Marx, social relationships influence the way people think, "knowledge" is limited and structured by the way we see to our material needs. Marx called this structured knowledge *ideology*.

To see knowledge as ideology is very different from seeing knowledge as reason. Thus Marx's view of knowing is very different from Descartes'. For Descartes, we can get knowledge by reasoning independently of worldly experience. For Marx, ideology develops in response to economic forces. Descartes is thinking about knowing from inside the mind, asking what the mind can do entirely on its own; Marx is thinking about knowing from outside society, asking how economic forces shape the way people think.

In this chapter, we've talked about how different philosophers deal with the issue of epistemology—through reason, experience, logic, and dialectic. We'll come back to these ideas when we look more closely at particular philosophies. First, though, we'll look at one other major philosophical concept, ethics, or acting, in the next chapter.

The Least You Need to Know

➤ Different views of knowing include rationalism (for example, Descartes), empiricism (Bacon and Locke), idealism (Kant and Hegel), and ideology (Marx).

➤ Different logical techniques for acquiring and testing knowledge are induction, deduction, and dialectic.

Chapter 4

How to Act

In This Chapter

➤ The group vs. the individual

➤ Western individualism

➤ Is and ought

➤ Responding to convention

Philosophers use the terms "morality" and "ethics" to refer to how people should act. A moral act or an ethical act is the right thing to do. An immoral or unethical act is wrong. Questions about how to act, then, are also questions about good and bad.

The field of ethics is a vital philosophical area today, as it was for the ancient Greeks. From questions concerning the Ten Commandments to genetic cloning, issues of morality and ethics concern not only people who think about these things for a living, but also everyday, ordinary people like you. Should judicial punishments be meted out based on a person's personal circumstances? Or, regardless of differing situations, are there ideal standards and judgments to be handed out across the board? Are people born with traits that cause them to act differently—maybe even immorally by some standards—than others? Philosophers approach these and other questions of morality based on their assumptions about reality and their priorities as philosophers.

Me vs. Us

Some of the most influential guidelines for how to act were set down by the Chinese philosopher Confucius around 500 B.C. In fact, Confucius's philosophy was centered on the idea of acting right. He thought about being and knowing, too, but these issues weren't as important to him as one's relationships with other people and the world as a whole. That's one reason for starting with him in this chapter.

Good Harmony

Confucius taught that the most important thing about acting was what he called "harmony." If your actions are in harmony with the rest of society, then they are moral actions and you are a good person. Society, to Confucius, is like music. All the different parts should work together.

Philoso-Fact
Confucius has been widely revered as a religious figure like Moses, Jesus, Mohammed, or Buddha, even though his philosophy is strictly secular in the sense that it makes practical recommendations for behavior without referring to God or an afterlife.

According to Confucius, whether your actions fit in with society depends on what everyone else is doing. You are not alone, but are deeply connected to your group. Other people, then, determine how you should act. For Confucius, it is terribly important to fit in, no matter who you are.

Confucius also recognized, though, that people can fill various roles in society. Not only did people perform different jobs, but some people were more important than others in making society work harmoniously. When Confucius taught that we should act in harmony with society, he was thinking of a society that is hierarchical—a society in which people occupy different levels of importance, from the peasant farmers to the rulers.

For a peasant to act like a ruler would make for an inharmonious situation, sort of like if the drummer in an orchestra tried to play the part of the violinist, or the trumpet player stopped playing and began conducting. Acting right, then, depends on how you fit in with the rest of the group. By understanding how your group works, you can figure out how to "play your part."

The "We" Culture

Confucian philosophy, with its emphasis on social harmony, has been tremendously influential for centuries. The belief that social harmony is more important than individual desires is at work in many Asian cultures today. This belief helps explain the success of communism in China. It also helps explain the focus on teamwork found in Japanese auto manufacturing companies.

This is not to say that all Asians read Confucius. But Confucius' ideas are in step with a broad spectrum of Eastern culture, just as Judeo-Christianity plays a major role in Western thinking, even for people who don't consider themselves religious.

In general, traditional Western philosophy has focused less heavily than Eastern thought on society for its own sake. Western thought tends to be more preoccupied with the individual. As a result, people in the West tend to be more *individualistic*; they tend to think about themselves as free, independent individuals rather than as holding sharply defined social positions. People in the East, on the other hand, are more *collectivistic* in general; they tend to think of themselves in terms of their relationships with others. (See Chapter 10 for more on Confucius.)

A number of philosophers have thought about individualism. One of them is the 19th century French political philosopher, Alexis de Tocqueville. De Tocqueville said that individualism is especially prominent in the United States where there is a democratic political system.

> **Lexicon**
> **Individualism** is the view that individual rights and freedoms should form the basis of society. **Collectivism** is the view that the stability of society is more important than individual rights and freedoms.

Democratic values like "freedom" and "equality" reflect Western individualism. These values suggest that people should be able to do what they want and not worry too much about what society expects them to do. This means they don't try to look to other people to figure out how to "play their part," but instead look inside themselves to find what they want. They also look at rules that they think should apply equally to everybody.

Me First

The downside of individualism is that individualists sometimes forget how important other people are in their lives. We all need help from other people whether we realize it or not, even if we think we are independent. Say, for example, a person becomes successful partly because of opportunities resulting from personal connections. If this person is an individualist, he or she is likely to overlook the social connections involved and take the full credit for his or her success.

Not only might this person be ungrateful, he or she is likely to be unsympathetic toward people who don't have the right connections themselves. Individualists tend to look at those who are unsuccessful as being at fault for their lack of success. When they see a homeless or an unemployed person, they don't say to themselves, "That person needs more help,"—they say "That person should have tried harder to succeed."

Wisdom at Work
Use **individualism** (if you don't already) to explain why you are so great and to account for all the good things that have ever happened to you. Say it isn't just that you happened to be in the right place at the right time, but that you have the special qualities of grit and determination that got you where you are today.

This is only one of the problems with individualism. Another is that it encourages people to be competitive rather than cooperative. Individualists tend to be out for themselves, often at the expense of others.

Still, this doesn't mean that it's always better to emphasize the good of society over the good of the individual. In China there is a serious problem with people being exploited—made to work long, hard hours for very little pay. The state benefits from their efforts, but is it worth living in a state like this where the same thing could happen to you? Would you want to live in a society in which you had to sacrifice your freedom for the good of the state?

Why I'm So Important

A number of factors have promoted individualism in the West over the centuries:

➤ Western religion focuses on the *individual's* relationship to God.

➤ Western philosophy from Plato to the 17th century focuses on the *individual's* relationship to ideal truths.

➤ Western science has largely focused on the *individual's* relationship to physical laws of nature.

➤ Western capitalism has focused on the *individual* as an economic unit.

➤ American democracy sees all individuals as equal and free rather than connected to each other in any specific way.

All these things work together as a set of blinders that keep people from seeing the importance of society for its own sake.

Religion's Part in Individualism

Western individualism has partly to do with the influence of the major Western religions and their emphasis on the individual's relationship with God. By stressing the importance of the individual's responsibilities to God, Western religion has downplayed the role of society.

In fact, society is seen as a bad thing in many stories in the Bible. Egyptian society enslaved the Israelites. Then, during their exodus, the Israelites set up a bad society centered around a false god and were punished. Society in the cities of Sodom and Gomorrah were so evil that these towns were destroyed by the hand of God.

Religious dissatisfaction with society and its teachings didn't stop there. Jesus criticized the Pharisees and the Philistines who relied too heavily on conventional thinking and focused "on the letter of the law" rather than on its spirit. He also warned that family ties could get in the way of finding the right path.

Centuries later, the Christian bishops in Constantinople rejected the directives of the Church in Rome and split off to form the Eastern Orthodox Church. Later still, the Protestants split off from the Church, believing that it had lost touch with God's intentions. The point is that when ways of thinking become conventional, people in the West often react against the convention by stressing the importance of the individual.

REALITY ✓

Reality Check

Westerners aren't completely individualistic. There are plenty of people in the Western world who believe that strong communal ties are more important than individual accomplishment, including Amish communities and some big Italian families.

Later, many philosophers came to feel that religion in general exerted social pressures that enslaved people's minds. All this suggests that it's always possible to find things wrong with the ideas that hold society together. For centuries, religious thinkers and other philosophers in the West have tried to find a solution to human problems by looking beyond society—at God, at the natural world, and at the individual.

Truth and Me

Western individualism also has to do with the tendency in lots of Western philosophy to focus on *being* first, and *acting* second.

When Plato and his followers, for example, thought about how people should relate to each other, they used their ideal notions of the world as a measuring stick for behavior. Ideas about God can have the same effect on individualism as ideas about being. If you believe you are, first and foremost, accountable to God or to an ideal reality for your actions, then you will be less likely to focus directly on how your actions effect other people. St. Thomas Aquinas is one religious philosopher who emphasized the dependency of human action not on society but on divine truth.

Philoso-Fact
St. Thomas Aquinas said, "Human law is law only by virtue of its accordance with right reason, and by this it is clear that it flows from Eternal law. In so far as it deviates from right reason, it is called an unjust law and in such a case, it is no law at all, but rather an assertion of violence."

Aquinas's words suggest that the "eternal laws" and the "right reason" that determine how people should act exist independently of human society. People who think this way do not consciously look to others for clues about how they should act, but look instead to their own ideals.

Science and Me

Eventually, the philosophical views of Plato and Aquinas gave way to a more scientific, empirical way of thinking, while the seeds of individualism continued to grow. Empirical science has helped to promote individualism in the West by marginalizing the role of society and spotlighting the individual. Science replaces the divine, eternal laws described by Aquinas with natural, physical laws. These laws are supposed to be understood "objectively"—independently of society and of the people who make it up.

Capitalism and Me

Finally, the economic practice known as capitalism—buying and selling stuff in a free, open market—also promotes individualism. Before capitalism, people filled pre-established roles in a feudal society. What you did depended on what your parents did, and you inherited their station in life as well as their possessions. There was almost no social mobility.

> **Philoso-Fact**
> In the Middle Ages, the word **estate** used to mean not only your property but what you did for a living. During feudal times it was unusual for people to change their estate, which they inherited from their parents.

In a capitalist society, anyone can make money by buying and selling things or services, so there is a lot of social mobility—people can improve their situation as individuals or lose what they had to begin with more easily than in collective economic systems. The fact that most people in the West have to go out and make money for their livelihood has encouraged them to think of themselves as independent, free individuals.

All these ideas behind the philosophy of individualism have influenced Western culture in its thinking about how to act. They help explain why so many Westerners believe that each person should pretty much take care of him- or herself and leave everyone else to take care of themselves in turn. Individualism, though, is not the only kind of Western philosophy. What's more, there is room even within individualism for many different philosophies about how to act.

Philosopher See, Philosopher Do

The choice between individualism and collectivism has a lot to do how you feel about social convention. Confucius believed social convention was vitally important. He associated it with what he called *the Tao*, or "the way." Other philosophers have come up with a variety of attitudes toward the issue.

Is social convention helpful or harmful? Here are different ways philosophers recommend dealing with the question.

➤ **Confucius** Follow it for the sake of a harmonious society.

➤ **Plato** Figure out whether it corresponds to ideal forms of virtue.

- ➤ **Descartes and the rationalists** Disregard it and obey reason.
- ➤ **Locke and the empiricists** Agree to follow it in order to avoid trouble.
- ➤ **Kant and the idealists** Obey the one true convention, namely, treat others as you want to be treated.
- ➤ **Kierkegaard and the existentialists** Look through it to the real you.
- ➤ **Marx** Figure out how it promotes the forces of production and rebel against it.
- ➤ **Foucault and the post-structuralists** Keep struggling with it; there's no way to escape its power.

So far we've looked at some key issues within the three main branches of philosophy in order to get an overview. The remaining chapters talk about particular philosophies—from ancient Greece, India, and China up to the present.

The Least You Need to Know

- ➤ Confucius based his ethical philosophy on the idea of harmony.
- ➤ People of the East tend to be more collectivistic than Westerners, who tend to be more individualistic.
- ➤ In the West, religion, philosophy, science, capitalism, and democracy have all promoted individualism.

Part 2
Ancient and Medieval Philosophy

The roots of Western philosophy are in ancient Greece, where changing, more complicated times gave rise to new ways of thinking about reality. First came the pre-Socratics who blended science with mysticism. Then came the Sophists who defined "wisdom" in terms of self-interest. In reaction to these spin doctors came Socrates who sought moral truth. Then came the great systematic thinkers, Plato and Aristotle.

These philosophers gave rise to the Hellenistic Age, a period when the influence of ancient Greek thinking was felt all around the Mediterranean and beyond. Philosophy became more structured and dogmatic—a way of life for many people, including the Stoics, the Epicureans, and the Skeptics.

In the period following the Hellenistic age, philosophy came into contact with the great Western religions, and the Middle Ages got under way. Neoplatonism—a blend of Plato, Aristotle, and religion—dominated philosophical thinking for centuries. Original religious thinkers like St. Augustine and St. Thomas Aquinas continued to modify the Greek influence. Science, religion, and philosophy went hand in hand.

But eventually, philosophers began to question the authority of the ancient philosophers and the religious thinkers who had adapted their ideas. A new humanism sprang up that paved the way for the modern age and the rise of empirical science.

Chapter 5

Golden Oldies

In This Chapter

➤ What the world is made of; the pre-Socratics

➤ How philosophy can go wrong; the sophists

➤ Reconciling knowledge and morality; Socrates

It was a long time ago when people first realized that wisdom—knowledge of what life is and how it should be lived—is something that needs to be worked at and developed. Although the first philosophers came up with a lot of ideas that we now know are untrue, they deserve a lot of credit for figuring out that wisdom doesn't just happen; you have to work at it.

These days, it's easy to overlook the importance of figuring out whether we're doing the right thing and seeing things the way they really are. When enough people realize this and try to do something about it, the result is philosophy. This happened for the first time in Milesia during the 6th century B.C.

Many of these early philosophers had heard legends about a golden age long ago when life was better. They wanted to bring that golden age back again. Others simply wanted to make gold for their own use and used wisdom as an easy way to do it. You've most likely heard some of the names of these philosophers of ancient Greece. Remember Pythagorus? The sophists? Socrates?

Their ideas for how to live took different forms. Some believed in seeking the truth by isolating themselves from society. Others thought that working with society was the way to go. Still others claimed that the answer was to make society fit in with an idealized vision of reality that united people, nature, and an unseen perfect world.

It's Not About Us

The first philosophers in ancient Greece thought about the world in a much different way than the mythmakers and story-tellers before them. The mythmakers, the epic poets, and the dramatists who preceded the philosophers saw people as the center of reality. Not only were the Greek gods very much like people themselves, but they were keenly interested in what people were doing. It was as if reality were set up with people explicitly in mind. The world was a place for human beings to have adventures and meet the challenges of survival.

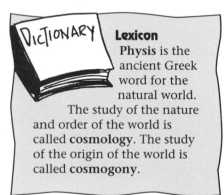

Wisdom at Work
Use the idea that reality isn't centered around people to see why there are so many disgusting things in the world like cockroaches, slime mold, leeches, viruses, bacteria, and TV commercials.

Lexicon
Physis is the ancient Greek word for the natural world. The study of the nature and order of the world is called **cosmology**. The study of the origin of the world is called **cosmogony**.

The first philosophers in ancient Greece, on the other hand, thought about the world in a new way. Their ideas show that they didn't think reality was necessarily centered around human beings. For them, people were just a small piece of the pie. These philosophers were interested in what the natural world is made of and how it works. They called this natural world *physis*, a term that gives its meaning to our word *physical*.

These first philosophers expanded their view of the world and began to think about it in a new way. The world for them was not primarily a place in which to travel, make war, fall in love, and build civilizations; rather the world became a source of questions: What is the world made of? How does it physically work? How did it come into being?

The early study of physis, the world, consisted of two areas: *cosmology* and *cosmogony*. Cosmology is the study of what the world is made of and how it is ordered. Cosmogony is the study of the origins of the world.

Earth, Wind, and Fire

These ancient Milesian philosophers proposed cosmologies and cosmogonies that had little to do with the daily lives of people. Thales said that the world is based on water. Water, in other words, is the source of all things; reality flows out of water. Thales speculated that the water has always been there and always will be. In fact, it seems that none of the first Greek philosophers thought much about the idea of creation. They didn't believe that reality ever had a beginning.

Heraclitus said the world was made of fire. Everything is essentially burning, just not necessarily as brightly or rapidly as actual fire. This burning involves a conflict of forms with their opposites. The result of this conflict is a state of impermanence; everything changes constantly. This idea of constant flux is an example of how Heraclitus left people out of the center of his philosophy. People are just forms that come and go like all other forms, made up of opposed forces that burn themselves out sooner or later. And then there was Anaximenes, who claimed the world was made of air.

Many of the pre-Socratic philosophers are referred to as *monists*. This means they believe the universe is essentially all one thing—it's all the same stuff.

Here are the different cosmologies put forward by the ancient Greek monists:

Wisdom at Work
Question: How many monists does it take to screw in a light bulb?

Answer: There's just one, stupid!

> **Thales**   The world is made of water.
>
> **Anaximander**   The world is made of substance called *apeiron*, which produces the basic elements of earth, air, water, and fire.
>
> **Anaximenes**   The world is made of air.
>
> **Pythagoras**   The world is an embodiment of numbers.
>
> **Heraclitus**   The world is made of fire.

Lexicon
The belief that the natural world is all connected into a single whole is known as **monism**. The belief that the world is made up of lots of separate, independent things is known as **pluralism**.

The Math and Music Man

Ancient philosophers found additional ways of thinking about the world as a place that is not centered around people. One of the most important pre-Socratic philosophers was Pythagoras, who taught that reality is based on numbers. He believed that numbers had a kind of magical power to shape reality.

Pythagoras was a brilliant mathematician as well as a philosopher. He is well known for having discovered the Pythagorean theorem, the geometric rule that says when you square two sides of a right triangle and add them together you get the square of the third side, the hypotenuse. He also discovered that harmonies can be made by plucking harp strings whose lengths are simple ratios of one another. For example, a string makes a fundamental harmony when it is plucked together with a string that is one third as long, or two thirds, or one quarter as long.

Pythagoras believed that the stars were arranged in a way that reflected this relationship between harmony and numbers. He said that they made music when they moved, and he called this "music of the spheres." He couldn't prove his theory, though, because this music cannot be heard by human ears!

Who's a Monkey's Uncle?

Pythagoras had a devoted following. In fact, he was something of a cult leader. His teaching and the activities of his students were kept secret from everyone else. If his students gave away any secret knowledge, they could be punished. It is said that he drowned one of his students for revealing the secret of irrational numbers to the outside world.

Philoso-Fact
Pythagoras' students followed strict rules. For one thing, they couldn't eat meat. This was because Pythagoras taught that when you die, your soul becomes reincarnated as another animal. Because we are spiritually connected to animals, he said, we shouldn't eat them.

Reincarnation is an example of how, for Pythagoras, human beings are only part of the big picture. Human souls can become non-human souls in the next life, so human beings aren't the only living thing of worth. Bugs and frogs and chipmunks are just as important.

Pythagorus shares this belief in reincarnation with Hindu philosophy from India. This belief reflects an understanding of people as intimately connected with both the natural and spiritual worlds.

Out of His Senses

Another philosopher who thought about the world in impersonal terms was Parmenides. He applied an impersonal attitude to thinking itself as well as to the rest of the world. Parmenides said that there is no difference between what people think and what actually exists. As a result, Parmenides believed that it made no sense to say something does not exist. He said everything exists, it always exists, and it never changes. Change is an illusion of the human senses.

Virtue's in the Eye of the Beholder

Although the first philosophers in ancient Greece focused on cosmology and other issues that were not directly related to people, it wasn't long before philosophers in Greece began concentrating on human-oriented ideas.

Democracy in Athens was gaining momentum and every free adult male was expected to participate in government. In Athens, the democratic system involved more participation and responsibility on the part of its citizens than American democracy today. Assemblies, consisting of large groups of the city's populace, frequently met to debate and decide courses of action. In this climate, in which many Greek citizens were expected to give great attention to society and political action, a group of philosophers emerged known as sophists. *Sophist* is the Greek word meaning *expert*.

The sophists were primarily interested in ideas that were politically useful. They thought about how people, acting as individuals, could best benefit themselves in their interactions with others. They believed that people should do whatever is necessary to be successful in life. This form of behavior, they thought, could be different for different people. In other words, the sophists did not believe in a natural set of rules for all of human behavior.

It's All Relative

The idea that different individuals and groups of people can have different standards for how to act is known as *relativism.* The sophists are widely regarded as the first relativist philosophers. One of them, known as Protagoras, said, "Man is the measure of all things." By this he probably meant that people decide what is true for themselves and act accordingly. It isn't nature that decides how people behave; rather, individuals themselves make these decisions.

Protagoras said we can't be sure about whether the gods exist. As a result, he believed people should do what they think is best for them without looking to a higher power. He saw human laws and nature as separate and basically unrelated things. Although this view was rejected throughout the Middle Ages, it anticipates modern empiricism.

The relativism taught by the sophists raised an important moral problem. If there was no set way that people should behave, what is to keep them from imposing their beliefs, priorities, and desires on others? How is the entire political system supposed to work if everyone is just looking out for himself? (Not herself—women did not participate in ancient Greek democracy.)

This relativism was especially significant since Athenians defended themselves whenever they were tried for wrongdoing. It was important to be able to persuade others by making things seem true, whether or not they were in fact true. Persuasion became more important than the truth. In fact, for all practical purposes, persuasion amounted to the same thing as truth.

Philoso-Fact
The sophists did not merely speculate on human behavior; they also acted on their beliefs. One of the sophists, Hippias, believed that people should be independent and see to their own needs. He demonstrated his own independence when he appeared at the Olympic Games dressed in clothes he had made himself. He even made the ring he wore!

Double Standard

Relativism, then, can pose a moral problem. It may lead to injustice and suffering. It can pose a logical problem as well, especially for teachers of philosophy, who may teach one set of rules for behavior and act according to completely different rules. This problem is known today as the *double standard*. The double standard is a form of hypocrisy in which what is supposed to hold true for everybody only holds true for some. The sophists in

Philoso-Fact
Protagoras' view that individuals will ally themselves with society willingly was restated in the 17th century by the English philosopher John Locke. Locke called this idea "the social contract." Locke said that society works when people agree to get along, regardless of what they actually believe.

ancient Greece were often guilty of holding double standards, teaching ideals of behavior that they did not live up to themselves, and finding tricky arguments to explain away their own behavior.

At the same time, though, many sophists did hold philosophical positions that made pretty good logical sense. Protagoras believed, for example, that individuals would recognize the advantages to being a member of society. Because they would be safer and more powerful as a group than as individuals, people would willingly curb their own selfish desires enough to cooperate with the rest of society. This is a logical way of saying that we can live with relativism. Things will balance themselves out because no one benefits by taking things too far—by being too greedy and selfish.

What's Fair is Fair—or Is It?

Not all the sophists, however, felt as Protagoras did. The sophist Thrasymachus believed that social order is imposed on everyone else by the people who have the most power. He said, "Justice is nothing else but the advantage of the stronger." By this he meant that those who are stronger than everyone else decide what they want "justice" to be in accord with their own preferences.

Wisdom at Work
Use relativism to explain why it's so hard to decide between two options. Should you become an insurance salesman or an environmental activist?—make money, or protect the planet? Different groups of people think different choices are good depending on their relative priorities. You can probably relate to both sets of priorities and that's what makes it so tough to decide between them.

Thrasymachus had a powerful and disturbing point. People who are in a position to make the rules tend to do so in a way that maintains their own advantages, making it hard for those who are already at a disadvantage to do anything about it. Disadvantaged people have to break the rules and risk punishment if they want to be better off. According to this view, there is no such thing as "fairness." Fairness is merely what the powerful want it to be.

This problem leads to additional difficulties. Even though "fairness" may not really exist, it is still influential, leading people to fool others—and themselves—into thinking they ought to act according to the idea of fairness. What's more, this can happen without people realizing it.

Here's an example of how power affects people's thinking: Suppose you grew up in a poor neighborhood. Because the people there have never had a say in government, they were never able to fight for their fair share of tax money to pay for good schools and other services. As a result, they weren't able to learn how to improve things. Suppose for some reason you are able to get a good education in spite of all this. Looking back, you'd be likely to blame the problems you grew up with on the people who live in your neighborhood, because your education is likely to have taught you that the people you grew up with don't know how to take care of themselves.

You would probably use your education to get a good job and move away. In turn, the people in your old neighborhood may resent you for selling out and turning your back on them. This may make you look at them as stupid or stubborn.

So, because you grew up in a poor neighborhood, you have to make a choice between doing what your neighbors think is fair and doing what the more wealthy, powerful, and educated people think is fair. In between these two versions of fairness there may be all kinds of room for double standards. If there is an absolute truth that doesn't simply reflect different people's points of view and economic interests, how can we tell what it is?

Politics as Usual

In general, the sophists did not believe in natural or divine standards of behavior, but thought that people should look out for themselves as individuals. At the same time, though, they were not afraid to say things that were to their personal advantage. As a result, history has given them a reputation as people whose wisdom cannot be trusted.

Of course, people who use knowledge to manipulate others for their own ends are not limited to the ancient Greek sophists. This is a problem that continues to play a big part in our society in present-day America. Today, specialists in many fields use their knowledge unfairly. There are lawyers who encourage people to say they've been injured in an accident in order to file law suits, mechanics who charge people for repairs they didn't do, doctors who overcharge for treatment; the list goes on and on.

> **Philoso-Fact**
> The sophists flourished under ancient Greek democracy, where the art of putting your own spin on things was an important skill to learn for every member of the polis, or city-state. In fact, our word politics comes from the ancient Greek word, *polis*.

Do politicians belong on this list of modern-day sophists? To a big extent, the rules of democracy allow them to pretend to do what's right for everybody while just looking to their own advantage. It's how democracy works. Politicians are supposed to look to their own interests—and to the interests of their constituents. It's their job. The only restraint placed on them is that they are supposed to follow rules that apply to everybody.

The tricky thing though, is that it's also their job to keep changing the rules in order to make their constituents happy. So they want to be as persuasive as they can, using ideas that people want to hear, whether they actually believe them or not. Of course, everybody knows this. We put up with it in the hope that the different positions will balance out into something we can all live with.

"Knowledge Is Virtue"

Not all philosophers believed that justice is just an empty word and that people are basically self-centered. Socrates, in particular, stands out as an opponent of sophistic thinking. In fact, he has been idealized for centuries as a wise and selfless seeker of the truth.

Socrates has even been seen as a kind of secular (non-religious) version of Jesus Christ because he was condemned for his teachings and, faced with the choice of death or renouncing his work, chose death. (Although Socrates won many devoted followers, most notably Plato, he also made enemies in high places.) His heroic decision has been memorialized by the famous neo-classic French painter, Jacques Louis David (*Dah-VEED*). In David's painting, *The Death of Socrates*, Socrates, bathed in sunlight, calmly accepts a cup of poisoned hemlock from a grief-stricken attendant and, facing his disciple Plato who sits at his feet, points to the sky as if to say, "The truth is up there!"

The Death of Socrates.

In fact, we know very little about the real Socrates. Moreover, we can't even be sure about what he said, since he never wrote any of his ideas down. What we know of him comes mostly from Plato, his student, who wrote down discussions between Socrates and many sophists and other Athenians. It's hard to say how accurate Plato's presentation of

Socrates is. There are times, though, when Plato seems to be putting words into Socrates's mouth in order to express his own ideas.

Socrates, a Pain in the Protagoras

Socrates is remembered not so much for what he said, but for how he taught. His famous *Socratic method* involved asking questions about what others thought. Through continued questioning, he was always able to poke holes in other people's ideas.

The Socratic method of teaching by asking questions involved an early form of what the Greeks called *dialectic*: talking about things and moving back and forth between points of view in order to see how well ideas hold up. As Aristotle pointed out years later, this method was the first systematic use of logic. Socrates was always looking for consistency or contradiction among propositions.

Philoso-Fact
According to legend, when someone asked the Delphic Oracle who the wisest man was, it answered Socrates. When Socrates learned of this, he went around asking people what they knew. He found that they all claimed to know things that, in fact, they didn't know. So Socrates concluded that he really was the wisest man, since he *knew* he knew nothing while everyone else mistakenly thought they knew something.

Socrates's interest in definitions was not simply logical; it was moral as well. This was particularly significant in discussions he had with the sophists, since he exposed their pretenses for what they were. He got them to say one thing about a concept as it applies to a particular situation, and then got them to say the opposite thing about the same concept in connection with a different situation. In this way, he exposed their double standards.

Rebuilding Knowledge

It's sometimes said of Socrates that his philosophy is more about tearing down other people's ideas than putting up ideas of his own. After he got done with the sophists, in other words, philosophy became a big empty space waiting for Plato to come along and fill up.

Even so, Socrates left a good foundation for Plato to build on. He drew attention to the importance of logic and dialectic and consistency of terms. He also set a strong moral example, even dying for his philosophical cause.

Socrates, then, was not simply a philosophical wrecking ball, but a builder as well. He admired the craftsmen of Athens who made things and he looked to them as a model for what wisdom was. He saw wisdom as a practical skill that was related to the workings of nature. Unlike the sophists, he believed that human law should be dependent on natural reality. He also believed that it took a special skill to be able to make good laws. He saw politics as an art to be practiced by those who knew how to do it right, and felt that those who did not know should keep out of it. He wasn't happy with democracy.

Reality Check

Socrates is the most famous reality checker of all time. Here's a section from Plato's dialogue, *Protagoras*, in which he persuades Protagoras that he has been wrong in saying that courage can be due to ignorance:

"Then the ignorance of what is and is not dangerous is cowardice?"

He nodded assent.

"But surely courage," I said, "is opposed to cowardice."

"Yes."

"Then the wisdom which knows what are and are not dangers is opposed to the ignorance of them?"

To that again he nodded assent.

"And the ignorance of them is cowardice?"

To that he very reluctantly nodded assent.

"And the knowledge of that which is and is not dangerous is courage, and is opposed to the ignorance of these things?"

At this point, he would no longer assent, but was silent.

"And why do you neither assent nor dissent, Protagoras?"

"Finish the argument for yourself."

The Least You Need to Know

➤ The pre-Socratics were the first philosophers in ancient Greece. They proposed theories about the nature of the universe (*cosmologies*) and about its origins (*cosmogonies*).

➤ The pre-Socratics were not especially interested in people and how we should act. The sophists, on the other hand, were keenly interested in people.

➤ The sophists were philosophers interested in using knowledge to their own advantage. They tended to believe that truth and virtue are whatever people make of them (*relativism*).

➤ Socrates became famous for getting people to think more carefully about their ideas of virtue. He was seen as a threat to society and chose to die rather than renounce his beliefs.

Chapter 6

The Philosopher King

In This Chapter

➤ Why you should know about Plato

➤ Plato's ideal reality

➤ How we know ideal forms

➤ Plato's ideal government

What's so great about Plato? Along with Aristotle (who you'll read about in the next chapter), he's the most important of the ancient philosophers. As a matter or fact, the English philosopher Alfred North Whitehead characterized the entire history of Western philosophy since the ancient Greeks as just "a footnote to Plato." Plato, who lived in ancient Greece from 428–347 B.C., was the first philosopher to take all the main aspects of philosophy—being, knowing, and acting—and put them together in one coherent system.

Being is especially important to Plato; he bases his whole philosophy on being, but he includes a complete set of ideas about knowing and acting too that make sense in light of his view of what being is. His ideas hang together logically, and he thought about a wide range of topics. What's more, Plato was an extremely talented writer. His works are clear and entertaining. Plato, then, is something of a king among philosophers. In fact, he believed that philosophers *should* be kings!

Politics' Loss Was Philosophy's Gain

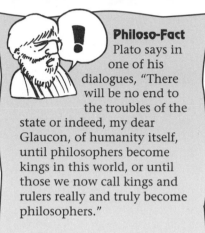

Philoso-Fact
Plato says in one of his dialogues, "There will be no end to the troubles of the state or indeed, my dear Glaucon, of humanity itself, until philosophers become kings in this world, or until those we now call kings and rulers really and truly become philosophers."

Plato

Plato was always trying to see the big picture, but as a young man he was especially interested in politics. Plato shifted away from politics, though, when he came to believe that politicians didn't think clearly enough about the proper relationship between political order and the ideal truth. He became especially disillusioned with politics when Socrates was forced to die. Even so, he remained hopeful that philosophy could have a positive influence on government.

Socrates was a major influence on Plato's thinking, but not the only one. He was especially impressed by math, and by geometry in particular, and hoped that he could find ways of making all philosophy as reliable as geometric principles. He was also influenced by the political order of the Egyptians. He visited Egypt while traveling after Socrates' death and admired the stability of Egyptian government.

Plato hoped that philosophy would come to play a strong part in government. In fact, he tried to use philosophy to influence government during his travels to Sicily, where he was visiting a friend whose cousin was a dictator of Syracuse. He tried to teach the young dictator philosophy and geometry, hoping to help make him a better ruler, but was unsuccessful. The dictator and his cousin, Plato's friend, became enemies and Plato's friend was eventually killed.

Philosophy Through Dialogue

After returning to Greece, Plato founded an important school known as the Academy, which is said to be the first university. He taught at the Academy for the rest of his life, and wrote a lot of philosophy in over two dozen works called "dialogues," which present his ideas in the form of discussions among his friends.

Plato's dialogues are important in the way they present his philosophy. Rather than say, "Here is what I think," Plato presented his ideas in the form of discussions of philosophical topics between two or more people. Socrates is the leading figure in most of the dialogues.

The dialogue form makes Plato's philosophy storylike. Although ideas themselves are of central importance, the characters of the people talking also enter in. And Socrates often raises particular philosophical issues with people who have a personal interest in those issues. For example, he discusses bravery with someone who prides himself on his courage, or piety with someone who thinks of himself as especially pious.

Not only are the characters of those who talk relevant to the ideas being discussed, but sometimes the setting and situation of the dialogues have dramatic significance. Socrates and those he talks to may be in the city surrounded by lots of people, or walking in the countryside, in the Academy, or in prison. The dialogue form, then, provides a way of showing how the ideas Plato talks about relate to the lives people actually lead.

Philoso-Fact
"Plato" is actually a nickname meaning "broad-shouldered one." His original name was Aristocles.

What's the Big Idea?

A key aspect of Plato's thinking is the idea of the *idea*. Ideas for Plato are not just notions that pop into people's minds that get them to do nutty things like have the couch reupholstered in pink leopard fur. Ideas for Plato really exist in a world of their own. Ideas are *forms* that give their shape to ordinary reality. What's more, they are always right. It's the physical world—the world of becoming—that can be mistaken.

Of course, for most of us, it's just the other way around. The physical world is always right but ideas tend to lose touch with the truth. The pink leopard fur on the couch is just what it's supposed to be; it's the idea that was a big mistake.

Wisdom at Work
Perhaps you have felt the same way as Plato about ideas. Have you ever had an idea that you knew was a good one even though it didn't work out as you had expected? Plato would have said that your idea exists in an ideal realm of being, a world that is too perfect for this fickle world we call reality.

Finding the Ideal

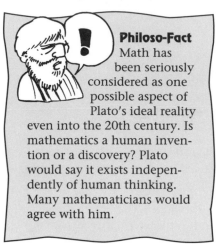

Philoso-Fact
Math has been seriously considered as one possible aspect of Plato's ideal reality even into the 20th century. Is mathematics a human invention or a discovery? Plato would say it exists independently of human thinking. Many mathematicians would agree with him.

Because he places ideas above the changing world of things, Plato is often called a rationalist—someone who believes we can know true ideas without ever learning them from experience. Just because we *can* know the truth, though, doesn't mean we necessarily do know the truth. In fact, because physical reality isn't the basis of truth for Plato, this truth can be a real challenge to discover.

The difficult task of the philosopher, according to Plato, is to figure out what this ideal world is like and to teach others to recognize it and to regulate their lives and thoughts in accordance with it. These tasks are difficult for a couple of reasons. First, it's hard to see the ideal world for what it is; second, it's hard to act in keeping with its perfection.

Understanding the Ideal World

Not everyone would agree with Plato that there is an ideal reality. In fact, Plato came up with this concept in reaction to the sophists who were spreading the notion that truth is whatever you make it. Plato defied these relativists, arguing that right and wrong are different things and we need to figure out what they are.

So how can we tell? If the ideal world is not actually physical, how do we know it's there? Two ways, said Plato: one way is logical, the other, intuitive.

It's Logical

The logical way of figuring out what the ideal world is like picks up on Socrates' work of examining concepts dialectically in order to make sure they get used correctly. We need to ask what one particular example of a concept has in common with all the other examples. Take, for example, courage. Is it just a word or is there really a thing called courage that some people have?

To answer this question, Plato looked at specific examples of courageous acts. By thinking about what these examples have in common, says Plato, we can understand the idea of courage as it always is, apart from specific, changing situations. This universal idea of courage is the true courage, according to Plato, the kind that exists regardless of the situation, without being influenced by other considerations.

To Plato, the *idea* of courage is the universal characteristic that all specific instances of courage have in common. By looking at particular examples, you can figure out the general idea which, for Plato, is true. This logical process is known as *induction*. Induction, as you saw in Chapter 3, is the logical process of working from particulars to generalities.

Through induction, you can find the nature of universals, ideas that hold true, no matter what the situation.

Notice that Plato's view is only one way of looking at courage. You could say instead that there is no such thing as courage except as an idea people have invented in order to get certain kinds of people to act in a certain way. The idea of courage has a practical use: it gets soldiers to fight well and it keeps them from complaining about things that scare them. It does this in effect by rewarding them for conquering their fear. Everyone knows war is scary. If you have to go to war anyway and you put up with your fear, people will compensate you with praise by saying you have courage.

This is the difference between Plato's *ideas* and Marx's *ideology*. Ideas are true and really exist. Ideology is invented to get people to behave in certain ways.

REALITY ✓

Reality Check

Plato said that philosophers would make the best kings. One reason for this is that real philosophers are more interested in the truth than in their own importance. Is this idea true, or merely an expression of Plato's unrecognized desire to be important?

I Think, Therefore It Is

Plato connects his ideas about how people should act not simply to his view of how society should work, but to his view of reality in general. He said that universal ideas are the source of the physical world and the things that happen in it. Visible reality *emanates*, or comes from, the ideal world. This idea leads to the second way of figuring out what the ideal world is like, the *intuitive* way. What this means, quite simply, is that the ideal world *thinks* the physical world into shape.

The Light at the End of the Tunnel

To illustrate how this works, Plato made up a little story known as the parable of the cave. A parable is a story that has to be interpreted for its unstated meaning. The parable appears in Plato's famous dialogue, *The Republic*, where Plato has Socrates tell it to a group of young men who want to hear his ideas about the education of a ruler.

Socrates says to imagine a cave in which prisoners have been chained since early childhood by some nasty ogre. Their heads are propped so they can only

Philoso-Fact
Plato frequently included myths and parables in his dialogues to illustrate his ideas. They show that understanding the truth can be a challenge, requiring us to think about things in new and strange ways.

look one way—at a wall of the cave. There's a humongous fire burning behind the prisoners, and between them and the fire there are people walking back and forth, carrying things.

The prisoners, because they're facing the other way, cannot see the fire, the people, or the things they are carrying. They can only see shadows of these things on the wall, cast by the firelight. Socrates says that these prisoners would probably imagine that the shadows on the wall of the cave were real things.

Imagine how a prisoner would feel if he were taken out of his chains and shown the fire and things the people were carrying. Socrates said that he would think that the unfamiliar things were imaginary, since he would be used to the shadows that he believed were real. What's more, the fire would hurt his eyes and he would turn away from it.

Now imagine the prisoner being taken outside into the light of day. Wow, is the light bright! If this poor prisoner were made to look directly at the sun, which, says Socrates, is the source of all things, his eyes would hurt and he wouldn't know what he was seeing.

Wisdom at Work
Use Plato's idea that the world of appearances is illusory to explain why you have no clue what's going on. If someone asks you what happened at a meeting you slept through, say "These passing shadows we call reality provide only the merest hints of an invisible truth."

The point of this story is to show how hard it is to understand ideal reality. The shadows on the wall of the cave are like the representations of things. A picture of something or a reflection of something is not the thing itself, although we might believe it to be. Similarly, the shadows in the cave are not the things that cast the shadow, although they may help us figure out what these things are.

These things—the things being carried around in the cave—are like the things of our ordinary experience. The world outside the cave represents the ideal world of forms. They can be hard to see if you are used to the dim light of the cave. The sun represents the ideal form of goodness itself. It is the source of everything, but it's hard to look at directly, even though it's what gives everything life and makes everything visible.

Here's a likely interpretation of Plato's parable of the cave:

➤ Shadows on the wall stand for echoes, perceptions, reflections, and other images.

➤ Things being carried around in the cave stand for things in the physical world.

➤ Things outside the cave stand for ideal forms.

➤ The sun stands for the ideal form of all goodness.

The parable of the cave suggests that it can be difficult understanding ideal reality because we get accustomed to thinking that apparent reality is all there is. To be a philosopher and learn to do the right thing in any situation, you need to see through appearances and act according to the ideal truth.

Remembering Truth

Plato had still more to say about how we can understand ideal reality through intuition. He said that we are all born with an understanding of ideal reality. The problem is, most of us forget what we were born knowing because we get fooled by the appearances of things.

Although we may forget ideal reality, we can sometimes remember it again. Plato called this process of remembering *anamnesis*. Anamnesis explains how we can know things even if we have never experienced them.

Wisdom at Work
Use Plato's concept of **anamnesis** (recollection of what we knew before we were born) to explain why you don't like something you've never tried. It's how you already know you do not like mountain oysters even though you've never had them.

Immortal Souls

To prove anamnesis really works, Plato told this story: Socrates asked a young Greek slave what he knew about geometry. "Not much," was the reply. Socrates then gave him a mini-geometry quiz, and he got a big fat 0 on it. Socrates next had the slave draw lines in the sand with a stick. The lines represented the geometric forms Socrates was asking about. After working through a series of questions, guess what? The slave was able to correctly answer Socrates' original questions.

Plato says this shows that we know things that we have never experienced and can remember them if we think about them clearly. This is proof that the human soul is immortal. The thinking goes that we must have existed in some form prior to this life if we are able to understand things that we've never actually learned about. This idea went a long way with the neo-platonic religious philosophers of the Middle Ages; they loved it.

The True Sciences

Plato applied his ideal reality to a number of different subjects. The true sciences, he said, are arithmetic, geometry, astronomy, and music because they only involve figuring out ideal relationships; their purpose is not to be practical. Studying these things teaches us about form and doesn't confuse us with questions like how much things cost or who has the most influence, or how you can come out ahead. These sciences are the proper study of the philosopher king, revealing the most about the ideal goodness—their perfect, unchanging source.

Philoso-Fact
Plato was not the first to say, "I'm trying to think, don't confuse me with facts," but he would have been able to relate to this statement.

Living Up to Perfection

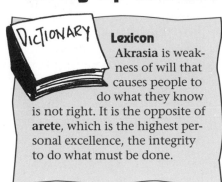

Lexicon
Akrasia is weakness of will that causes people to do what they know is not right. It is the opposite of **arete**, which is the highest personal excellence, the integrity to do what must be done.

Plato said that when people understand how they ought to behave but don't do it, they have a special kind of weakness he called *akrasia*. Akrasia is weakness of will that takes place when you give in to your short-term, selfish desires rather than doing what you know is right.

Philosophers need to guard not only against ignorance, but against akrasia. Doing so makes them special people, fit to rule others who are naturally more ignorant and weak willed. They must possess the quality Plato called *arete*—the integrity and strength of character to behave in accordance with ideal goodness.

The Republic—Plato's Paradise

Plato believed that not everyone has equal amounts of akrasia and arete. Some people are just better than others. Plato took this idea of natural inequality when he wrote his famous dialogue, *The Republic*, which includes his recommendations for what the ideal government should be like.

If everyone were equally virtuous, there would be no need for government; people would be able to govern themselves. They would live in small groups and help each other voluntarily, making their own basic necessities and sharing them freely. People would recognize that material possessions serve no useful purpose beyond basic survival and they wouldn't want anything more. There would be no need for wealth, so there would be no greed or jealousy. In turn, there would be no need for an organized government, or for police or soldiers to protect people's material possessions. Sounds heavenly, doesn't it?

Rulers, Soldiers, and Tradespeople

The problem is, most people do not realize that the real truth and goodness is only to be found in ideal reality. Instead, most people want a lot of worldly possessions. Such desire leads to an imperfect society made up of special groups of people to make luxury items, doctors who will give them medicine when they make themselves sick by overindulging, and rulers and soldiers to protect their property from those who would try to take it from them.

In order to take care of all these needs, Plato theorized a republic divided into three classes of people: rulers, soldiers, and tradespeople. Just guess who get to be rulers? The philosophers, of course! They understand ideal reality—including truth, goodness and justice—most clearly, so they are in charge. Also they have the fewest selfish desires, not needing many material possessions. They don't even need to have families, since they regard everyone under their rule as part of their family, loving them all equally. Most important, they don't form special attachments; the rulers are guided in all things by their intellect.

Next come the soldiers. The soldiers, like the philosopher-kings, are unselfish and virtuous. All they want is to protect the state from outside hostility and inner conflict. Their characteristic virtue is courage.

That leaves everybody else to become tradespeople. The tradespeople are motivated mainly by their appetites. They may be more or less courageous or intelligent, but they don't have to be; it's their appetites, their desire to get material possessions, that make them good tradespeople. They can be as greedy as they want up to the point of causing trouble for others. At that point, the rulers and soldiers step in and make sure that no one gets either too rich or too poor.

Philoso-Fact
Plato said that we could think of the three classes of people in his republic as having souls made out of three different kinds of metal. The rulers' souls are made of gold, the soldiers' souls are of silver, and the tradespeoples', of iron or lead.

The three classes in Plato's republic correspond to the three main characteristics Plato saw in every individual: wisdom, courage, and appetite. Although people naturally have all of these characteristics, people have varying amounts of each one. So, people are tested when they are children to see whether they are naturally wise, courageous, or appetitive. Wise children are trained to become rulers, courageous children to become soldiers, and appetitive children to become tradespeople.

Better Than Democracy or Tyranny

The point of the republic is to promote maximum stability in government, given the characteristics of human nature as Plato understood it. It provides a theoretical alternative to the existing forms of government in Greece: democracy and tyranny. Plato was happy with neither of these forms. He believed that both of them let selfish people have too much power. Plato thought that philosophers should run things because they are unselfish and would look to the good of all people.

The Least You Need to Know

➤ Plato turned to philosophy when he was disillusioned with politics.

➤ Plato believed that the world of appearances is only a shadowy emanation of an ideal reality.

➤ We can come to know the ideal world of forms through inductive reasoning and by "remembering" what we've always known (*anamnesis*).

➤ In Plato's ideal republic, philosophers rule with the help of soldiers, keeping the tradespeople in line.

Chapter 7

A Sense of Purpose

In This Chapter

➤ Aristotle's view of change

➤ Aristotle's view of the Soul

➤ The logic of how things happen

➤ Why we should act in moderation

Throughout the Middle Ages and into the early modern period, Aristotle was referred to simply as "the philosopher," the most respected authority on almost everything. He wrote on all sorts of subjects including ethics, politics, physics, metaphysics, psychology, biology, logic, even literary criticism.

Aristotle's broad scope has a lot to do with his continued importance down through history. He had something to say about almost everything, so those who came later naturally looked back to him as the one who laid the foundations. What's more, his way of looking at various things enabled him to tie them all together and make them seem relevant to human existence.

Aristotle

Two factors in particular stand out in Aristotle's philosophy. One is his view that everything has its own purpose that is part of a larger purpose. His philosophy consists largely of trying to figure out what these purposes are and how they fit together.

Another key aspect of his thinking is his logic, the way he looks at words and gets them to do what he wants them to. He used his logic to separate truthful ideas from erroneous ones.

In these ways, Aristotle's sense of purpose helped him come up with new ideas and new ways of thinking about them. One of the most significant new ideas he came up with was his answer to the question many philosophers of his day had been wrestling with: how things change.

ARISTOTELES STAGIRITA·CLAR·OLYMP·105
*Magnus Aristoteles caufas exquirere rerum,
Sed quâ quâ naturae caufa fecunda patet.*

Bad Form

The two main aspects of physical reality for Aristotle are *substance* and *essence*. Substance is what everything is made out of, and essence is what everything actually is. To an extent, Aristotle's theory parallels Plato's ideas about the world of forms and the material world of appearances. Aristotle's substance is like Plato's material reality and his essence is something like Plato's forms. But there's a big difference.

Plato's theory of forms provided an answer to the question of how things got to be the way they are. He said that it wasn't matter, but an unchanging, invisible form that determines the shapes of all things. Aristotle, on the other hand, believed that form and matter do not exist separately from one another. Form exists *in* matter, or essence exists in substance. Form is not invisible and unchanging but an actual part of what things are. There is no ideal world of forms, only this world of visible, physical things. What you see is pretty much what you get.

Change Has Purpose

For Aristotle, change is not a bad thing. It does not show how imperfect the world of appearances are. Change is natural; it happens through the natural course of things. In fact, it is necessary in order for things to fulfill their potential.

The most important kind of change for Aristotle is determined by essence. The essence of something is what makes it what it is, as well as what it should become. The essence of an acorn makes it become an oak tree. The essence of a rock makes it sit there for eons until wind and rain crumble it to dust.

Philoso-Fact
Most philosophers abandoned the idea of a built-in purpose for humanity in the 19th century. This led the 20th century French existentialist philosopher Jean Paul Sartre to say, "Man is condemned to be free."

Change, then, for Aristotle, can have a purpose. This was a whole new way to think about change. Existence was actually getting somewhere. Philosophy was getting somewhere too, because Aristotle was doing more than others had done to explain how things are.

Aristotle's attitude toward change continued to influence philosophers and scientists for centuries, until the English scientist Charles Darwin came up with his theory of evolution through natural selection in the 19th century.

Changing Beliefs About Change

Look how Aristotle's attitude about change is different from his predecessors' and from Charles Darwin's, who was the first to really offer us a good alternative to Aristotle's views.

➤ **Heraclitus** Change is the natural result of things colliding with their opposites.
➤ **Parmenides** Change is illusory; it only looks like things change. In reality, everything is always the same.
➤ **Plato** Change shows how inferior things are to their unchanging, ideal forms.
➤ **Aristotle** Change can have a purpose. It happens when things become what they should be.
➤ **Darwin** Change occurs randomly, but changes may be passed along through natural selection.

Aristotle vs. Darwin

One of the main things that separates Aristotle from modern scientists is his idea of things having a purpose. Most scientists today see it as a mistake to talk about natural things as if they have a purpose.

We might say, as would Aristotle, that a bird has wings in order to fly. A scientist would say, though, that a bird's wings evolved through a series of random variations and mutations that turned out to be adaptive. This is Darwin's theory of evolution.

Imagine, for example, whatever sort of animal that evolved into a bird. Say it was a lizard with feathers but no wings. Over the centuries, thousands of these creatures were hatched, all with slightly different characteristics. Some had eyes that bugged out, others had feet with big warts on them, and so forth. If these variations helped the creatures survive, they got passed on to the next generation.

Eventually, feathered lizards were born that could flap their arms and get off the ground—not because they were supposed to, but just because this was one of a million random changes in the way these creatures were hatched. But, because they could flap themselves off the ground, they got to all the best food first and they escaped their enemies before their brothers and sisters who couldn't flap. The non-flappers died off, while the flapping lizards survived and gave birth to more flapping lizards. So, a scientist would say a bird has wings because of a lucky accident, not according to some plan.

Darwin's theory explains how life forms can change without a larger purpose behind it. Very simply, change occurs randomly. But natural selection determines which changes stick, that is, which become adaptive characteristics of a species. So, according to Darwin, there was no necessary purpose that caused human beings to evolve out of apes—it's just that human characteristics happened to be the ones that enabled our species to survive and reproduce under the particular environmental conditions we were up against.

Born to Think

Aristotle had no such conception of random, purposeless change. The whole world is made up of interrelated parts all joined with interrelated purposes. He saw people as part of this purposeful world, with their own particular purpose for being the way they are. He saw things as having a point to them, including human behavior. We were meant to be

> **Wisdom at Work**
> We can use Darwin's concept of adaptive change to explain changes in philosophical thought throughout the centuries, as well as the mutation of living species. Why was Aristotle's philosophy so influential for so long? Not because he was "right"; most people today would disagree with him. He was influential because his ideas were well adapted to the ways people live in society, where it helps to have a sense of purpose.

> **Wisdom at Work**
> Use Aristotle's idea that thinking has an essential human purpose as an excuse to slack off from work. Say, "I'm not goofing off, I'm thinking about things and by thinking I'm fulfilling my purpose as a rational creature."

the way we are, and we were meant to think. Reason, the ability to think about the world, has a purpose. And Aristotle believed that people should keep their purpose in mind as they lived their lives.

For Aristotle, thinking is something we were meant to do. It feels good to think. In fact, we were meant to be philosophers who appreciate the wonder and complexity of existence. It is part of being alive as people.

Natural Soul

Because of his special attitude toward human purpose, Aristotle's thinking is consistent with a lot of the religious thinking that came after him. In fact, religious thinkers relied heavily on Aristotle for centuries to come. But Aristotle's thinking was different from religious thinking in some important ways. For one thing, he didn't believe in an afterlife or the immortality of the soul. Like all living things—plants and animals—human beings have souls, he said, but they die with the body. So we'd better enjoy our dose of reality while it lasts.

Reality Check

The religious philosophers of the Middle Ages tended to ignore Aristotle's idea that the soul dies with the body. Although they revered him as an authority in most things, they held on to their belief in the immortality of the soul.

Our human soul enables us to reason. Reason, for Aristotle, is as organic a process as breathing and walking, and it can grow and develop just like our physical bodies. It's part of our biological nature. The soul, for Aristotle, is not separate from the body; it is an aspect of the body. Your soul *is* you; it makes you who and what you are. When you die, says Aristotle, your soul dies with you.

This fits in with the idea that, where living things are concerned, change can be a good thing if it is an aspect of development. This development has a purpose. When the development has achieved its purpose, it gives way so that new purposes can be achieved by other living things. Change for a purpose is natural and inevitable.

The idea of purpose is especially important in Aristotle's philosophy. Still, purpose is only one of Aristotle's explanations of change. In fact, Aristotle realized that change can be thought about in a number of ways, so he broke down the idea of change into a number of different parts. Taken together, these parts make up his view of causality.

Philosophy*

For a Good Cause

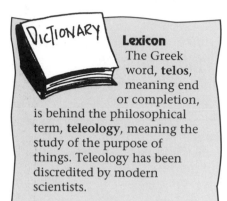

Lexicon
The Greek word, **telos**, meaning end or completion, is behind the philosophical term, **teleology**, meaning the study of the purpose of things. Teleology has been discredited by modern scientists.

Cause for Aristotle is not just what happens as a lead-up to an event; it is also a goal being realized, a sense of purpose. Aristotle called this sense of purpose a *telos*, the Greek word meaning "end." It's as if the outcome is already there ahead of time, pulling reality along with it.

So essence seemed like a good idea that could explain a lot about the way things are. But how can we tell the difference between a change that has a purpose—or is essential, in Aristotle's way of thinking—and one that isn't essential? Lightning could strike an oak tree, causing one of the limbs to fall off. That would be a different kind of change from the purposeful change that caused the oak to grow out of an acorn.

Why It Happened

To explain why things are the way they are and why they change, Aristotle identified four kinds of causes:

➤ **Material cause**: the matter or substance that things are made out of that allows change to take place

➤ **Efficient cause**: the event that precedes and leads to an outcome

➤ **Formal cause**: the internal, essential propulsion leading to change

➤ **Final cause**: the external end or purpose served by a change

What Aristotle did in describing cause in these ways was to identify all the ways we can think about why something happened. His approach to the problem is extremely logical, attempting to account for physical reality in terms of all possible explanations.

Reality Check

Some people think that Aristotle got carried away with his logical descriptions of physical reality. The early modern English empiricist philosopher, Francis Bacon, said that Aristotle "made his natural philosophy a mere bond-servant to his logic, thereby rendering it contentious and well nigh useless." Bacon meant that Aristotle was too concerned with logical possibility and not concerned enough with actual physical things and events.

Aristotle's Mental Breakdown

Aristotle had no tolerance for the logical tricks of the sophists, whom he felt were just playing with words. How did they play with words? To give you an example I could say, "Your mother is 50 years old. The woman who gave birth to you was only 25. Therefore, she could not have been your mother, but must have been some other woman."

To expose this kind of thinking as false logic, Aristotle divided up into categories all the different kinds of things we can say about something. One category refers to what a thing is. Another category refers to how old a thing is or how long it's been around. Aristotle would say that the reasoning about your mother confuses these categories. Saying what (or, in this case, who) your mother is, is different from saying how old she is. Each statement uses the concept of being in a different way.

Reality Check

The pre-Socratic philosopher Heraclitus said "You can't step in the same river twice." Aristotle would say he made a categorical mistake, confusing the set of facts that make the river a river with the particular water that happens to be coursing past. Heraclitus had a point, though. Not only water, but language—even categorical language   has a tendency to wash away into something else.

Aristotle's Categories

Aristotle divided everything up into ten categories. Since two of these have meaning only in ancient Greek, and I assume you don't know that language, here's a list of the eight remaining categories:

➤ **Kind:** What is a thing?
➤ **Quality:** What are its characteristics?
➤ **Quantity:** How many are there or how big is it?
➤ **Relation:** How does it relate to other things?
➤ **Location:** Where is it?
➤ **Time:** When is it or how old is it?
➤ **Action:** What is it doing?
➤ **Reception:** What is being done to it?

61

Aristotle wanted to break down all the different kinds of things it is possible to say about anything and keep them sorted out so people could better understand what they were talking about. He wanted to avoid the kinds of logical confusion the sophists were spreading around.

Aristotle's categories were all the rage in schools for centuries. If you wanted to be a scholar, you had to learn them and use them. These days, though, most philosophers agree that this kind of formal logic doesn't really tell us much about things. It relies more on how language works than on what things are really like. For example, how can we tell the difference between the category of kind and the category of quality? If you think about it, things get categorized into kinds because of the qualities they have.

Wisdom at Work
Use Aristotle's concept of categories whenever you want to miss the point of what someone is telling you. Say, "Your statement that I need to learn to be a more effective worker confuses the categories of *what* working is in itself with the *quality* you attribute to working."

Empiricists in the 17th century reacted against this kind of thinking and criticized Aristotle for imposing artificial categories on things. In complaining about his logic, they forgot a good deal about his contributions to philosophy in all areas. In fact, much of Aristotle's thinking made their way of thinking possible.

Aristotle's logical approach to reality resembles Plato's in that it brings ideas with it to reality that aren't, strictly speaking, there already. All the different ways we can *think* of change occurring are not necessarily the same as the change we actually *see* occurring. As in Plato, there is a tendency in Aristotle to run together the way we think and the things we think about.

Even so, Aristotle didn't rely on as much invisible, ideal explanations as did Plato. In some ways his thinking resembles that of a modern scientist because he made careful studies of living things, collecting specimens and observing their natures. In this respect he occupies a philosophical middle ground between Platonic idealism and what we now call modern science.

The Golden Mean

The greatest purpose people have, according to Aristotle, is to live life well. For him this involves using the virtues we were intended to use, including, chiefly, reason, but also courage, honesty, and moderation in pursuing pleasure. In fact, all these things are tied in with one another.

An important feature of Aristotle's ethics is that he recognized that too little or too much of anything could be bad. Every good thing, according to Aristotle, exists in between two bad things. This idea applies to enjoyment as well as to morally good behavior. In fact, for Aristotle, moral goodness and enjoyment of life are pretty much the same thing.

There is no reason for a good person to deny himself (again, Aristotle is focusing on men) anything he wants, just so long as he doesn't go overboard.

For Aristotle, then, what's bad is simply what's bad *for* you. When you do wrong, you're only hurting yourself here in this life. If you overindulge in physical pleasures your health will deteriorate. If you abuse power over other people, they will no longer respect you and you will suffer the consequences. On the other hand, if you can enjoy things in moderation, you will be happy. This, Aristotle would say, is your purpose as a human being.

This idea of avoiding extremes is known as the *golden mean*. A mean is a middle way or a medium degree. The golden mean is a rule that says you shouldn't do anything to excess.

Aristotle was not the first person to think of the golden mean. It has been attributed to King Cleobulus of Rhodes some 200 years before Aristotle. It was also made famous by the Roman poet Horace who helped make it popular down through the ages, especially among wealthy people.

In fact, Aristotle's ethics are especially appropriate for rich people who can have pretty much anything they want. They need to remember just what Aristotle tells them: don't get carried away with the things you like. It figures that most of Aristotle's students were well off; they're the only ones who had the time and money to study philosophy all day!

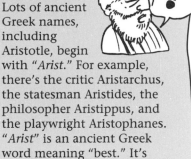

Philoso-Fact
Lots of ancient Greek names, including Aristotle, begin with "*Arist.*" For example, there's the critic Aristarchus, the statesman Aristides, the philosopher Aristippus, and the playwright Aristophanes. "*Arist*" is an ancient Greek word meaning "best." It's where we get the word "*aristocracy,*" meaning "rule of the best."

Wisdom at Work
Use Aristotle's concept of the golden mean to explain why it's actually good that you are mediocre at something. Say, "Of course I'm not an outstanding athlete. The whole purpose of athletics is ruined when it is taken to excess."

Aristotle also realized that how we act is an integral part of who we are. We can't simply *decide* how to be, we must *learn* how to be so that purposeful actions are second nature to us. The best way to lead the good life as Aristotle described it is to grow up learning how to live it so one can develop as a person, emotionally and intellectually as well as physically.

A Legacy Up for Grabs

Although Aristotle was perhaps the most influential philosopher ever, he may well have disapproved of much of what the future ages would do with his work. Because he was such a thorough and systematic thinker, he became an important authority on almost everything. As a result, people used his ideas in ways he never intended.

Followers of Plato wanted to believe that Plato and Aristotle agreed on the most important points, so they tended to ignore differences between the two. Religious philosophers wanted to think that Aristotle's ideas were in keeping with what they thought about God and the soul.

What's more, the universities of the Middle Ages got carried away with Aristotle's logic and used it as an answer for everything. As a result, the scientists of the 17th century blamed him for being a logic chopper even though their science was greatly indebted to him.

Because of all this, the real Aristotle is hard to see through the haze of time, in spite of—or because of—his tremendous importance as a philosopher.

The Least You Need to Know

➤ A key element of Aristotle's philosophy is his view of the purposeful nature of things. The study of purpose is known as *teleology*.

➤ Aristotle used his idea of purpose to explain the development of living things, including people.

➤ For Aristotle, the soul is not separate from the body; it ceases to exist when the body dies.

➤ Partly as a reaction against the sophists, Aristotle broke down the reason things happen (causality) and existence into logical categories.

➤ Aristotle advocated the *golden mean*, the idea that a moderate existence is the way to happiness.

Ancient Hardheads

In This Chapter

➤ How to cope with hard times

➤ The tough-guy approach: the stoics

➤ The feel-good approach: the Epicureans

➤ The who-knows? approach: the skeptics

Philosophy became increasingly important after Plato and Aristotle had made their mark. They helped give rise to the "Hellenistic age," a period when ancient Greek philosophy spread to all the countries surrounding the Mediterranean Sea during the time when Alexander the Great was conquering the entire area.

The spread of Greek philosophy benefited from the fact that people looked to it as a way of helping them live their lives. People wanted to be "wise" in order to know how to live. As a result, philosophy became more structured and dogmatic. Several different schools of philosophy arose for people to choose from.

The more important of these were *stoicism, Epicureans*, and *skepticism*. You're probably more familiar with these than you are with many other types of philosophy, not because these three are any more important to the Big Picture—they aren't—but because they've worked their way into our modern language.

These philosophies are less idealistic than those of Plato and Aristotle. They have less to do with figuring out cosmic truth than with coming to terms with the ups and downs of day-to-day life. The question is not "what is reality?" but "what's the best way to cope with reality?" Stoicism, Epicureans, and skepticism provide three different answers.

Who Cares?

Do you ever have good or bad things happen to you and not really care about them one way or another? You may be a stoic. Stoics accept that much is beyond our control. And since we can't control things, there's no sense getting all worked up about them.

Are you feeling sad? You're a jerk; stop wallowing in self-pity and get on with life. Or don't. It really doesn't matter.

That's stoicism. It originated around 300 B.C. in Greece with a philosopher named Zeno, who spread his ideas to his followers. They in turn spread them further, particularly in Rome where stoicism became especially popular. Some famous Roman stoics are Seneca, Epictetus, and Marcus Aurelius.

Wisdom at Work
Use stoicism to cope with anything unpleasant that you can't do anything about. If you get sick at the beginning of your vacation and have to spend the whole time in bed, say "That's the breaks."

In fact, stoicism has been so influential that it's still around today. You probably already know exactly what I'm talking about. You might even know a stoic individual or two. They put up with whatever comes along without complaining.

Stoicism is a philosophy for hard guys. The point, though, is not just to be macho, but to adopt a way of life that's appropriate for the unpleasant reality of things. Bad things happen, and we shouldn't let them get to us.

It's All in the Mind

In fact, Zeno and the other stoics noticed that a lot of the problems and hardships people undergo seem to disappear when they simply decide not to be bothered by them. Unhappiness, discomfort, and even pain are all in the mind. Block them out and it's as if they were never there. Even though you can't control what happens to you, you can control your attitude toward such events.

A famous example of this stoic attitude comes from Epictetus, a Roman slave, who was tortured by his master. Like all good stoics, Epictetus refused to groan under torture, but he also seemed not to feel the pain at all. He simply commented in an offhand way, "If you keep twisting my leg like that, you're sure to break it." And he was right, his leg did break. When he realized this, he said in the same tone of voice, "What did I tell you? It's broken."

People Are Scum

It's worth noting that Epictetus not only shrugged off an incredible amount of pain, he also put up with the fact that his master was a sadistic nut-case. In fact, stoics generally have a low opinion of people. They see most people as stupid, weak, sneaky, and selfish.

This is all the more reason for stoics to believe that whatever happens doesn't really matter. If you care about something, it only shows that you are weak and foolish, so you deserve the bad things that happen to you. If you're one of the few wise and deserving people around, then you know enough not to care what happens, so, again, it doesn't matter.

Reality Check

Some see stoicism as one of the main reasons people can be so nasty and screwed up. If you think you're not supposed to let out your feelings of sadness, they can come out later in the form of cruelty to others. Your mind tells itself, "I suffered, so others should have to suffer also!"

A Twist on Fate

Even if something does matter, the stoics believe that there isn't anything people can do about it. Fate determines all things. Ironically, though, stoic fatalism didn't mean that the stoics refused to accept responsibility for their actions. They believed that when you *can* take control of a situation you should. They were not trying to change fate, but to act in accordance with fate's decrees in living up to their responsibilities.

If they had a job to do, they just did it. And this is why stoics, like many others, were involved in trade, politics, and family life.

Philoso-Fact
Even though he was not a Christian, Seneca was supposed to have written letters to, and received letters from, the Christian apostle Paul. Because of his willingness to die for his principles, Seneca has been numbered among the Christian saints by St. Jerome, one of the church fathers.

This attitude had a significant influence on Roman law, which relied on people to carry out their assignments without playing favorites or showing pity to people who were to be punished. This rule applied even in the most extreme circumstances, for example, if you were told to kill yourself. Many stoics—including the Roman statesman and philosopher, Seneca—did just this.

Don't Worry, Be Happy

At about the same time that Zeno founded stoicism, another philosophy emerged in ancient Greece that, like stoicism, proposed a way of dealing with the idea that some people are scalawags and life can play dirty tricks. This philosophy is called *Epicureans*, named after the philosopher Epicurus.

Epicurus said that the point of life is to be happy. It's no big secret that indulging in bodily pleasures like eating, drinking, sex, and lying around on the couch are ways of being happy. In fact, these sorts of pleasures have come to be associated with Epicureans.

The association, though, between Epicurean philosophy and sensual pleasure that has developed over the centuries is a little misleading. Although the original Epicureans were certainly not opposed to sensual pleasure, they were more focused on avoiding pain.

Reality Check

Today an *epicure* is someone who appreciates fine food and drink. The original Epicureans, though, were not members of a gourmet society, but rather a school of philosophy interested in mental tranquility.

Why Suffer?

One reason that the Epicureans were misunderstood may be that they were in competition with other groups like the stoics and the Christians who disagreed with their beliefs. Compared to the rigors of stoicism and early Christianity, Epicureans might seem preoccupied with sensual pleasure, but this isn't the main point the Epicureans wanted to make.

In fact, the Epicureans noticed a problem with sensual pleasure: namely, that pain often goes along with it. Going after pleasure for its own sake doesn't always work out. Drinking a lot, for example, can be extremely pleasurable—at least for a short time. The morning after, though, can be an entirely different story.

Lexicon
In the years following Plato and Aristotle, much philosophy focused on achieving the goal of **ataraxia**, the Greek term for mental tranquility.

In avoiding pain, the Epicureans may seem to have completely different ideas about life from the stoics. In reality though, the two philosophies are not that far apart. Both of them recognize that the importance of pain depends a lot on your mindset. It's important to have the right attitude toward life in order to be at peace in your mind. The ancient Greeks called this inner peace *ataraxia*, the state of being detached from the cares of reality and at peace with yourself.

The Epicureans and, to some extent, the stoics, were interested in achieving ataraxia. The main difference between the two schools is that stoics were more concerned with living up to social responsibility while the Epicureans focused more on individual freedom.

Yes, the Epicureans wanted to avoid physical pain, but it doesn't take an especially deep philosophy to teach people to do that. What interested Epicurus and his followers in particular was the problem of avoiding *mental* pain. They believed that people unnecessarily suffered from mental pain because of their own beliefs. They saw peace of mind as philosophy's most important goal.

The Gods Make Us Crazy

Many people in and around ancient Greece believed that gods were watching over them, getting ready to punish them if they made a wrong move. Epicurus noticed that people could get pretty stressed out trying to figure out both what the gods wanted them to do and then actually doing it. He taught that the gods do not pay any attention to what people do, and so instead of worrying about what they want, we should enjoy life while we can. Superstitious beliefs, said Epicurus, cause needless suffering.

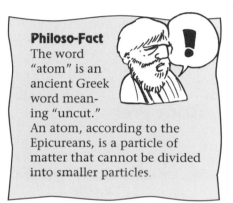

Philoso-Fact
The word "atom" is an ancient Greek word meaning "uncut." An atom, according to the Epicureans, is a particle of matter that cannot be divided into smaller particles.

Since Epicurus didn't believe the gods cared one way or the other about people, he needed to explain how the world full of people came to exist if the gods didn't create it. So he looked back to a contemporary of Socrates, the philosopher Democritus, who theorized that the world was made entirely of atoms.

It's All in the Atoms

Building on Democritus' cosmology, Epicurus said that the world was formed by the accidental collisions of atoms. Originally, all the atoms were simply falling straight through space. Some of the atoms, though, had random sideways movements that caused them to knock against other atoms, making them bounce around in turn. In time, the bouncing around of the atoms resulted in the world as we know it, full of rocks and water and trees and…parking lots.

Since the world is made by atoms and not by gods, people don't have to worry about whether the gods are going to punish them for their actions on earth. People themselves are only a bunch of atoms stuck together anyway; our souls, as well, dissolve into separate atoms when we die.

Because we are made of atoms, we have no reason to worry about death. Because our souls will dissolve, there will be no life beyond the grave, good or bad, that we need to worry about. What's more, death won't hurt, because, when you die, you won't exist anymore. There won't be any *you* around to feel pain, just a bunch of atoms coming loose from one another. Life will be over before you know it, so why worry?

Like the stoics, the Epicureans thought physical pain was vastly overrated. It never lasts longer than a little while before it goes away, often leaving you with a sense of relief that's pleasurable. Even being sick doesn't have to be so bad. Sickness has a bad reputation because it often leads to death, so people are afraid of it and worry about it. Without the worry of death, though, sickness is no big deal.

Born Free

Because the Epicureans were unconcerned about death and the afterlife, they felt free to enjoy life. Their belief in personal freedom sets them apart from the stoics, who believed in fate. Stoics accept the idea that all things are governed by destiny and there isn't anything people can do about it.

The freedom the Epicureans believe people enjoy is modeled after the motions of the atoms that make up the universe. Originally, the atoms were falling through space at the same speed and in the same direction. Because they moved freely, some atoms veered sideways and began the ricochet effect that resulted in the world as we know it. Human beings are similarly free to bounce around however they wish.

Wise people, then, will decide which way to bounce based on how happy they will be as a result. The trick is to figure out what pleasures lead to unwanted pain later on and what pleasures come with no strings attached.

Not Their Scene

Many of the strings attached to pleasure have to do with social customs such as marriage and political life. Epicurus advised against getting married because he saw it as an obstacle to peace of mind (so do some people today!). Also, he believed, participating in politics interferes with your tranquility. It involves trying to achieve imaginary goals, rather than looking to your own peace of mind. Both marriage and politics involve focusing too much on what other people want you to do; these are better avoided, taught Epicurus.

Friendship, on the other hand, was important to the Epicureans. In fact, Epicurean philosophy was very much a group effort, with whole schools of Epicureans getting together to talk about how to achieve tranquility. Epicurus' school, called the Garden, became more popular than both Plato's school, the Academy, and Aristotle's school, the Lyceum.

Alma Maters

Here's a list of the most important philosophical schools of ancient Greece during the Hellenistic period:

➤ **The Academy** Founded by Plato in Athens around 385 B.C., it continued in various forms under successive teachers until A.D. 529. At this time it was closed down by Christian religious authorities who condemned it as a source of paganism. At one point, the Academy was dominated by skeptical philosophy.

➤ **The Lyceum** This school was founded by Aristotle in 335 B.C. It was also called the Peripatos, a word meaning "covered walkway," which connected the buildings. The students and teachers supposedly rambled through such a walkway while discussing philosophy. The Lyceum continued into the 3rd century A.D.

➤ **The Stoa Poikile** The name of this school means "painted porch," a place where discussions were held. This is where the word "stoic" comes from. The school was founded by Zeno around 300 B.C. and continued into the 3rd century A.D.

➤ **The Garden** This school was founded by Epicurus around 300 B.C. Its name refers to a garden outside Epicurus' house where he taught. The Garden was not only a school, but also a kind of commune where students lived in isolation from society in pursuit of Epicurean pleasure and peace of mind.

Epicureans was a successful rival of Platonism and Aristotelianism for centuries, until the Christian philosophers modified Plato and Aristotle in accordance with their religion. At this time, Epicureans died out. It came back into favor centuries later during the 17th century when scientists began to take the idea of atoms seriously again. Seventeenth century scientists were impressed by the empirical tendencies of Epicurean atomism—both Epicureans and 17th century scientists understood reality in physical terms as something that can be sensed and tested.

Reality Check

Although atomistic philosophy came back into style in the 17th century, it encountered a lot of resistance from philosophers who saw God as an important influence on reality; they interpreted the idea that their world was formed by the accidental colliding of atoms as atheistic.

Who Knows?

The third important Hellenistic philosophy after stoicism and Epicureans is skepticism. The skeptics believed that we can't know the truth. All we have are ideas that may or may not be true. To support this view, they said that we can't rely on our senses to tell us anything for certain. They also pointed out that we can't rely on what other people say either, since different people are frequently in disagreement with one another.

Wisdom at Work
Use skepticism to disguise the fact that you don't understand something. Imagine a colleague tells you that you can run a new application on your computer if you reconfigure your start-up file to run in expanded memory. You have no idea what this means, but you don't want your boss to know what a computer nitwit you are. You can say, "I'd need proof before I'd believe that would work."

Skeptics practice different degrees of skepticism. Some believe that we can know some things for certain but not others. Others take the extreme position that nothing is certain.

The first full-fledged skeptic philosopher was Pyrrho of Ellis, who taught that there is nothing we can be sure of. He borrowed from the thinking of Socrates and the sophists, all of whom went around pointing out that people are often wrong about what they think is true. Pyrrho systemized the sort of doubting that Socrates and others practiced into a whole way of thinking and acting. Although he starts with the idea that we can't know things, he is especially concerned with what this tells us about how we should act.

Are You Hallucinating?

One of the main skeptical arguments about why we can't be sure of anything is that anything anyone thinks may simply be imaginary. In fact, you may be dreaming right now and not realize it. You may only *think* you are reading this book, although, in reality, who knows?

You say you can pinch yourself to see if you're awake? Maybe you're only dreaming that you're pinching yourself. The point is that the ideas you have about reality in your mind are just ideas, nothing more. For all you know, people may well see and hear completely differently from one another. Just because you experience a sensation doesn't mean that sensation is true; it may just be something your mind and body does.

Just as we can't trust our own senses, we can't trust other people either. In fact, the skeptics pointed out that all the authorities people look up to are in disagreement with one another. Maybe they're *all* hallucinating!

Curb Your Dogma

The skeptics were particularly opposed to the dogmatic thinking of the other philosophers, especially the stoics, who acted as if they were certain about reality and how people should act. *Dogma* is any idea or system of ideas that gets expressed as if it were the truth.

Although the skeptics were opposed to the dogmatic teachings of the other philosophers, they had an important idea in common with many of them. This was the idea of *ataraxia*, or inner tranquility. Skepticism, then, was not intended just to be a way of criticizing everyone else's ideas; rather, it was supposed to help people get used to the fact that a lot happens that is beyond our control. If we realize that nothing is certain in life, it makes it easier to throw out our expectations of how things should be. As a result, we won't be disappointed when things don't turn out the way we've planned.

> **Lexicon**
> **Dogma** is any way of thinking that is accepted as true. It comes from an ancient Greek word meaning "belief." Skepticism is the idea that something someone *thinks* is true may in fact *not* be true. Skepticism comes from an ancient Greek word meaning "seeking."

In fact, it was probably Pyrrho who introduced the idea of ataraxia to the other Hellenistic philosophers, including Epicurus. Pyrrho may have picked up this concept on a visit to India, where philosophy tends to focus on renouncing worldly desires and detaching oneself from the cares of life. (See Chapter 11.)

Pyrrho himself was so detached from the world that he didn't bother to write down his philosophy. He left that job to his followers. He did, however, run the Academy, the school founded by Plato, for a number of years.

The Seeds of Doubt

Although hardly anyone goes along with extreme skepticism—the idea that we can't trust *any* of our own ideas—skepticism in modified form has been an important and influential way of thinking. Modern science, for example, is based largely on skepticism.

The first modern scientists took almost nothing for granted. They questioned their own existence, their senses, and people in authority. Science, of course, was not a philosophy that accepted nothing as true, but a way of testing ideas and events that constantly takes into consideration the possibility that the hypotheses we use to explain things might be wrong.

This kind of science didn't get off the ground until centuries later. The ancient Greek philosophers, though, laid a good foundation for science that would be rediscovered in the 16th and 17th centuries. In the meantime, philosophers became preoccupied with developing a religious view of reality.

> **Philoso-Fact**
> Tradition has it that Pyrrho the Skeptic was so careless about his own life that his pupils had to watch over him like a baby to keep him from hurting himself.
>
> One of Pyrrho's students had to push him out of the path of a runaway cart. Although Pyrrho was staring directly at the cart, he was too busy "suspending judgment" about the cart's existence and trajectory to act.

The Least You Need to Know

➤ Philosophy after Plato and Aristotle became more dogmatic and was directed toward the question of how to live your life.

➤ This philosophy, originating in Greece, is known as Hellenistic philosophy, and it spread throughout the Mediterranean.

➤ Stoicism is the philosophy of not caring what happens.

➤ Epicureans is the philosophy of avoiding mental pain.

➤ Skepticism is the philosophy of doubting your own thoughts and the statements of those in authority to protect yourself from false expectations.

Chapter 9

God and Knowledge

In This Chapter

➤ Philosophy in the Middle Ages

➤ Sorting out philosophical reason and religious faith

➤ Why old writings were so important

➤ Interpreting reality for hidden meaning

➤ The debate over what's real

➤ The unstated message behind medieval logic

During the final days of the Roman Empire and throughout the Middle Ages, God was popping up everywhere. All around the Mediterranean and on into Europe, people were convinced in the belief in a single, all-powerful, righteous God. While this idea replaced the pagan religions of the Greeks, Romans, and North Africans, it did not replace philosophy. But it affected it drastically.

Philosophy in the West and in the Middle East was dominated by three powerful influences: Plato, Aristotle, and religion. Jewish, Islamic, and Christian philosophers were reconciling philosophy with religion—reason with faith.

For centuries, a blend of Plato's philosophy and religious thought, known as neo-platonism, enabled philosophers and religious authorities to see eye to eye. There were some exceptions, as a few daring thinkers came up with ideas that did not sit well with established religion, but for the most part, neoplatonism made everyone happy.

Later, Aristotle was revived in a way that didn't make too many waves with religious authorities. Aristotle, Plato, and religion provided a broad framework for most of the philosophical ideas of the Middle Ages. This framework remained in place well into the Renaissance when it was slowly and gradually replaced by the rise of modern science.

Faith Meets Reason

The basis for medieval philosophy was laid in ancient times. The empire of Alexander the Great had fallen apart, and the Roman Empire attained unprecedented power before falling in the 5th century. During the time of Roman dominance of the Mediterranean region, religious ideas began to exert a powerful influence on philosophy, in spite of the fact that some religions were often suppressed by the Roman emperors.

> **Philoso-Fact**
> Roman emperors were typically deified—made gods—by official decree. The stoic philosopher Seneca ridiculed this process, calling it "pumpkinification."

One of the first philosophers to combine ancient Greek philosophy with established religious teaching was the Jewish philosopher, Philo (30 B.C.–A.D. 45). Philo noticed a similarity between Plato's desire to apprehend the ideal form of the good and the desire of many Jews for a mystic connection with God.

Philo said that the ideal good and God were the same thing. In saying this, he anticipated a key element of neoplatonism that remained useful for centuries in the ongoing attempt to square philosophy with religion: the belief that understanding and faith point in the same direction.

God Thinks of Everything

> **Wisdom at Work**
> Use the idea that you have a mystic connection with God to explain why you are staying at home in bed all day when you're not sick. Say God wants you to take it easy.

Philo said that God, the ideal of goodness, is a oneness that underlies all things. We can appreciate this oneness both through philosophical reasoning and through religious faith. This oneness, God, is like a universal mind, and the other ideal forms described by Plato can be understood as God's thoughts. These "thoughts" of God give order to the material world so that it can be understood by people, whose minds are made in the image of God's mind.

Because people's minds are modeled after God's mind, we can understand God through reason—to a point. The problem is, though, that people are also tied up with material things like food and clothes and VCRs and their physical bodies, which can distract and prevent them from understanding God. This connection to material things limits people's abilities to reason, so we also need faith to achieve a mystic connection with God.

Words Get in the Way

Also, because material things are an obstacle to understanding God, we need to think about God in negative terms, in terms of what he *isn't*. This holds true for all the ways we can think about God. Not only is God *not* a corkscrew or a horned toad or your brown pair of pants, he is also not what you might actually think he is. Philo said that God is like a mind, but he is also not a mind. The idea that God is like a mind is only an *approximation* of what God is—an image that helps us get closer to understanding the truth. The truth requires a mystic vision, rather than a set of words or images, to be grasped.

In other words, words themselves are material things that can stand in the way of our understanding. We have to look at them as approximations of the truth and learn to see through them and past them to really grasp what they represent.

The Hebrew Bible Goes Greek

Philo believed that even the words in the Bible are only approximations of the truth they point to. Accordingly, he interpreted stories in the Bible as metaphors for Platonic forms. For example, Philo said that the serpent in the Garden of Eden represents lust, which means that the serpent's seduction of Eve shows how lusting after material things gets people into trouble. Plato had a similar attitude toward the desire for material things. Philo's reading of the Bible, then, helped show that Greek philosophy and Judaism were essentially on the same track.

This way of reading the Jewish Bible turned out to be extremely influential for Christian theologians, who looked for metaphors for Christ and Christian teachings as they read it. Christians read the Hebrew Bible much as Philo did, except that where Philo looked for symbols and imagery that would point to Platonic ideas, Christians looked for things that would point to Christian beliefs.

Getting a Read on Things

This way of reading came to be known as *allegory*. Allegory is a way of interpreting a story so as to make it mean what you want it to. Allegory is a way of writing too, when the writer uses one set of things, usually concrete pictures, to represent another set of things or ideas that are often more abstract.

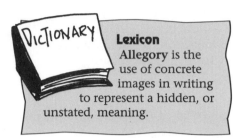

Lexicon
Allegory is the use of concrete images in writing to represent a hidden, or unstated, meaning.

For example, in the allegory called Psychomachia, or "Battle of the Soul," by the early medieval writer Prudentius, characteristics like lust and chastity are represented as opposing knights who battle each other.

Allegory was an important way of writing and interpreting throughout the Middle Ages. It was also an important part of the way neoplatonic philosophers understood the relationship between material and ideal things: Material things are not the same as ideal things, but they can point to ideal meaning.

In reading the Bible allegorically, then, Philo helped combine Plato with religion and, in so doing, influenced Christian, as well as Islamic, philosophers. Philo's reconciliation of Greek reason and Jewish faith suggested to him that God inspired the Greek philosophers as well as the Jewish prophets to write and teach.

If It's Written Down, It Must Be Important

Philoso-Fact
Philo went to Rome from his native city of Alexandria in Egypt to request a special favor from the emperor Caligula on behalf of his Jewish community: They wanted permission not to worship Caligula as a god. We don't know if he was successful, but we do know that Philo helped establish that Caligula was insane!

Neoplatonism, like religious thinking of the time, placed great importance on writing, regarding the written word as special, magical, or even divine. By studying other people's writings, philosophers of the late ancient and medieval periods hoped to learn about the hidden oneness that words point to. This oneness, revealed as words, was called *logos* in Greek.

This fixation with written words is one reason why medieval philosophers prized the ancient philosophers so highly. Rather than coming up with radically new philosophies, they revered philosophies already established and written down. As a result, many neoplatonist Christians came, like Philo, to see Greek philosophy as divinely inspired.

Time Warp

In Renaissance Italy around the 14th century, there came to light some forgotten philosophical writings from an unknown writer. The philosophy described in these writings was a mix of Greek philosophy, religion, and magic. The people who found them, including the neoplatonist philosopher Marsilio Ficino, thought they had stumbled on an inspired Gentile philosopher who dated back to the time of Moses. They believed he was Egyptian and called him Hermes Trismegistus, meaning "three-times great Hermes," and they called his philosophy Hermetic philosophy.

Ficino thought that Hermes Trismegistus received the word of God, together with instructions to teach God's word to the Gentiles, just as Moses had been instructed to spread the word to the Jews. This is how the neoplatonists came to explain the religious ideas they found in Plato. Plato got them from Hermes Trismegistus, who in turn got them straight from God. The Hermetic philosophical writings seemed to prove this theory because of the way they incorporated religion and Greek philosophy.

Reality Check

Neoplatonists refuse to admit that everything may not fit together into a mystical unity. If they think something doesn't fit, they assume it's because they're not understanding the hidden connection between it and the rest of the world.

The fact is, though, that Ficino and the others were fooling themselves. Hermetic philosophy was actually written around Philo's time or shortly afterward, when a number of philosophers began bringing together religion and Greek philosophy. What had seemed like a divinely inspired anticipation of Greek philosophy turned out to be a dating mistake. Ficino was about 13 centuries off in estimating the date of the Hermetic writings!

Ficino's mistake shows the tendency in neoplatonic thinking to make all words, ideas, and things part of a single idealized picture of reality. Everything fits together. Contradictions get explained away with the notion that they point allegorically to a unified, but hidden, meaning. When neoplatonists interpreted things, they tried to explain how everything fit in with their idea of unified oneness.

It All Adds Up to One

The next important philosopher after Philo was the Egyptian Plotinus (205–270). Plotinus is often said to be the first neoplatonic philosopher, although his ideas resemble Philo's in many respects. Plotinus elaborated on the connection between the divine oneness and material things. He saw material things and ideal forms as divine creations. For him, the world was a kind of work of art, expressing divine being.

This account of creation is known as the *emanation theory*. Reality emanates from the One, the divine being, like heat from a hot iron. Because the One is a kind of artist, or creator, we can commune with the divine being through art as well as through meditation. The point is to see beyond the barriers that separate you from everything else. Your separateness, your individuality, is essentially an illusion. If you can lose track of the difference between yourself and other things, you can experience the One.

A Private Line to God

For Plotinus and the other neoplatonists, knowledge depends not on the testing of material things and real events, but on the mystical apprehension of a transcendent

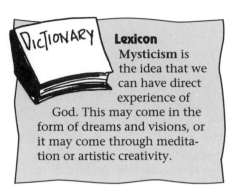

Lexicon

Mysticism is the idea that we can have direct experience of God. This may come in the form of dreams and visions, or it may come through meditation or artistic creativity.

Oneness. In fact, mysticism was a common element in neoplatonism and the religious and magical cults as they were practiced during the waning years of the Roman empire. It was an important element of philosophical and religious life throughout the late ancient and medieval periods.

Mysticism is the idea and the practice of achieving unity with God. It usually involves some form of sidestepping ordinary reality, taking oneself out of connection with ordinary material things, out of day-to-day reality. For some people, mysticism involved avoiding words, or even thought. For others, working oneself into a state of deep thought played a key role in mystic experiences.

You Can't Blame God

Thinking and mysticism went together for the North African neoplatonist, Augustine of Hippo, who became a Christian saint. St. Augustine, though, was a mystic only up to a point. He believed that people were limited to the degree to which they could commune with God in this life on earth.

People, said Augustine, can only get just so close to God without actually dying and going to heaven. If we really want to experience God, we'll just have to wait until our lives end, when our souls can experience divine reality without being tied down to physical reality.

This view puts people at a distance from God and makes God seem all the more perfect and powerful, while making people seem all the more weak and sinful. If things aren't to our liking, it's our own fault.

Philoso-Fact
The statement, "I believe in order to understand," is often associated with Augustine. It means that human reason is limited and requires God's help in the form of divine revelation through scripture. The statement underscores that Augustine's philosophical ideas are largely derived from his Christian beliefs.

Even so, just because we can't experience God fully or directly doesn't mean that we shouldn't try to understand divine truth in this life, said Augustine. He was intensely concerned with the relationship between God and the human soul as a key to understanding divine truth.

Augustine began as a Skeptic, someone who did not believe in oneness, or much of anything else, for that matter. He dealt with his skepticism much as the French philosopher, Rene Descartes, did many centuries later: He turned inward to see if anything was in there that he could be sure of. He decided that, even if he were wrong about everything else, he could be sure that *he* existed. From this he concluded that the relationship between the inner self and God was of primary importance.

The Reason for Evil

One of the big things that had previously prevented Augustine from accepting the idea of divinity is the fact that there is evil in the world. If there was a perfect divine creator, why would that creator make evil along with everything else?

Augustine reasoned that evil per se doesn't really exist. At any rate, it was not created by God, but happens only as a result of God's distance from material reality. God is more or less present in all things, but where he is less present evil has a good chance of setting in. Unlike good, evil doesn't happen on purpose; instead, it just happens, like dust settling when you don't vacuum regularly.

Augustine believed that many people get caught up in this evil dust of life, mistaking it for what's really important. He believed that these people will find out the truth when they die, and realize that they had missed the whole point of existence.

Getting with It, or Get in the Way

Augustine believed that people have a choice of whether to get with the program God planned, or to just get in the way. Even though this means that a lot of people will be in the way, this free will is actually a good thing, because it lets people take part in God's creative, active, deciding nature.

Because we can choose how to be, we are more like God than doorknobs and other things that can't choose. The downside of this is that, paradoxically, we can choose to be even less like God than doorknobs by deciding to be evil. For Augustine, this meant giving yourself up to the pursuit of worldly pleasure.

Even so, we can't simply choose to be good and be sure God will reward us after death. We need God's help, or grace, in order to move beyond our nature, which Augustine saw as essentially sinful. This reliance on a combination of free will and God's grace ties back in with Augustine's partial mysticism. Just as we can partly know, and commune with, God, we can only partly choose good on our own. We have to hope God will do the rest.

Augustine's thinking amounted to a severe divvying up of responsibility between God and individuals. We have some free will and are responsible for avoiding sin if we can, but we can't take all the credit for doing this, since we need God's help. This means we can't blame God if we give in to our selfish desires to do evil things. Even though we can't take a whole lot of credit if we do good, we take all the blame if we do evil.

Philoso-Fact
Augustine was so convinced that we are unable to choose good without grace from God that he used his influence as a Bishop to get the opposing view declared a heresy. Under his leadership, the church fathers opposed anyone who thought that people can be sinless and attain immortal life without God's grace.

Neoplatonism, then, as it was described by Plotinus and Augustine, and anticipated by Philo, became an important aspect of the way officials in the early Christian church understood the way things are.

Philosophy Goes to School

While church officials looked to Plato for wisdom and insight, teachers and university scholars often looked instead to Aristotle. The first medieval Aristotelian, or scholastic philosopher, was Boethius (480–524). Scholastic philosophy has tended to focus on Aristotle's logic rather than the other aspects of his work because Boethius translated, and thus preserved, those writings of Aristotle's that deal with logic.

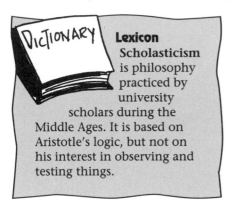

Lexicon

Scholasticism is philosophy practiced by university scholars during the Middle Ages. It is based on Aristotle's logic, but not on his interest in observing and testing things.

Boethius' writing treats issues of faith and issues of reason as two separate things. In fact, much scholasticism focuses on reason without contradicting religious teaching. In general, one of the main things that separates scholasticism from neoplatonism is that where neoplatonism tries to unify everything under a single mystic truth, scholasticism tries to chop things up into lots of tiny logical distinctions. Such logic chopping took place in universities where scholasticism was practiced.

Although scholastic logic chopping often went to absurd lengths by applying rigid and seemingly arbitrary rules to decide irrelevant questions—like whether slush is a kind of snow or a quality of snow—it provided scholastic philosophers with a way around neoplatonism. They could focus on how words work without having to accept or refute neoplatonic thinking.

Aristotle Goes Islamic

Scholastic philosophy got a big boost in the 10th century from a number of Islamic philosophers. Thanks to the Persian empire, Arabic people ruled much of the area around the Mediterranean that had been most strongly influenced by Greek philosophy. This influence rubbed off on the Arabs who practiced the Islamic faith.

Islamic philosophers rediscovered important lost writings by Aristotle and spread his ideas to Christian and Jewish philosophers. These ideas included interpretations of Aristotle's metaphysics as well as his logic. Ibn Sina (980–1037), known as Avicenna to the Latin speaking world, for example, made categorical distinctions between levels of ideal being and intelligence that span the distance between God and material reality.

Ibn Sina was influential in spreading scholasticism all around the Mediterranean, in spite of the fact that some of his ideas ran contrary to Islamic, as well as Christian, teachings. He believed, for example, that God had only an indirect, general knowledge of living creatures, which challenged the idea of divine providence, or fate, decreed by God.

Another influential Islamic philosopher was Ibn Rushd (1126–98), known outside the Arabic speaking world as Averroes. He wrote extensive commentaries on Aristotle's works and was a respected authority all over Europe. Like Ibn Sina, Ibn Rushd had ideas that disturbed religious authorities. Some of his writings suggest that he followed Aristotle in thinking that the human soul is not immortal, but rather, dies with the body.

Proving God Exists

While tensions remained between philosophy and religious faith, a number of philosophers used Aristotelian logic to demonstrate the existence of God. One of these was St. Anselm of Canterbury, whose "ontological proof" that God exists has become famous. This proof says that if something is perfect, it must exist, since non-existence is a sign of imperfection. The most perfect thing we can think of is God. Because God is perfect, he must be exist.

Lexicon
St. Anselm's **ontological proof** of God's existence says that if something is perfect, it must exist, since non-existence is a sign of imperfection. God is perfect, therefore he must exist.

St. Thomas Aquinas is another influential philosopher who put forward logical proofs of the existence of God, coming up with five altogether. Aquinas also provided the most complete philosophical explanation of the relationship between God and humanity that had been developed so far. He explained not only how humans and other creatures were created by God as derivations of God's perfection, but also how we could return to oneness with God both through his power to assimilate us and through our desire for him.

He did this by drawing on Aristotle's concept of causality. Everything has a purpose and, for Aquinas, this purpose pertains to God. Aquinas incorporated neoplatonic ideas into his thinking as well. For example, he saw the human soul as the Platonic form of the self.

Logic Chopping

Aquinas also drew, like the other scholastic philosophers, on Aristotle's logical concepts and procedures. This logic has become notorious for being convoluted and unnecessary. As a result, medieval scholars have a reputation for being self-absorbed and obsessively fixated on the use of obscure terminology.

Although Aquinas made successful and influential use of Aristotelian logic, a number of philosophers were combining Aristotle and neoplatonism in ways that led them to absurd conclusions. They became so fixated on Aristotle's logical terminology that they came to believe this terminology determined, rather than just reflected, the way things are.

This led them to engage in seemingly pointless arguments about categories and causes, what they were, and how they should be applied. The idea that the *logos*, or word, could lead to a vision of oneness was getting lost amid bickering over words that had little connection to anything in reality.

83

A Real Controversy

One important thing did come out of all this bickering—something that would prove to be significant for the future of philosophy. This was the question of universals raised by the French philosopher, Peter Abelard (1079–1142). *Universals* are concepts that can be applied to any number of particular things, or qualities, as Aristotle had called them. They include colors like redness, and characteristics like hardness and roundness.

The question is, do universals have an actual existence that are independent of the particular things that exhibit them? Does redness, for example, exist anywhere outside of all the things that are red?

Philoso-Fact
Abelard was a famous lover as well as a famous philosopher. He secretly married one of his students, Heloise, and ran off with her. This made Heloise's uncle so angry that he had Abelard castrated. Poor Abelard spent the rest of his life in a monastery.

Although this may seem like more pointless logic chopping, it really gets to the heart of the whole question of neoplatonism. Although the scholastic philosophers generally didn't want to admit it to themselves, they were asking if there really were such a thing as the ideal truth that everyone was making such a big deal about. If universals don't exist, in other words, the whole notion of an ideal oneness is challenged.

Abelard described three different positions one could take in response to the question of universals. The first and most widely held view was *realism*. Realists believe that universals are real and that they actually exist independently of particular things and independently of the people who think about them.

Lexicon
Universals are concepts that can be used to describe any number of particular things. **Realism** is the view that universals *actually exist* as more than names and more than mental impressions. **Nominalism** is the view that universals exist only as *names*. And **conceptualism** is the view that universals exist as *concepts* in the mind.

Now, this gets confusing, but the realists are also sometimes referred to as *idealists*, since they believe in ideal reality. Their view is opposed to *nominalism*, which holds that universals are merely names used to describe particular things.

Abelard tried to square realism and nominalism. In his attempt he paved the way for a third position, known as *conceptualism*. Conceptualism is the view that universals exist in the mind. This position emerged only gradually, because in Abelard's time, "the mind" was something that existed not only in people's heads, but more generally in ideal reality.

As we've seen, the idea that God is more or less "mind" is a basic idea of neoplatonism. God is like a mind and the ideal forms of things are his thoughts. Before conceptualism could emerge as a recognizable position, people had to decide whether "mind" was universal or particular. If mind is universal, then conceptualists are realists too. If not, they are more like nominalists. (Are you still with me?)

Sidling Up to the Big Questions

Does the question of universals seem profoundly unimportant? In a way, that's what the nominalists wanted people to think. Who cares? What does it matter? It's just a bunch of niggling about abstract logical concepts.

This niggling, though, disguises deeper questions that the religious philosophers of the Middle Ages couldn't face head on: Does God exist? Is the material world really just a debased reflection of ideal reality? Are we really doomed by our physical natures to be cut off from an ideal oneness until we die?

Shaving Explanations

In time, the nominalist reaction to the problem of universals helped lead philosophy out of the Middle Ages and into the Renaissance. And William of Ockham (1285–1349) was the guy most responsible. Ockham said that many philosophers were getting hung up on categories and classifications.

Ockham argued that when we're trying to explain the nature of something, we should use the fewest ideas of things as possible. We should avoid using more concepts than we need in explaining things. The simplest explanation is most likely the correct one. This argument became a rule known as "Ockham's razor."

> **Lexicon**
> **Ockham's razor** is the logical rule that says the simplest explanation for a situation is more likely to be correct than a more complicated explanation. This rule challenged the universalizing tendencies of neoplatonism.

Ockham's razor helped get philosophy focused on observable things instead of on words for ideas and classifications. In so doing, Ockham helped prepare the way for modern science. As a nominalist, Ockham helped focus attention on the important distinction between words and things. Not everyone jumped on the Ockham bandwagon right away, though; it took years for neoplatonic realism to subside.

The Least You Need to Know

➤ Medieval philosophy was largely about reconciling reason and religious faith.

➤ One dominant philosophical view was neoplatonism, which saw material reality as an imperfect reflection of a mystic oneness.

➤ Another dominant philosophical current was scholasticism, which focused on Aristotelian logic.

➤ The focus on logic sparked debate about whether ideas exist other than just inside the mind or just as names. Ultimately, this debate brought philosophy back in touch with material things and guided it into the Renaissance.

Part 3
Eastern Philosophy

…Meanwhile, on the other side of the planet, philosophy has been taking an entirely different course. For many Westerners, Eastern philosophy seemed superior to their own philosophy, because it was more in tune with nature, with human nature, and with the nature of human society.

This being in tune has to do with the fact that Eastern philosophy tends to lack the complicated metaphysics developed in the West, which in many people's eyes gets in the way of what reality is all about. Also, Eastern philosophy tends to lack the sharp distinction imposed by much Western philosophy between subjectivity and objectivity. As a result, in Eastern philosophy there is less of an attempt to control reality and more of a recognition that we are all part of reality.

There are three main traditions of Eastern philosophy: one from the Far East, one from India, and one from the Middle East. They represent important traditions in and of themselves, and have had an important impact on the way Westerners think.

Chapter 10

Far Eastern Philosophy

In This Chapter

➤ The two major philosophies of China: Confucianism and Taoism

➤ How Confucian philosophy tries to improve society

➤ The idea of ceremony as it applies to daily life

➤ Taoism's oneness with nature

Much Western philosophy is strongly influenced by religion. In the Far East, it's the other way around: religion is strongly influenced by philosophy. Philosophy has had as profound an impact on Asian cultures as religion has had on European cultures.

In fact, Eastern philosophy has influenced Westerners too. People in Europe first started hearing about Eastern philosophy in the 17th century, and Western philosophers have been borrowing from the East ever since. As a result, Confucius is at least as familiar as Plato to most people in the West, and the Eastern concept of the *Tao* (*the way*) is just as familiar as the Western concept of empiricism (see Chapter 3).

Confucianism and Taoism form the two main strands of Far Eastern philosophy. Although they are very different from one another, they both begin with the basic idea that nature and culture should work together.

A Gentleman and a Scholar

Confucius, the name given by people in the West to the philosopher known in China as K'ung fu-tzu (551–479 B.C.), was especially concerned with the problem of corruption in government. He noticed that China's ruling class, the aristocratic nobility, took advantage of the people they governed, imposing heavy taxes to support their luxurious lifestyles.

Confucius

Philoso-Fact
When Westerners first discovered Chinese philosophy, it was customary to latinize the names of important people, so they called K'ung fu-tzu "Confucius." Other famous latinized names are "Christopherus Columbus" for the Italian explorer, Christoforo Colombo, and "Nicolaus Copernicus" for the Polish astronomer, Mikolaj Kopernik.

Because of the extreme difference in wealth between the few rulers and the rest of the population in China, most people had very little to live on and led a sorry life. As a result, no one trusted anyone. The people didn't respect the rulers, who in turn bullied them into submission. Things were pretty miserable all around.

We're All in This Together

Confucius, who had the people's best interests at heart, developed a way of thinking that he believed would help solve China's problems. His approach was intended to get rulers and government officials to stop taking advantage of the common people and to win their respect without using force. His ideas, which were directed toward governmental problems, actually wound up solving a lot of other problems as well.

Confucius' idea of good government involved everybody, not just the rulers. Although some people in China (particularly those with blue blood in them!) believed that only people who had aristocratic roots should rule, Confucius thought that was hogwash. Those most capable of governing should govern, whether they were born with silver chopsticks in their mouth or not.

This was an important new idea. Up until then, it was widely believed that ruling families were selected by heaven itself. This belief was coming under attack, though, since it was easy to see that the rulers were not particularly good at taking care of things and that they depended on military force, not divine intervention, to maintain power.

Still, the idea that only people of a certain family should rule persisted, especially since it tied in with China's tradition of reverence for one's ancestors. It was expected that children be like their parents and carry on tradition.

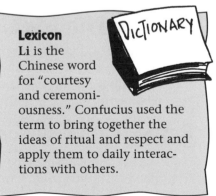

Philoso-Fact
Confucius wanted to become a government official himself but was not willing to obey the unjust commands of his superiors. So, instead of governing, he spent his life teaching others—and many of them became government officials.

Confucius' idea that the job of governing should simply go to those most capable broke with the long-standing tradition of inherited family rule. Confucius knew that if he made big waves with his new idea he wouldn't get very far, so he said that the family of rulers should remain as figureheads and leave the job of governing to those who were best qualified.

Leading by Example

People don't need to be threatened and bullied into obedience, argued Confucius. They will show respect and loyalty to rulers who, through experience and study, have learned to govern well, and who understand people.

For Confucius, the idea of influencing people by example worked both ways. Not only should rulers be good role models, the people should also *show* the leaders how to lead by being loyal followers. This meant that the people should use their judgment and refuse to obey foolish or evil orders, while loyally obeying all other commands.

Governing Wise-Li

Confucius' good governing is based on a principle known as *li*, behaving with courtesy and ceremoniousness. In his time, the word was frequently applied to the practice of worshipping one's ancestors. Ancestry was considered extremely important; in fact, it was a common practice to make sacrifices to dead ancestors. Confucius did not interfere with this practice but instead tried to turn it to more productive use. He said that people should take the respect that they showed their ancestors and show it to one another.

Lexicon
Li is the Chinese word for "courtesy and ceremoniousness." Confucius used the term to bring together the ideas of ritual and respect and apply them to daily interactions with others.

Just a Little Respect

For example, Confucius said that if someone comes to visit you, you should treat them with all the respect you would show if you were presiding at an important ritual sacrifice. Convention, ritual, and respect should always be observed in interactions with others.

But Confucius' emphasis on convention didn't mean that people shouldn't think for themselves. Even though he believed that everyone should be taught to appreciate the conventional ways of doing things, and to fill their place in society, he did not think people should follow convention blindly, or just for the sake of show. Flashy, insincere displays of respect were not as good as simple, heartfelt demonstrations. What's more, it's okay to depart from convention if you have a good reason.

Working with Tradition

For example, if it's customary to have plum sauce with special family dinners, but you hate plum sauce, you can use cranberry sauce instead. The point is people can decide to influence and change tradition. In fact, Confucius believed that it's important for everyone to be involved in what's going on. If you're unhappy with the conventional way of doing things, you don't have the right to isolate yourself from them; you should work with convention to try to find a way of doing things that makes sense and is satisfying to you.

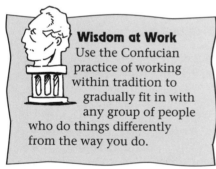

Wisdom at Work
Use the Confucian practice of working within tradition to gradually fit in with any group of people who do things differently from the way you do.

In this way, everyone is involved in *li*, working out a way of doing things that all can be happy with and recognize as important. This is just what Confucius did in his attempt to reform Chinese government. Although he had a lot of ideas about how things should be changed, he never said the old ways were bad. He drew on tradition as far as he felt he could. For example, he didn't say it was a waste of time making sacrifices to dead people. Instead, he recognized the value of devotion and ceremony, and saw that it could be used for practical purposes.

A Good Mind-Set

The value of *li* is not just that it shows respect for other people; it also gets people mentally prepared for the task at hand. The things people do are important and require concentration and awareness if they are to be done well. This is especially important in conducting affairs of state, but it applies to other aspects of life too.

Respecting What You Do

The idea of *li* means not only doing things respectfully, but in their proper time and place, according to custom. If you have a lot of stuff to do and it doesn't seem particularly important or interesting, then you are likely to rush through it, doing a shoddy job in the process. Additionally, you'll be thinking about other things while you're working, thus being inefficient. You'll be unhappy while doing the work and unhappy with the result. What's more, you may look for ways out of doing the work, for example, by getting someone else to do it or by leaving it unfinished, even if this causes problems for you and for others down the road.

> **Wisdom at Work**
> Apply the concept of *li* to the work you have to do. This will help you to appreciate its importance and to become mentally prepared for doing it well.

If, on the other hand, you take the time to get mentally prepared for what you have to do, the work will go more smoothly, be more enjoyable to do, and the result will be more satisfying for everybody. The way to do this, instructed Confucius, is to think about why the work is important, and about how and when you are going to do it.

This is where convention kicks in; it can help you decide how and when to do things. If, for whatever reason, convention gets in your way more than it helps you, you can simply change the convention without making a big deal about it.

Confucius vs. Confusion

By doing things both thoughtfully and according to convention, people can make less trouble for themselves and for others. Everyone is on the same page, with a common understanding of what's important, but they can decide for themselves how best to accomplish them. Think how well everything would go in a world where everyone had this attitude.

Confucius thought such a world would work much better than the world he lived in, so he taught people his philosophy. Although it was new in many respects, it was also based on old ideas that people in China were already familiar with. One of these ideas is the *Tao*. Tao is a Chinese word meaning "way," or "path." For Confucius, the Tao involved finding the right mix of convention and personal awareness.

The concept of Tao is not usually associated with Confucius, even though he used its concepts in his teaching. Instead, the Tao has come to form the basis of Taoism, a major branch of Chinese philosophy that is often opposed to Confucianism. Taoism differs from Confucius' teachings in that it focuses on being in tune with nature, rather than being mainly concerned with the practical matters of relating to others.

> **Philoso-Fact**
> Although Taoism and Confucianism are separate philosophies and in opposition concerning many matters, they are both based on the idea of "the way."

Philosophy for the Well En-Tao'd

Like Confucian philosophy, Taoism grew from a number of traditional Chinese ideas during the 6th century B.C. The ancient philosopher Lao-tzu (which means "the old master") is credited with establishing and teaching Taoism.

Unlike Confucius, who believed in the importance of convention, Lao-tzu taught that convention was often a bad thing because it interferes with our natural ability to live in harmony with the Tao. For Lao-tzu and the Taoists, the Tao is natural, rather than social, and many Taoists have isolated themselves from others in order to live a more natural existence.

The point of Taoism is not to create an ideal society, but to achieve oneness with the Tao, "the way," which is understood as a natural principle. The person who is able to blend in with "the way," who can detach himself from the worries of society, will be happy and healthy and live for a long time.

Going with the Flow

Lao-tzu taught that the best way to live according to the Tao was to follow a principle called *wu-wei*. Wu-wei can be roughly translated to mean "receptivity." To abide by wu-wei is to accept things as they come, go with the flow, and try not to assert yourself or change the natural course of things.

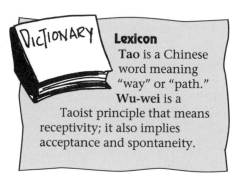

Lexicon
Tao is a Chinese word meaning "way" or "path." **Wu-wei** is a Taoist principle that means receptivity; it also implies acceptance and spontaneity.

Say, for example, that there is something you want to buy that you have had a hard time finding. Finally, you talk to some people on the phone who say they have what you're looking for at their store, which is ten miles out of town. So you make a special trip to go and pick it up. When you finally get to the store, it turns out that the people you talked to misunderstood what you said you wanted. You explain again what you want, and it turns out that they don't have it after all.

If you're like many people, you might get mad, complain, argue, and generally let those people know that they screwed up and put you to a lot of trouble for nothing. If, on the other hand, you follow the principle of wu-wei, not only would you not get upset, but you would look at what happened with detached amusement.

A Taoist would consider, in the grand scheme of things, that it really doesn't matter whether you achieve your goals or not. The important thing is just being part of the process of life. For this reason, Taoists love nature. Nature works spontaneously, and whatever happens in nature always works out right.

This view of nature separates Taoism from Hellenistic stoicism (see Chapter 8). Both Taoists and stoics believe in detaching oneself and putting up with whatever happens, but Taoists believe in a benevolent nature whereas stoics believe in a hostile "fate."

In fact, if you think things go wrong, it's only because of your point of view. To you, it may seem bad that you wasted a trip out of town. To the Taoist, it doesn't make any difference. Life goes on. As long as you're out of town, why not take a walk in the woods and notice how all things in nature exist together in a state of constant change?

Worry Less, Live Longer

Things live, grow, and die. Even death is not a bad thing; it is part of what happens. That fact that our consciousness ceases when we die shouldn't bother us. We should be receptive and accepting of death, in the spirit of wu-wei. The Taoists believed that the more accepting you are of death and other natural processes, the healthier you will be and the longer you will live. By not worrying about the course nature takes, you can more fully become a part of nature.

This paradox—that the less worried you are about death, the longer you will live—is typical of the way Taoists think. Taoist teachings are full of paradoxes. In fact, Taoists believe that the Tao can never be explained in words, since words, like everything else, exist in a state of constant flux.

The Taoists believe that everything that exists is always in a state of becoming its opposite. Life is always turning into death, and death is always becoming life. Wet things are always becoming dry; dry things, wet; strong things, weak and weak things, strong. Summer and Winter keep trading places. The world is held together in a shifting state of balance.

The More Things Change, the More They Stay the Same

This condition of shifting, balanced opposites illustrates the Taoist concept of *yin and yang*. Yin and yang are opposed principles that are really part of the same thing. The whole made up by yin and yang is represented by a familiar symbol.

In this symbol, the black shape and the white shape form a circle, representing completeness. They look like they are moving toward one another, as if trying to become their opposites. In addition, the black shape has a white dot in the middle of it, just as the white shape has a black dot. This shows that things are made up of their opposites.

Taoists see the world as made up of things that can be classified as being either yin or yang. Yin is female: the

Wisdom at Work
Use the principle of wu-wei when you're in a situation where you don't know what to expect. Rather than feel anxious, you'll be ready to accept whatever happens and respond in a spontaneous way.

Lexicon
A **paradox** is a statement that combines two seemingly opposite ideas, yielding a more subtle truth.

Lexicon
Yin and yang are complementary Taoist principles. Yin is the female aspect and yang, the male.

earth, water, and winter. Yang is male: the sky, fire, and summer. The Taoists believe that learning to recognize the interplay of yin and yang can help us fit in harmoniously with the process of change constantly taking place.

Philosophy or Fortune Telling?

The concepts of yin and yang are used by Taoists to understand natural processes. Some Taoists apply this understanding of nature to the social world as well, seeing social situations and practical affairs in terms of intermingled characteristics of yin and yang.

One expression of the way yin and yang can be applied to social life is in the ancient book known as the *I Ching*, or the *Book of Changes*. This book combines practical advice on etiquette and management with inspirational thoughts about the natural world, together with an orderly system for reading into the future.

Using the *I Ching* is something like reading a Western horoscope, except that instead of figuring out the alignment of stars and planets to tell your fortune, you read a particular combination of yin and yang characteristics.

Philoso-Fact
According to tradition, Confucius didn't begin studying the *Book of Changes* until the ripe old age of 70.

Using a broken line to represent yin and a continuous line to represent yang, the *I Ching* is based on 64 different possible combinations of six yin and yang lines. Each combination of six lines, known as a hexagram (not to be confused with a hexagon), represents a different situation that can be applied to your life and interpreted. The meaning of each hexagram can be explained by poetic and philosophical interpretations. After selecting a hexagram by chance, you can apply its interpretations to any personal situation and draw conclusions as to how you should deal with it.

Many of these interpretations are thought to have been written by Confucius himself. The *I Ching*, then, represents a combination of practical Confucianism and natural Taoism, as well as a combination of philosophy and fortune-telling.

The Least You Need to Know

➤ Confucian philosophy emphasizes that people are all responsible for doing their part in society.

➤ Confucius worked for gradual change within traditional ways of doing things.

➤ *Li* is the concept of courtesy and ceremony that Confucius applied to daily working and interacting.

➤ Taoism emphasizes oneness with nature.

➤ Wei-wu is the Taoist principle of receptivity and acceptance.

➤ The Taoist world view, symbolized by yin and yang, sees things in a constant state of change.

➤ The *I Ching* is an ancient book that combines Confucian and Taoist wisdom as well as philosophy and fortune-telling.

Chapter 11

Indian Philosophy

In This Chapter

➤ How Indian philosophy works toward release from suffering

➤ Karma and respect for all living things

➤ Philosophy and the caste system

➤ Buddhism and release from selfhood

➤ Gandhi's philosophy of passive resistance

Philosophy in India is at least as old as ancient Greek philosophy and it continues to influence millions of people today, including Westerners. You're probably already familiar with the concept of karma—the idea that the things you do today could have an influence on seemingly unrelated things that happen to you sometime down the road.

You may also have heard about attempts to achieve a higher state of consciousness through meditation or yoga. These ideas come from Indian philosophy. And some of the important Indian philosophers whose names you may have heard include Siddhartha Gautama (the Buddha) and Mohandas "Mahatma" Gandhi.

Most Indian philosophy stems from ancient writings known as the Vedas. The thinking expressed in the Vedas—known as Vedanta—has been reworked, revised, and restated in different forms throughout the centuries, resulting in one of the most important philosophical traditions in the world.

Above the Suffering

One of the main ideas behind Indian philosophy is that existence, which is full of suffering, can be transcended—we can rise above it. This state of transcendence is often associated with bliss and peace; it results when the individual is released from reality as we ordinarily experience it. The Hindus call this state *moksa* and the Buddhists call it *nirvana*.

Philoso-Fact
Nirvana literally means "blowing out," as in blowing out a flame. Specifically, it refers to blowing out the flames of selfish desire, resulting in a state of bliss.

Many Hindus and Buddhists believe that it is possible to transcend worldly cares in this life through study, meditation, *yoga*, or a combination of all three. (Yoga is a form of discipline for controlling the mind and body.) This idea of transcendence stems from an older idea that one is released from worldly cares only after death and after having lived wisely and renouncing the world during this life.

According to this older idea, the best thing we can hope for when we die is to be released from worldly existence. We are all tied to existence through *karma*, the principle that our actions determine what happens to us. If we live well, we can be released after death. If we don't live well, we will be reincarnated in a new life. The new life will be determined by the karma we practiced in the previous incarnation.

Lexicon
Most Indian philosophy is based on ancient writings known as the **Vedas**. Out of the Vedas developed the Hindu idea of **moksa**, or release from suffering, which the Buddhists call **nirvana**. Another important vedic idea is **karma**, the totality of one's actions that determines what will happen to you in the future. **Yoga** is a form of mental and physical discipline that many Hindus believe can help lead to moksa.

Karma Chameleons

Your karma determines not only whether you will be reincarnated or not, but what sort of existence you will have if you are reincarnated. You may come back as a bird or a tree or a stink bug, depending on how you lived your previous life.

Many Hindus and Buddhists regard all living things as having souls that are essentially equal and connected to one another. As a result, they feel it is wrong to kill any living thing. Even killing an insect can result in bad karma, since, as a living being, that bug is essentially as important as a person. This respect for all living things is expressed in the principle of *ahimsa*, or non-violence.

Lexicon
Ahimsa is the Hindu and Buddhist principle of non-violence that encourages respect for all living things.

Although Vedantic thinking sees all living things as essentially equal, all things are different from one other. This is especially true of people, who, traditionally, hold different positions in Indian society that are determined at birth. In fact, the Vedas say that your karma determines what place you will hold in society. Indian society has been structured through the *caste system*, in which people were born into one of four groups. The lowest caste was made up of servants and laborers, then came the merchants, then the soldiers, and finally, at the top, the priests.

Hindu Castes

It was thought that if you were born into the priestly caste rather than the laborer caste, it was due to better karma because of your actions in a previous life. If you were in a low caste, you could hope to improve your status in your next life by living well—towing the line and not making trouble.

➤ **Brahmins** Priests and scholars

➤ **Kshatriyas** Warriors and administrators

➤ **Vaisyas** Merchants

➤ **Sudras** Servants and laborers

Practice Makes Perfect

The Vedas supply a set of rules for how both people and the many Hindu gods should live; this is known as *dharma*. Your dharma, which describes your duty to gods, neighbors, family, and yourself, is determined by your caste, your occupation, your age, and your position in your family. Even though dharma is a unifying principle that connects people to one another and to the gods, everyone can practice dharma in a different way. By faithfully following your dharma, you can get released from the cycle of karma.

Lexicon
The **caste system**, which says that everyone is born to hold a particular position in society, has defined the social structure in India for centuries. Each caste has a different way of satisfying **dharma**, the duties we must fulfill to the gods, our families, our neighbors, and ourselves.

Hindu Duty

The specific way you should follow dharma depends not only on who you are, but where you are in your life. The dharma that is appropriate for you changes with your age. Typically, when you are young, you should devote yourself to studying. When you are older, you should focus on your occupation and on raising a family. And when you are older still, you should retreat from society to meditate and perhaps practice yoga. In this way, by the time you reach the end of your life, you will have mastered your worldly desires and, hopefully, will be ready to be released from worldly existence forever.

If you follow dharma carefully, you can hope to achieve the state of moksa during this life and be released from the cycle of reincarnation back into this world of suffering. In addition, you will be following rules for existence that are woven into the fabric of reality itself.

Is Karma a Good Idea?

There are many benefits that come from believing in karma, in following dharma, and in trying to achieve moksa. If you have a hard life, you will be better able to detach yourself from your problems and see beyond them. And you are unlikely to make trouble for other people, since you will be focused on your own inner peace.

Wisdom at Work
Use the idea of karma to explain why good things happen to you, seemingly by accident. Say that you lived an especially virtuous existence in a previous life, so you are being rewarded with good fortune in this one.

At the same time, believing in karma encourages people to put up with difficulties rather than work to change them. This is especially true of those who belong to the lower castes. These people are taught, essentially, that they are considered socially inferior because of their own mistakes made in a previous life. Thus many see the traditional concepts of karma and dharma not only as untrue, but also unfair.

REALITY ✓ **Reality Check**

Many people think that the idea of karma has helped maintain an unjust caste system in India for centuries. Are the people who are forced to hold the worst jobs being punished for what they did in a previous life? Or is karma a way of blaming the victims?

The Awakened One

One of those who wanted to make changes in Hindu beliefs was Siddhartha Gautama, the teacher who came to be known as the Buddha. Although many of Buddha's ideas stem from ancient Hindu philosophy, he added some important innovations. Most significantly, Buddha rejected the caste system. In addition, he believed in renouncing not only worldly pleasures as taught in the Vedas, but even in renouncing the idea of the self.

Buddha was an Indian prince who grew up living a sheltered life of luxury. Wanting to learn more about life, he went out into the world and was shocked at the suffering he saw. Everywhere he found people who were poor, hungry, sick, old, and resigned to a life of hard labor. Motivated by the need to relieve such suffering, he devoted himself to religion. He mastered all the religious techniques he studied, including meditation and *asceticism.*

Legend has it, that, still not satisfied, he sat under a tree to meditate. At last, the answer came to him: The right way to live was neither to pursue pleasure nor to deny oneself physical necessities, but to attain the wisdom that allows us to see past the misleading idea of the "self." The Buddha grasped this wisdom and spent the rest of his life teaching it to others.

The Buddha

The term, buddha, means "awakened one," or "enlightened one." The emphasis in Buddhism is not on having faith in an unknowable God or afterlife, but in knowledge that focuses on transcending the self.

Freeing the Self from Itself

Like much Hindu philosophy, Buddhism starts with the idea that all life is suffering. Even the gods suffer. According to Buddhism, suffering is part of the make-up of reality; we're all tied to suffering by our desires.

The problem is not only that we are unlikely to get what we want out of life, but that even if we do get what we want, we are not going to be truly happy as a result. Satisfying our desires will only lead to new desires; ultimately, we will never be satisfied. Instead, we will just tie ourselves more closely to the suffering involved with unending desire, and we will continue to be deluded with the idea of self.

If you are concerned about yourself, you will be especially prone to experience suffering. Desire is essentially selfish and only leads people to think that they are important as individuals rather than as part of a suffering reality that can be transcended. To the Buddhists, the self is an illusion that keeps people from achieving nirvana.

> **Lexicon**
> **Asceticism** is the practice of denying oneself physical comforts and necessities, usually in order to move beyond material needs and desires and focus on loftier things. It has been practiced through the ages by many Hindus and many Christians.

> **Philoso-Fact**
> Siddhartha Gautama, the Buddha, is only one of many buddhas, or "awakened ones," recognized by Buddhists. According to them, there have been many buddhas—enlightened teachers—in the past, and there are many more to come.

The way out of suffering, then, is to eliminate selfish desire. To show people how to do this, Buddha described what is known as the *Eightfold Path*—eight steps to achieving enlightenment and freeing the self from itself and its cravings.

The Eightfold Path

- ➤ Right seeing
- ➤ Right thinking
- ➤ Right speaking
- ➤ Right acting
- ➤ Right lifestyle
- ➤ Right effort
- ➤ Right mindset
- ➤ Right meditating

Different Buddhists provide different interpretations of what it means to be "right." The Eightfold Path is not a dogma, rather, it's intended to help you focus on enlightenment.

Philoso-Fact
Buddhism declined in India during the Middle Ages as Hinduism and Islam became prominent. At this time, however, it spread further east and became extremely popular.

Philoso-Fact
The Indian poet, Rabindranath Tagore, described Gandhi as "the great soul in beggar's rags." The word he used for great soul was "Mahatma," a name that stuck.

Following the Eightfold Path, according to the Buddha, can help you achieve nirvana, and be released from the chain of suffering that defines existence.

Budding Buddhism

Buddhism has spread throughout India and from there to Thailand, Burma, Tibet, China, and Japan. And many people in Europe and America practice Buddhism, both as a religion and a philosophy. Its popularity is partly due to the fact that Buddhism can coexist easily with all kinds of practices and beliefs.

Although many revere the Buddha as a kind of saint, he himself stressed that his ability to transcend selfhood did not make him divine. He did not believe that there was anything particularly godlike about himself, but felt he understood things more clearly than others. As a result, Buddhist rituals, which include chanting and meditation, are intended to help people focus their minds and bodies rather than demonstrate faith, as many Christian, Jewish, and Islamic rituals are intended to do.

Fighting with Peace

India has had a long and difficult history in which Indians have been forced to submit to rule by foreigners, including the Aryans back before the time of Buddha, the Persians during the spread of the Persian empire in the Middle Ages, and finally, the British during the years of British colonialism.

Some see Indian philosophy as partly responsible for its centuries of subjugation. Its focus on self-denial and the transcendence of worldly suffering encourages people to put up with hardship—including foreign rule—rather than work to change things.

Indian philosophy, however, has proved useful as a tool for change, change that has lead to self-rule for its people. In particular, self-denial and the idea of release were important features of the movement for India's independence from British rule in the 1940s and '50s, which was spearheaded by the philosopher and social activist Mahatma Gandhi.

You've Got to Admire His Moksa

Mohandas "Mahatma" Gandhi (1869–1948) grew up practicing a form of Hinduism that emphasized self-denial and included fasting and other ascetic practices intended to lead to *moksa*, the state of liberation or release. He also was taught the principle of *ahimsa*— non-violence toward all living things—a practice that was observed throughout India.

These ideas became important to Gandhi when he became an activist against foreign rule. He applied the idea of moksa, or personal liberation, on a political level, arguing that people should pursue political as well as spiritual freedom. His non-violence emphasized the moral significance of his cause and helped him win the support of Indians and non-Indians alike.

Gandhi also drew on his training in self-denial to emphasize the morality of independence for India. He was not afraid to lie down in the street in front of on-coming cars or go on long hunger strikes to draw attention to his cause. Revered by millions, he achieved great success in working toward independence for India. His methods have since been adopted by Martin Luther King, Nelson Mandela, and peaceful protesters all over the world.

The Least You Need to Know

➤ Indian philosophy focuses on the release from suffering.

➤ Karma is the idea that what you do influences what happens to you in the future— and in your future lives.

➤ Your dharma, the Hindu and Buddhist conception of duty, depends on your caste, your place in your family, your occupation, and age.

➤ In Buddhism, selfhood is an illusion, and you transcend suffering by eliminating selfish desire.

➤ Gandhi, the 20th century philosopher and social activist, used ideas of Indian philosophy to work for Indian independence from Great Britain.

Chapter 12

Middle Eastern Religious Philosophy

In This Chapter

➤ How Judaism, Christianity, and Islam are related

➤ How believing in one righteous God formed a foundation for equality and justice

➤ How Judaism, Christianity, and Islam interpret sin, evil, and salvation

The Middle East gave rise to three of the world's great religions: Judaism, Christianity, and Islam. Underpinning these distinct religions are some shared philosophical ideas that have had a deep and widespread influence.

All three embrace the idea of a single, all-powerful God who is righteous and cares about humanity. This belief leads to powerful philosophical views of good and evil, justice and equality, and history.

One God

The belief that there is only one God is known as *monotheism*. In the Judeo-Christian and Islamic traditions, God, who is all-powerful and good, created the universe. He has ultimate divine authority, but he has separated himself from human authority here on Earth. With monotheism, human authority may be seen as good or even willed by God, but it is not seen as divine itself.

Who's Got the Power?

This idea that human authority is not part of God's authority undermines certain ancient Roman and Egyptian attitudes toward kings and emperors, who were often thought of as gods themselves. Think about it: when there is only one all-powerful God, it makes it awfully hard to go around saying that you are a god yourself!

Lexicon
Monotheism is the belief in a single all-powerful God. Judaism, Christianity, and Islam are all generally considered monotheistic religions, even though they sometimes recognize additional divine or powerful beings, such as the Christian trinity, Christian and Islamic saints, and, in all three religions, the devil.

Monotheism, then, planted the seed that has grown into the Western ideas of justice and equality. Because God created everyone equal, God cares about everybody equally and places equal value on all, no matter who may be in charge on Earth.

The separation of earthly and Godly power means that people who don't have power on Earth may be as good as, or even better than, human rulers and other important people. You can see why justice, which places equal value and rights on all, is an important feature of government in monotheistic societies. We have to be fair in government because God cares about everybody equally.

But despite its built-in sense of justice, monotheism has not completely eliminated the problem of earthly inequality. Throughout history, many who believe in a single God have assumed that those who do not believe ought to be converted to their religion or defeated in battle.

Somebody Up There Likes Me

Philoso-Fact
Judaism, Christianity, and Islam are the major, but not the only, monotheistic religions. Monotheistic beliefs were also put forward by the Persian prophet, Zarathustra (c. 628–520 B.C.), and by the Egyptian Pharaoh Amenhotep IV, "Akhenaton" (14th century B.C.).

Jews, Christians, and Muslims (the followers of Islam), have all traditionally believed that, because of their religion, they are especially important to God. The Jews have referred to themselves as God's "chosen people," the ones who are chiefly responsible for carrying out God's purpose for humankind on Earth. More than a little of this attitude has rubbed off on Christians and Muslims and has caused all kinds of problems and upheavals, including "holy wars" waged in the name of God and all three religions.

By the Book

Justice in monotheism is based on a set of written rules that apply to everybody. These rules, as well as beliefs, myths, and histories, are found in the holy books that form the foundation of each of the three major religions: the Jewish Bible (the Old Testament), the

Christian Bible (the Old and New Testaments), and the Muslim Koran. These rules, or laws, show what God wants from the people who believe. Living by these rules shows obedience to God for its own sake and also maintains righteousness among people. Despite the many different and often conflicting interpretations of these holy books, they are traditionally regarded as the ultimate source of truth.

Sharing the Wrath

Failure to obey the rules laid down in holy writ makes God angry and may bring down divine punishment on those who disobey. This punishment may take place in this life—you may be struck by lightning or smitten with plagues—or it may be waiting for wrongdoers after death. Some Jews—and most Christians and Muslims—believe in an afterlife in which people will be rewarded or punished for their actions on Earth.

> **Philoso-Fact**
> The Islamic Koran is not only the revealed word of God, it is *the* word of God, since an exact copy is said to exist in heaven. For this reason, it is considered reliable only in the original Arabic language.

> **Reality Check**
> Sometimes too, people take it upon themselves to punish wrongdoers in this life. They think they know what God wants, and they impose and enforce rules accordingly. The Salem witch trials are a notorious example. In this way, monotheism has had a big influence on legal practice in general, both good and bad.

Evil Ways

In religions that believe in a number of gods, evil may be the result of arguments among the gods, or it may be caused by the fact that not all the gods care about human well-being. In such religions, evil isn't necessarily the fault of people.

In monotheism, though, because God is good and God's laws are good, anything bad that happens must result somehow from people who break God's law. This law-breaking is known as sin. In Christianity and Judaism, the original sin of disobedience on the part of the first man and woman, Adam and Eve, is responsible for all evil in the world, including disease, death, and having to work for a living.

> **Wisdom at Work**
> Use the idea that having to work is the result of original sin as an excuse for working less. Say you want to experience reality as God intended it to be before the fall of humankind.

107

Explaining Evil Under a Just God

What evil is and what should be done about it is a central problem of monotheism. Why would a good, all-powerful God allow so much evil to exist in the world? Monotheists have come up with many answers:

➤ We don't know what God wants; the evil we experience shows how dependent we are on God.

➤ Satan, the devil, is the source of evil.

➤ We can only appreciate God's goodness if we have experienced evil as well.

➤ God wants us to see how unimportant earthly reality is in comparison with the kingdom of heaven.

➤ Evil results from the accidental leftovers of creation—it is the absence of God.

➤ God is testing us so we can learn to be more like him by taking responsibility for how things are.

➤ Human evil allows God to demonstrate his forgiving and merciful nature.

➤ God's plan will unfold and be fulfilled over time, so that what is evil now will be eliminated or transformed to good.

Many of these explanations for evil, taken together, point to a paradox at the heart of monotheism concerning the importance of earthly existence. On one hand, human beings and their existence on Earth are unimportant in comparison with God and the perfection of heaven. As a result, what seems horribly evil to us from our earthly perspective may be no big deal to God in heaven. Evil, then, is here to help us look past worldly existence in anticipation of the afterlife.

On the other hand, humanity and the lives we live are very important. God cares about us and wants us to exercise our free-will in order to resist evil so that we can help bring about a transformation of earthly existence.

REALITY ✓

Reality Check

Evil is not always someone's fault, but the idea is often used as an excuse to blame certain people for problems everyone has. This process is known as "scapegoating," named for the ancient Hebrew ritual of symbolically pouring all of society's sins onto a goat and then sacrificing it or chasing it away.

The End Is Near

One especially important explanation for the problem of evil has to do with the idea of human destiny. Evil is part of a situation that will change over time according to God's plan for humanity. Different versions of this plan say that human beings are getting progressively better and better, or more and more sinful.

In either case, the idea is that at the right moment in history, or at several moments, something really important will happen: an *apocalypse* will take place in which the world as we know it will end, leading to the *millennium* when all good people will be rewarded, when the *Messiah* will come and save us from evil. This idea of human destiny is common to Judaism, Christianity, and Islam, and gets worked out in different ways by each religion.

Lexicon
Apocalypse, the Greek word for "revelation," has come to mean the time when the world as we know it will be destroyed. In Christian thinking, this will be followed by the **millennium**, when Christ will rule on Earth. While Christians recognize Jesus Christ as the **Messiah**, the savior of mankind, Jews do not, and are still waiting for the Messiah to appear for the first time.

History Is Us

History is an important aspect of monotheistic thinking in general. This is especially true of Judaism, with its many rituals celebrating events in the history of the Jewish people. These rituals emphasize the unique identity of the Jews as a people, and the importance of Jewish society as a religious community.

Jews not only celebrate past events, they also look forward to a future event: The coming of the Messiah, or anointed one, when God's purpose for humanity will be made clear. In the meantime, though, it isn't known exactly what God is up to. God has chosen the Jews as his own and given them strict laws to obey. He's promised them a land of their own (which has come to be Israel); but what God has planned for the future is something of a mystery.

You Always Hurt the Ones You Love

One of the main indications that God cares so much about the Jews in particular is that they have had to go through so much trouble on God's account. The hardships the Jews have undergone throughout history are often taken to mean that God cares specially about them. Even when the enemies of the Jews defeat them in battle, God is said to be punishing his people for not obeying properly. Many Jews believe that, in a way, this punishment is better than God not caring about them at all.

Wisdom at Work
Use the idea that God punishes people he cares about to explain why bad things happen to you. If you get fired from your job as vice president of a major corporation, tell yourself that God has been keeping track of how much junk food you've been eating and isn't happy about it.

The tendency of the Jews to blame themselves—or, at any rate, one another—when things go wrong is the subject of the Book of Job in the Jewish Bible. God decides to test Job, who is faithful and devout, by destroying all his property and killing members of his family. Job's friends jump to the conclusion that Job had done something wrong, and they blame him for his misfortune.

One moral interpretation of the story is that we can't always tell what God is up to when things don't go the way we want them to. Another moral, though, is that God may be testing people when he gives them a hard time. In any case, Jews traditionally believe that God cares especially about them in spite of—and because of—the hardships they have undergone.

Brand X: Newer, Bigger, Brighter

Christianity, one of many outgrowths of Judaism, interprets the Jewish Bible—or the "Old Testament"—in its own way, and has added a new set of scriptures to it, the "New Testament."

Come Again?

Like the Jews, Christians believe that God's purpose will be fulfilled through history with the coming of the Messiah. The Christian Messiah, Jesus Christ, has already come once and, according to the Book of Revelation, will return to rule over his kingdom on Earth.

Since, for the Christians, the Messiah has already come and saved them from sin, they don't have to wait for the millennium, but get to go to heaven as soon as they die.

Philoso-Fact
There is a long-standing debate among Christians about just what it takes to get into heaven. The two main contenders are faith (believing in God and Jesus) and good works (behaving well and doing good, which includes getting others to believe).

The thinking goes that even though people are inherently sinful, God is merciful and sent his son, Jesus, down in human form to atone for human sin. Because Jesus made everything all right with God, good Christians can get into heaven. Evil is still a problem, but only a temporary one for those who receive God's mercy.

Christians recognize many of the laws that the Jews abide by, but they interpret them much more loosely. They see God less as laying blame than as forgiving. As a result, the idea of communal responsibility and social identity tends to be less important to Christians than to Jews. Personal salvation becomes more important.

Feeling Their Pain

This emphasis on personal, as opposed to historical, identification with religion affects the way Christians interpret the stories in the Jewish Bible, or Old Testament. They see these stories not only as law, prophecy, and religious history—as the Jews do—but also as metaphors for personal hardship and salvation.

Jews, for example, interpret the story of Moses leading the Israelites out of Egypt through the wilderness and into the promised land literally, as the story of what happened to their ancestors. Christians see it this way too, but also interpret it as a metaphor for personal salvation from sin.

According to Christian interpretation, bondage in Egypt is like being enslaved to whatever sin you are guilty of. Wandering in the wilderness is like the uncertainty of the individual's belief in Jesus. Arriving in Canaan, the promised land, is like accepting Christ and being saved.

The Latest Word

Islam, like Christianity, is based on Judaism. According to the Muslims, though, instead of choosing the Jews as his people, God, who is called Allah, chose the Arabs. Even so, Muslims see the Jewish prophets as prophets of God, and they see Jesus as a prophet too.

> **Philoso-Fact**
> Both the Jews and the Arab Muslims trace their lineage back to Abraham. The Jews look on Abraham's son Isaac as the one chosen by God to continue the line, while the Muslims see Abraham's other son Ishmael as the chosen one.

Islam was founded by the prophet Muhammad (570–632 A.D.). Muhammad is the most important prophet of Islam. Although he is not considered divine by orthodox Muslims, he is worshipped and prayed to by some. According to Islamic tradition, Muhammad went out into the hills around Mecca, his native city in Arabia, to meditate. There he was visited by the angel Gabriel and filled with the word of Allah, which was later written down in the Koran.

The Five Pillars of Islam

Central to the Koran are "The Five Pillars of Islam," the basic rules every Muslim must follow:

➤ Affirm that there is no god but God, and Muhammad is his prophet.

➤ Pray daily while facing Mecca.

➤ Give alms to the poor and be generous to anyone in need.

➤ Observe the holy month of Ramadan by not eating or drinking during daylight.

➤ Make a pilgrimage to Mecca at least once in your life.

The five pillars, in stressing ritual observance, promote obedience and community. In stressing charity, they promote the idea of the basic equality of everyone, regardless of his station in life.

One God, Many Points of View

Like the Jews, Muslims place great importance on law and the religious community. They are strong believers in justice and in punishing those who disobey. At the same time, like Christians, Muslims emphasize the free will of the individual believer and the importance of the inner struggle to believe.

These conflicting directions of Islamic thinking have led to disputes throughout the history of the religion. They lie behind arguments about the rights of individuals and the power of the community, about the relationship between the law as it is set forth in the Koran and as it is imposed by the government, and about how the Koran should be interpreted and who should interpret it.

Islam is like Judaism and Christianity in that it has experienced inner disagreement and has splintered off into a number of different sects. In fact, these three religions can be seen as one religion that has been split into three main parts, and from there into any number of little parts, all based on the belief in a single god.

The Least You Need to Know

➤ Monotheism is the belief in a single, all-powerful, righteous God.

➤ The three major monotheistic religions are Judaism, Christianity, and Islam.

➤ Monotheism tends to place the blame for evil on human beings, while it emphasizes law and justice.

➤ Because Jews consider themselves God's "chosen people," they have a strong sense of social identity and responsibility.

➤ Christians emphasize God's mercy, and personal salvation through faith and good deeds.

➤ Muslims place great importance on community and obedience, but also free will and personal struggle.

Part 4
Making Progress

Western philosophy really came into its own in the early modern period, starting in the Renaissance during the 15th century and continuing into the Enlightenment of the 18th century. Philosophers had a lot of cards on the table, and many fascinating ways of shuffling the deck. Religion remained a key influence, but it gradually lost its dominance over thinking in general. In its place, science rose to the forefront of human thought.

Even so, science left a lot of philosophical problems unsolved, and it created new ones for people to wrestle with. What's more, scientific thinking didn't take hold right away. It had to be worked out gradually and squared with other kinds of ideas— religious and moral ones.

In the process, philosophy emerged as a possible solution to conflicts between science and religion and between science and morality. Philosophy attained a new-found importance, not only for university and church types, but for people in general.

More people were becoming educated and they needed philosophy to help them deal with the complicated circumstances that faced them. New possibilities for human existence were emerging, and philosophy provided new explanations for these possibilities.

Chapter 13

Renaissance Humanism

> **In This Chapter**
>
> ➤ Renaissance philosophy squares new thinking with old ideas
>
> ➤ Neoplatonism inspires human creativity and accomplishment
>
> ➤ The revival of skepticism
>
> ➤ Erasmus and peaceful doubting
>
> ➤ Machiavelli and tyrannical doubting
>
> ➤ Montaigne and personal doubting

During the Middle Ages most Western philosophy was religious philosophy, which tended to emphasize how little people understand without the help of God, Holy Scripture, and the church. During the Renaissance this attitude was gradually replaced by a general feeling that people aren't so helpless after all.

This feeling is often referred to as *humanism*, the idea that all of the things people think and do are important, interesting, and valuable pretty much for their own sake, in addition to whatever they may say about the relationship between people and God.

By the 14th century Western civilization had taken root and the countries of Europe had formed themselves into strong kingdoms. The political and economic stability that followed gave people the opportunity and motivation to explore and create, to delve into a wide range of areas practical, theoretical, and artistic. The growth in human experience and knowledge was remarkable. The Renaissance became a real turning point in the history of philosophy in the West, marking a shift from a religious to a scientific world view.

At the same time, though, the old religion and philosophy maintained by the Church and the universities continued to have a strong influence on people's thinking and actions. Emerging new ideas caused a fair amount of commotion you can be sure, but many of them gradually became incorporated into the old ideas so that they didn't seem quite so radical anymore.

Philosophy Reborn

The schools of thought that had had strong influences on medieval philosophy, namely neoplatonism, Aristotelian scholasticism, and religion, continued to thrive and influence Renaissance philosophy. But renewed interest in the philosophies of ancient Greece and Rome put a new spin on the thinking of the time.

Philoso-Fact
The word "Renaissance" means rebirth—a revival of the philosophy and arts of the classical period in Europe in the 14th, 15th, and 16th centuries. Some scholars argue that the idea of the "Renaissance" is misleading for various reasons: For one, art and philosophy were very different in ancient times and, for another, they didn't exactly "die out" during the Middle Ages.

The neoplatonists had paved the way for this humanistic thinking. In fact, there was a sizable upswing in the popularity of neoplatonism early in the Renaissance. The Renaissance neoplatonists, including Pico de la Mirandola, Marsilio Ficino, Giordano Bruno, and Nicholas of Cusa, had a more positive attitude toward life and the world than their medieval predecessors. They looked at the world not so much as an inferior reflection of an ideal reality, but rather as something created by God that was beautiful in and of itself and that reflected God's power and benevolence.

Where do people fit into this new world view? On the one hand, they are God's creations. As such, they may be beautiful, but they don't necessarily have a clue as to what creation is all about. On the other hand, people are creators themselves, and their creativity connects them to God. The idea that people are both important and clueless is a paradox at the heart of much Renaissance philosophy.

"Learned Ignorance"

This paradoxical view of the relationship between people and God is evident in the work of the German philosopher, Nicholas of Cusa (1400-1464). Cusa said that God is unknowable. At the same time, God is the only reliable truth. Observable reality is full of contradictions that show how little we humans know. The more you learn, said Cusa, the more you see how ignorant we are. Cusa called this ignorance *learned ignorance*, and said it was all the knowledge we can hope to have in this life.

Learned ignorance, though, doesn't mean we should stop thinking. Instead, we should think about ideas not as true things, but as created things. This notion contradicted the concept of knowable, absolute truth. And if we can't know the truth, then all the religious dogma that had been popular throughout the Middle Ages takes on a different meaning. Those religious doctrines are just ways of thinking—among many other ways that may be equally valid.

> **Wisdom at Work**
> Use Cusa's concept of *learned ignorance* to explain why it's actually good that you know so little. Say, "I understand reality so well that I see how little we can really know."

Cusa was himself religious—in fact he was a cardinal in the church—but he saw religious ideas as being relative: not the last word on reality, but approximations of the truth.

Will the Circle Be Unbroken?

To show how all knowledge is approximate and the truth is unknowable, Cusa used the idea of infinity to illustrate the nature of God and reality. Infinity, said Cusa, is present in everything. Each tiny point has the essence of infinity inside it. At the same time, infinity is unknowable. Think, for example, of a circle. A circle has a circumference and a center, and may be either very big or very small.

> **Philoso-Fact**
> For many philosophers of the Middle Ages and the Renaissance, including Nicholas of Cusa, the circle was a mystic symbol of perfection and completion.

Now think of a circle that is infinitely large. Cusa said that the circumference of such a circle would be a straight line that would meet at either end. Hard to picture, huh? This infinite circle represents God and reality.

The center of this infinite circle is everywhere. This makes a kind of logical sense, but it's impossible to imagine. It is a paradox that shows how hard it is to understand God, but it also suggests that the Christian notion of the church being in the central theological position on earth is misleading. The church can't be the only center, since the center is everywhere!

> **Reality Check**
> Paradoxes—ideas that seem to be logically impossible—often cut two ways at once. They suggest, on one hand, how inadequate the human mind is in attempting to understand reality. On the other hand, they suggest that ideas about reality are inherently misleading!

If everywhere is the center of this circle, then all of the medieval ideas about how the world is organized go out the window. In fact, all ideas are pretty much as good as all other ideas, especially if we realize that these ideas are not "true," but only approximations, or creative expressions.

Cusa's idea that God and reality are like an infinite circle had a similar effect on the rising status of humans as did the discovery that the sun, not the earth, is the center of the universe. If there is not a single, absolute center of both the human and the physical universe, then reality must be more flexible than people had previously thought. This means we have more leeway in deciding how we want to behave. We can take more responsibility for ourselves and for our own ideas.

This new view of the universe suggested to people that there is plenty of room for new ideas. Ideas about the world can be understood as if they were works of art created by people, just as God created the world. Humanity is a work of art, too, and is therefore not depraved, but beautiful. One of the particularly beautiful things about humanity is that we, like God, can be artists and make things.

We Are the World

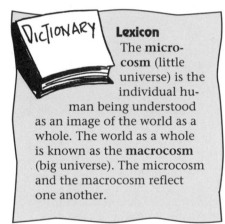

Lexicon
The **microcosm** (little universe) is the individual human being understood as an image of the world as a whole. The world as a whole is known as the **macrocosm** (big universe). The microcosm and the macrocosm reflect one another.

People are creative because they have all the aspects of reality inside them to draw upon. A human being, according to this view, is like a little world unto him- or herself. We are all the center of our own universe. The philosophical term for this view of the human being is the *microcosm*. The microcosm is the individual person understood as an image of the entire world, the *macrocosm*.

This means that things people do are, in a way, examples of the kinds of things God can do. This revelation is in no small way responsible for the many accomplishments and creations that the Renaissance became noted for: painting, sculpture, and literature, as well as advances in science, medicine, engineering, and philosophy.

Change Across the Board

This new vision of the connection between God's creativity and human creativity compelled people to challenge and ultimately change many old ideas. There was Polish astronomer Nicholaus Copernicus' momentous discovery that the earth revolved around the sun, not the sun around the earth.

In medicine, the physician Theophrastus Paracelsus rejected old notions about treating diseases as symptoms of sinful behavior. He saw diseases and injuries as natural problems that could be healed naturally, and he used medicines and techniques designed to assist nature.

Even bigger changes took place in theology. Many began to complain of church teachings and practices that encouraged superstition and corruption. They felt that they were not in keeping with Christianity as God intended it to be. The German monk, Martin Luther, felt so strongly about the need to rethink religion that he rejected the Catholic Church altogether and founded Protestantism.

> ## Reality Check
>
> Some Protestants left the Catholic Church for reasons other than restoring "true" Christianity in the face of corruption and superstition. Henry the VIII, King of England, introduced Anglicanism—the Protestant Episcopal Church—into his country so that he could break from Catholicism when the Pope would not grant him a divorce from one of his six wives.

There were big changes in the arts, too, especially in painting and literature. Artists and writers looked back to the classics for inspiration. They found new relevance in the non-Christian ancient writings of Greece and Rome, and found more flexible ways of blending ancient art and thinking with Christian beliefs.

Counterbalancing this whole new way of thinking, though, was the older view that said "do what you're told to do and believe what you're told to believe." This more conservative attitude continued to influence philosophers, as well as everyone else, throughout the Renaissance, even the enlightened humanists.

Believing in Belief

One of the major elements of humanism during the Renaissance was a resurgence of interest in the classics—the writings of the ancient Greeks and Romans. This was more than just an antiquarian interest in old things. It also involved a new-found respect for old philosophical ideas, including ideas of the Hellenistic philosophers—the Stoics, Skeptics, and Epicureans—who emphasized practical and social concerns rather than the spiritual, other-worldly concerns that preoccupied philosophers during the Middle Ages.

Philoso-Fact
The humanistic view of sacred beliefs as socially important resembles Confucius' view of the importance of ritual (see Chapter 10). Confucius, then, can be seen as a humanist, too.

The embrace of classical thinking did not result in the outright rejection of medieval philosophy, including neoplatonism and scholasticism, or in an outright rejection of religious thinking that emphasized the relative unimportance of earthly life compared with the afterlife in heaven. Instead, philosophers began to consider the social implications of these sacred medieval beliefs. They saw them as important not simply because they seemed true, but also because of the practical results of believing in them.

119

Three of the most important Renaissance thinkers who combined religious and philosophical ideals in this way were the Dutch theologian Desiderius Erasmus (1466-1536), the Italian political philosopher Niccolo Machiavelli (1469-1527), and French essayist, Michel de Montaigne (1533-1592). While these thinkers were respectful of the religious and philosophical ideals of the Middle Ages, they were critical of them, too.

Skepticism

Skepticism is a philosophical attitude that stems from Hellenistic philosophy of ancient times (see Chapter 8). It was revived and interpreted in different ways during the Renaissance—notably by Erasmus, Machiavelli, and Montaigne—and has continued to be an important influence on Western thinking ever since.

Gimme That Old-Time Religion

Erasmus was a monk and a scholar who was keenly interested in drawing on new-found classical knowledge in order to rethink religious ideas. He felt that the church had been encouraging people to overlook the original intent of religion and he thought that better translations of the Bible would help people recover its original message. The true message, according to Erasmus, was that people can live in peace with one another if they have faith in God and show love to God and to each other. All the issues that the theologians and the scholastic philosophers were arguing about, Erasmus maintained, are unimportant in comparison.

Philoso-Fact
Because Erasmus tended to go along with beliefs he did not hold rather than argue over them, he was sometimes seen as an insincere phony. It's probably more accurate to see him as peace-loving and open-minded.

Because we can't be certain about what we know, Erasmus believed that we have to understand the Bible on our own terms. It doesn't help just to go through the motions of doing what the authorities tell us to do. In recommending a more personal approach to the Bible, Erasmus sounded much like the Protestant reformer, Martin Luther.

Erasmus, however, didn't want to help start a whole new church. He felt Luther was wrong to make so much trouble for everyone. Arguments such as those Luther had started caused problems that were worse than the problems they were intended to solve. Change should be brought about more peacefully, within the established church structure.

Everybody Plays the Fool

Erasmus felt that because we can't really know anything for certain, it's pointless to argue about things. At the same time, he recognized that people tend to be argumentative and opinionated. Erasmus' best-known work demonstrates these views. Called *In Praise of Folly*, it satirizes all claims to knowing the truth. Such claims are all ridiculous, *even* the claim that the truth cannot be known. It suggests that all of us are foolish and that it's best to withhold one's personal opinions and try not to make waves.

Politics Is Torture

Like Erasmus, the Italian political philosopher, Niccolo Machiavelli, was skeptical about ideals based on the religious thinking of the Middle Ages. Unlike Erasmus, though, Machiavelli did not recommend detachment.

Involved in politics in Italy during a period of upheaval, he supported a republican government that took power for a short period of time, booting out the Medicis, a wealthy and powerful family. When the Medicis regained control, Machiavelli was thrown into prison and tortured. After he got out of prison, he wanted to get back into politics, but first he had to regain favor with the Medicis. He tried to do this by writing a book on how to rule called *The Prince*.

Prince Not Charming

The Prince is notorious for recommending that rulers resort to extreme measures in governing. These include both the use of force and the use of manipulation through lying and playing on people's beliefs and their ideals of goodness. At the same time, rulers should not hesitate to make people fear them.

Machiavelli's recommendations were intended to help the Medicis and Italy achieve a more stable government. The extreme measures were shocking to many readers, though, and Machiavelli's name came to symbolize the philosophy of ruthless and immoral lusting after power, *Machiavellianism*.

Doubting Fairplay

One thing that made Machiavelli's ideas shocking was his skeptical attitude toward the ideals of goodness that had been developed in the Middle Ages. Among these ideals was the notion of "virtue." To the Neoplatonists this idea meant acting with courage and wisdom, but also with justice. In fact, according to this medieval concept of virtue, you couldn't have courage and wisdom without justice.

> **Lexicon**
> **Machiavellianism** is a term that is often used to describe ruthlessness and deception in politics. More generally, the term is used to refer to anything someone doesn't like about anything political.

Machiavelli reinterpreted virtue to mean the courage and wisdom to pursue and secure power. If you are the ruler, it's less important to treat everyone fairly than it is to maintain your power over them. For this you need to be smart enough to know how to maximize your own advantage.

Unlike Erasmus, who recommended that everyone should learn to be skeptical in order to promote peace among people in general, Machiavelli thought that rulers in particular needed to be skeptical and on their guard in order to more effectively control the people they govern.

Another important humanist philosopher of the time was the French essayist Michel de Montaigne. Montaigne, too, was a skeptic who, like Erasmus, encouraged people to challenge accepted ideas, but, like Machiavelli, he recognized that it's human nature to adhere to one's established beliefs.

Try, Try Again

Montaigne is famous for his essays, written on a variety of subjects, but mostly about himself. In fact, Montaigne invented the essay as a new genre. The word *essay* means "try" or "attempt" in French, and Montaigne called his writings essays because he was experimenting with ideas, trying to see what he could figure out about himself and other people.

Philoso-Fact
Montaigne was the first person to refer to his writings as "essays." People have been writing essays ever since. They're short- or medium-length pieces that draw on various ideas, including personal experience, to explain rather than prove a position or point of view on a particular subject.

One of Montaigne's biggest revelations (at least to him) was how flexible he was. He could change his views, his attitude, and his mood depending on the situation. This "it-all-depends" attitude forms the basis of his skeptical approach to life. He recognized that different points of view could each be valid, up to a point, even though they contradicted one another.

Montaigne was skeptical about reason itself. He doubted that natural human reason was really superior to the way animals think and feel. What really separates humans from the animals, said Montaigne, is divine grace. Therefore we shouldn't be too positive about what we think we know as people. Paradoxically, he suggests that one of the things we shouldn't be too positive about is our religious knowledge.

Montaigne's skepticism didn't mean that he wanted to revise other people's way of thinking—like Erasmus—or control other people— like Machiavelli. Instead, Montaigne said that the smartest thing to do is to just fit in with other people, even though the things they do are no better than other ways of doing things.

This means that, although Montaigne was capable of thinking in revolutionary ways, he acted conservatively. He believed in thinking deeply and honestly about the world, people, and himself, but not in making a splash or causing a spectacle. In this way Montaigne, like all Renaissance philosophers in general, reconciled new ideas with old ways of thinking and acting.

Montaigne and his essays helped put philosophy on a new track by making it more speculative and less definite. Thanks largely to Montaigne, it became okay to write your ideas even if you didn't know whether they were true. This helped philosophy separate itself from religious thinking without actually refuting religious ideas.

The Least You Need to Know

➤ Most Renaissance philosophy involves reconciling a new humanist attitude with older medieval ways of thinking.

➤ Renaissance neoplatonism took a new, positive attitude toward human creativity, which encouraged the arts, science, and philosophy to flourish.

➤ Skepticism played a big part in helping to reconcile old and new ways of thinking.

➤ Erasmus promoted peaceful change within the established church.

➤ Machiavelli reinterpreted the medieval concept of virtue, and advocated the use of cruelty and deception to secure power.

➤ Montaigne wrote the first essays, mostly about himself and his flexible way of relating to others. These helped make philosophy more speculative without directly challenging religious thinking.

Chapter 14

Science Rises from the Mud

In This Chapter

➤ How science grew from the idea that knowledge is a group project

➤ How people tend to get hold of mistaken ideas

➤ Why some philosophers didn't like science

➤ Descartes' thoughts about the mind and the passions

➤ How ideas about the mind are related to ideas about government

➤ Newton's application of math to the study of physical things

Renaissance philosophers made exciting new discoveries in a variety of fields, not the least of which were medicine, astronomy, and chemistry. These discoveries contributed to the rise of what we now call modern science.

Modern science, a new way to study observable reality, was greatly encouraged by new technological developments of the Renaissance, which, in turn, greatly encouraged many more technological developments right up to this day.

But it was a gradual process, this development of modern science. In the early days of the 17th century, science was a mixed bag—a little religion, a little magic, a bit of philosophy, some social influences, and, of course, some new scientific ideas. At this time, science began slowly separating itself from some of these other areas and moved closer to focusing itself on the physical, or material, world.

Bringing Home the Bacon

One of the main factors in the rise of science as a distinct, systematic approach to finding out about reality was the work of the English philosopher Francis Bacon (1561–1626).

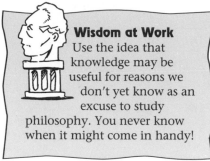

Wisdom at Work
Use the idea that knowledge may be useful for reasons we don't yet know as an excuse to study philosophy. You never know when it might come in handy!

Bacon was interested in knowledge in general, especially knowledge about the natural world. Like other philosophers before him, he recognized that knowledge could be extremely useful—more useful than anyone had yet imagined. This got Bacon very interested in knowledge for its own sake. He believed that the more we know, the more we will be able to help ourselves in the long run. For this reason, we ought to learn all we can, regardless of whether or not we see an immediate need for the knowledge.

A Man with a Plan

Bacon's interest in the possibilities for knowledge gave him a new perspective on the importance of avoiding mistakes. According to Bacon, being wrong was not just something that could interfere with your personal, individual well-being; it could prevent everybody from taking advantage of the potentially wonderful uses of knowledge. Bacon

Philoso-Fact
Many early scientists adopted the motto, "nullius en verba," *nothing in words*, to show how unimportant they considered words to be in the study of reality.

wanted everyone who took the time and effort to think about things to be right, and on the same wavelength, so to speak, so that everyone would be able to share in the same mission—putting knowledge to good use.

Because he had such big plans for knowledge, Bacon was extremely critical of all the learning that he saw as wrong. In particular, he criticized the Scholastic, Aristotelian philosophers, or "schoolmen" as he called them, for believing and teaching a lot of ideas based solely on words, rather than on a scientific investigation of material things in the natural world.

Idolizing Error

More generally, Bacon noticed that people tended to cling to mistaken ideas for a variety of reasons. He called these mistaken ideas "idols of the mind," suggesting that people worshipped their false beliefs as if they were false gods. He identified four different kinds of these mental "idols."

➤ **Idols of the Tribe** Mistakes caused by human nature. As people, we are a "tribe" whose perceptions and emotions are inherently unreliable.

➤ **Idols of the Cave** Mistakes caused by tendencies of the individual. Different people have different ways of understanding things. As individuals, we all live inside our own "cave" where we see things in our own way.

➤ **Idols of the Marketplace**   Mistakes caused by convention. When we communicate with one another, we often agree on things that have nothing to do with the truth. Instead, we "buy and sell" ideas because they seem socially valuable.

➤ **Idols of the Theater**   Mistakes caused by philosophical authorities. Philosophers like to show off and "play act" as sages who dispense wisdom, even though they may not have a clue what they're talking about.

Bacon believed that the "idols of the mind" had confused people so much that there was more mistaken knowledge around than good, reliable knowledge. So, he said that we should just throw all the stuff that passed for philosophy out the window and start over again, focusing this time on nature rather than words.

> **Reality Check**
>
> Bacon exaggerated the differences between his philosophy and Aristotle's. Even though Bacon complained that Aristotle's logic was wrong, many of his own ideas were actually based on Aristotle's way of seeing things. Both philosophers were firm believers in the importance of making careful observations of the natural world.

Don't Believe Everything You Read

Bacon reacted against the popular tendency of the times to take everything that was written down as truth, or knowledge. Many books on geography, history, and natural history, for example, written in the Middle Ages are a combination of facts and myths. People read without making any distinction between truth and fiction. It was all the same to them.

Bacon argued that we need to resist the temptation to say things we don't know to be true. Instead, we should be content to say only what little we do know in the hopes of someday being able to build on that. We should also be careful with our use of words by assigning them consistent, clear definitions. Then we should make sure we use our ideas logically, and test their accuracy by performing experiments. In Bacon's words, "If a man begins with certainties, he will end in doubts, but if he will be content to begin with doubts, he shall end in certainties."

Bacon's campaign was a bold one: people must pool their efforts to learn more about the natural world. They must sift out all the tons of misinformation that has accumulated over the centuries. Thanks to Bacon, philosophy began to clean up its act and set the stage for the beginning of modern science.

Science and Spirit

Still, there were a lot of bugs that had to be worked out before sufficient numbers of people could get together to agree on science. Scholastic philosophers were one of the stumbling blocks. They claimed that they had, in effect, figured out all that God wanted people to know in this life. Science, in trying to figure out how nature works, was just meddling into things that God intended to keep secret.

And then there was disagreement within the scientific community itself. Some scientific philosophers were interested in how the mind works. They concluded that the mind isn't like other things in nature and that, as a result, there is a lot that science, as Bacon envisioned it, can't tell us. One of the most notable of these philosophers was Rene Descartes (1591–1650).

It's All in the Mind

In many ways, Descartes pursued a scientific approach much as Bacon described it. He was intrigued by math and geometry and was a great physicist. He was also interested in anatomy and made careful studies of the human body. What's more, he was interested in the mind.

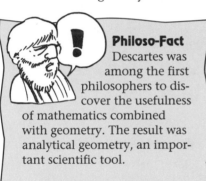

Philoso-Fact
Descartes was among the first philosophers to discover the usefulness of mathematics combined with geometry. The result was analytical geometry, an important scientific tool.

His approach to the mind was closely related to, but different from, the study of the natural world. The mind, according to Descartes, can do things that other things in nature can't do, like think and imagine and make conversation. Because of its special abilities, the mind, for Descartes, was not just something you could study like nature, which is purely physical.

The mind, said Descartes, is not simply made of material matter; it is also made up of spirit.

A Divided Mind

Descartes explained thinking by saying that it depends on two aspects, a body that works pretty much like a machine; and a mind that can't be explained in physical terms. If you've got a good memory, you'll recall from Chapter 2 that this view is called *dualism*.

Descartes carefully studied and described the physical aspect of the mind by dissecting the human brain and examining how it is connected to the rest of the body, including the eyes, ears, and nerves. At the same time, he studied the spiritual aspect of the mind by meditating, trying to see what made the mind able to know things. It was this focus on how the mind knows that separates Descartes' philosophy from Bacon's science.

The spiritual mind, according to Descartes, is always right, so long as it isn't misled, as it frequently is, by the material body. And everything that is capable of physical sensation comes from the bodily senses, which tell us what's going on around us—and which sometimes makes us do crazy things, unless the mind steps in and takes control.

A Passionate Affair

Our senses can mislead us by making us want things we don't really need, or by making us afraid of things that won't really hurt us, or generally by getting us to do things that we shouldn't do. Descartes referred to all of the feelings that can influence our minds in this way as *passions*. As you may remember from Chapter 3, the view that the mind can know things independently of physical reality is known as rationalism. Descartes is a preeminent rationalist.

The passions, said Descartes, can keep us from seeing the truth, making us act selfishly and thoughtlessly. We need to see beyond our passions with our spiritual minds in order to see the truth, which is not a matter of feelings, but, like math and geometry, is just the way things are.

Philoso-Fact
Descartes said that if the human body didn't have a spiritual "soul" inside it, it would work automatically, just like a machine. Many of Descartes' followers saw animals as machines—bodies without souls that worked automatically.

Keeping Government in Mind

Descartes' view of the mind and the passions was extremely influential. His thinking helped shift the responsibility for deciding how people should behave from the church and the government to the individual. Many people came to believe that, if they looked past their passions, they would see how they ought to behave. This idea made a big impact right at the time when the church and government were losing some of their influence and authority over people. It encouraged people to think for themselves—and govern themselves—without acting selfishly.

Philoso-Fact
Among those interested in Descartes' philosophy were women. Many of them drew on Descartes' thinking to argue that women are as rational as men.

His popularity in his own time was also due in part to the fact that his thinking helps reconcile religious and scientific ideas. Many people were concerned that scientific thinking ignored God by trying to explain the world in terms of natural principles. Descartes found a way to explain most of the world in terms of these natural principles, but he still left room for God and spirituality in the workings of the mind.

Even so, not everybody agreed with Descartes' view of the dualistic—spiritual and material—mind. One of the strongest opponents to the idea of spirituality was Bacon's friend, the Englishman Thomas Hobbes (1588–1679).

A Whale of a World View

Hobbes is most famous for his political philosophy, which argues that people ought to obey the king, even if he's a tyrant. If we don't, says Hobbes, we'll all end up killing and stealing from one another. We need a strong ruler to keep us in line and we must be loyal to this ruler even if he treats his subjects harshly. This argument is set forth in Hobbes' famous work *The Leviathan*.

A leviathan is a huge beast like a whale or a sea monster. Hobbes suggests that, without a strong ruler, human society is big and monstrous. In fact, according to Hobbes' view, society is pretty big and monstrous even *with* a ruler. In his words, "The condition of man…is a condition of war of everyone against everyone."

Not in the Spirit

This political philosophy is based on Hobbes' materialistic philosophy of nature and of the mind. Nature, according to Hobbes, is completely made up of material matter. There's nothing spiritual or magical about it. This view of nature is in keeping with the scientific view suggested by Bacon and later taken up by others.

> **Philoso-Fact**
> It is said that Hobbes used to sing in bed before going to sleep because he thought it was good for his lungs—a clear example of his mechanistic view of the human body.

The mind, according to Hobbes, is completely physical. Hobbes disliked the idea of spirit in the mind, because he felt it led people to cause trouble by claiming that they were directly in contact with God. In fact, during Hobbes' day, people were using spirituality as an excuse to disobey the government and the church.

These "enthusiasts" as they were called, did not like being told what to believe by the Church of England. They had an even bigger dislike for having to pay taxes to support the church. Frustration with established religion and with an authoritarian government came out in the form of fervent spirituality, or as they said, *enthusiasm*.

Hobbes did not say that all of these spiritual enthusiasts were deliberately trying to fool people. Instead, he said that their ideas about God had made them crazy. In response, he developed a philosophy based on the material workings of nature in which the mind is a physical thing.

> **Reality Check**
> Hobbes' view of religious enthusiasts helped promote the idea that people are crazy if their way of thinking benefits them socially and economically. Today, most people think the opposite is true—if your ideas don't help you, there's something wrong with the way you think!

Thinking Machines

Hobbes believed that all thoughts and sensations in the mind are produced mechanically by the senses and the brain. When we perceive something, let's say a dandelion, what is really happening is that light is bouncing off the plant and striking our eyes. The nerves and tissues in our eyes react to the light and send a signal to our brain, making us *think* we see the dandelion. What we really "see," though, is not the dandelion itself, but the effect the dandelion has on our senses.

Our senses and our minds, in other words, work like machines. The problem is, these machines don't always tell us the truth, they often tell us things that we want to believe or things that we are afraid might be true.

According to Hobbes, when an enthusiast feels connected to God, or feels moved by the Holy Spirit to reject the teachings of the established church or the commands of the king, he's only responding to the effects of his physical senses. People who think that God is speaking to them are mistaken; they are being led astray by their minds.

Weak Minds, Strong Ruler

Because, according to Hobbes, people's minds are not reliable, people can't be trusted to coexist peacefully with one another. They're naturally prone to fight with one another unless they have a strong government to keep them in line. Without government, said Hobbes, we would all be living in "the state of nature," a dog-eat-dog world where there is no peace. In Hobbes' famous words, life in the state of nature is "nasty, brutish, and short."

Therefore we need to be obedient to a strong ruler, the king, who will protect us from one another and from ourselves. In some ways, of course, this idea was very conservative, since it defended the traditional form of government.

At the same time, though, it put a new wrinkle into the idea of kingship. Hobbes revised the idea that kings ruled by "divine right." According to him, it isn't the king's majesty or God's will that make kingship what it is; it's the people who get together and say "be our king."

Hobbes' political views were more severe than Locke's. He recommended extreme measures in governing, much as Machiavelli did in the preceding century, to secure stability for his country, which was going through civil war. Hobbes wanted people to stop fighting and relinquish control to a single ruler.

Philoso-Fact
Hobbes' idea that the people should decide how they are to be ruled sets the stage for the "social contract" proposed some years later by John Locke. According to this concept, society makes a kind of contract with itself to give power to a ruling body. (See Chapter 16.)

Gentlemen Don't Fight

The early scientists, Hobbes' contemporaries, also wanted the fighting to stop. But unlike Hobbes, they didn't think a strong ruler was the solution. Rather, it was science and the rational mind that would come to the rescue. Once people stopped fighting and took time to think, they would come to a reasonable agreement. They used science as a way to practice working out problems and disagreements.

Thinking about—and also experimenting with—the natural world provided early scientists with a way of putting aside political disagreements. Scientific experiments required that people be detached and objective about things, leaving their own personal concerns and desires out of the picture. This way of thinking was especially appealing to aristocratic men who liked to think of themselves as unconcerned by personal disputes. They wanted to place themselves above all the wrangling that was going on.

> **Reality Check**
>
> Although science is widely associated with impartial inquiry, people have often used what they call "science" to further their own interests. For example, so-called scientific studies of racial and sexual characteristics have been used as evidence that certain groups of people are superior to others.

Originally, scientific activity was limited almost exclusively to aristocratic men. In fact, it was in their best interest to promote philosophical activities rather than make political waves. England had just been through a revolution and everybody's nerves were frazzled. Science fit the bill perfectly. Scientists made a point of being polite to one another and tried to be respectful of other people's views whenever they had disagreements.

Science, of course, became a big success and led to many important discoveries about how the world works. Part of the price of its success was that it had to leave aside questions about human nature and government that continued to cause heated disagreements.

Eye of Newton

Among the major triumphs of the early days of science were the laws of physics established by Sir Isaac Newton (1642–1727). Newton developed these "laws" by applying mathematical principles to the study of physical things.

Formulas for Everything

Scientific study of the natural world became especially fruitful when scientists learned to apply mathematical principles to things. Philosophers had been interested in mathematics for centuries, and had proposed all kinds of ways in which it might be relevant to philosophy. Before the 17th century, though, no one had really figured out how to apply math to the study of material objects.

Newton figured out mathematical formulas that described mechanical relationships between things. He is credited with developing calculus and a number of formulas that have become accepted as "laws" of physics. For example, he figured out an equation that describes the relationship of force, motion, and acceleration for all moving things:

$$\textbf{force} = \textbf{motion} \times \textbf{acceleration}$$

He also figured out a formula for describing the force of gravity. The impressive thing about these mechanical formulas is that they applied to all things, no matter what their size or weight.

Shedding New Light on Color

Newton went on to make further accomplishments, including his discovery that all light is made up of combinations of different colors. He found that beams of light can be separated by a prism into the colors of the spectrum: red, orange, yellow, green, blue, indigo, and violet.

This means that color isn't actually *in* the things we look at, but rather is the result of light that bounces off them. Things appear to have colors because they are made of materials that reflect certain colors of light. A rose is red, in other words, because red light bounces off it.

Philoso-Fact
Although Newton's physical formulas are recognized today as more significant than his work with optics and light, he was best known during his own lifetime for his work with light. It made a big impression because it was easy to understand and made people think in new ways about how they see things.

The Least You Need to Know

➤ Sir Francis Bacon's idea that knowledge should be a group project paved the way for modern science.

➤ Bacon identified reasons people cling to mistaken ideas, which he classified as the four idols.

➤ Some philosophers objected to science for religious reasons; others objected because it did not take the mind into account.

➤ Descartes believed the mind had a physical and a spiritual aspect.

➤ Hobbes saw the mind as completely physical; our thoughts and feelings are caused by material processes.

➤ Newton gave science a big boost by applying math to the study of things in motion.

Chapter 15

Men and Women of Substance

In This Chapter

➤ Different philosophical conceptions of substance: Spinoza, Leibniz, and Cavendish

➤ How substance relates to intellect

➤ How we can have free will even if God knows everything ahead of time

➤ Logic as a foundation for reality

➤ Conflict as a foundation for reality

Substance is the stuff reality is made of. Different philosophers had different ideas about substance. Some, namely dualists like Descartes, believed in immaterial, thinking substance and in material, non-thinking substance. Hobbes believed only in material substance that cannot think, but causes thinking in the human mind. Still others believed everything is made of a single material substance that can think.

Being in the Know

Among the more interesting and imaginative conceptions of substance were those developed by the English philosopher Margaret Cavendish, Duchess of Newcastle (1624–1674); the Portuguese-Dutch philosopher, Baruch Spinoza (1632–1677); and the German philosopher Gottfried Wilhelm Leibniz (1646–1716).

While the philosophy of each of these thinkers differs from the others in many respects, they are all similar in rejecting the dualistic, mind-and-matter view of substance suggested by Descartes. What's more, they all say that perception and awareness are not limited to human beings. Knowing is woven in with substance itself.

Spinoza's and Leibniz's philosophies provide different understandings of how reality is ordered. For Spinoza, reality takes shape out of the substance that makes up everything. For Leibniz, reality takes shape from an infinite number of monads that come together according to what he called a "pre-established harmony" determined by God.

God and Nature Are Us

Spinoza was born in Amsterdam, where his Jewish parents had fled from Portugal to escape persecution. Although Spinoza was raised as an Orthodox Jew, he was kicked out of his community because of his philosophical ideas, which challenged the religious views of Jews and Christians alike.

Lexicon

Pantheism is the belief that God is all things. This means that people and Nature are aspects of God and have divine power in and of themselves. Pantheism is a kind of *monism*, the belief that everything is one and the same.

Substance is a philosophical term for that which exists. Some 17th century philosophers used substance to mean material matter; others used it to refer to what is both material *and* spiritual.

Spinoza was a *pantheist*. This means that he believed God is all things. Spinoza's pantheism bothered religious authorities because he did not make a big distinction between God and Nature. Spinoza's God couldn't do anything that Nature couldn't do. Some of Spinoza's pantheist beliefs suggested that there is no immortal human soul, that human actions are determined ahead of time, and that there is no afterlife.

For Spinoza, all of God and Nature is a single substance. This substance is self-determined. It doesn't have to be explained in terms of other causes because there is nothing outside it that makes it what it is.

We can think about substance in two ways, said Spinoza. We can think about it as Nature, in terms of its physical properties and in terms of the fact that it takes up space. Or we can think about it as God, in terms of the fact that it reveals its intellect. These two ways of thinking about substance both refer to different "attributes" of substance. Spinoza called these two attributes *extension* and *thought*, respectively.

Thought is the idea of extension, and extension is the embodiment of thought. Even though these attributes refer to the same thing, they don't *appear* to be the same to us, Spinoza said. As human beings, we can't explain extension in terms of thought or thought in terms of extension. In other words, we can't talk about mind as if it were body, or body as if it were mind, even though they are actually the same substance.

Spinoza à la Mode

Even though everything is all the same substance, this substance takes different forms, or *modes*. Modes, unlike substance, need to be explained in terms of something else, since modes depend on substance for their existence. A mode is *in* substance, sort of like a wave is in the ocean or lumps are in oatmeal. People, animals, plants, and things are modes.

Modes account for why things take different shapes. As modes, we are all just a part of everything else, except that the substance that makes us up keeps trying to stay together as us. In fact, said Spinoza, all modes and everything that happens to them are predetermined by substance.

Reality Check

If everything that happens is predetermined as Spinoza says, then even the most horrible events are supposed to take place. All we should do, Spinoza suggests, is just accept things. This outlook may seem disheartening to many and discourage people from trying to improve their situation.

This is true, according to Spinoza, for both attributes of substance: thought and extension. Spinoza believed that everything happens as it must, according to the way that substance—God and Nature   shapes and changes itself as both mind (thought) and matter (extension).

Where There's a Will, There's a Way

Spinoza certainly had his critics. The idea that people have no free will—no control of their own lives and destinies—isn't one that everyone was quick to embrace. Spinoza argued that if there's no free will, then there's no afterlife or immortal soul either. (Think how his critics liked that one!) The reasoning goes that if there is no free will, people can't choose to be good and act right, and then there would be no reason for some people and not others to go to a heaven when they die.

Philoso-Fact
Spinoza worked for much of his life as a grinder of glass lenses. He died of tuberculosis, which was probably made worse from breathing particles of glass.

Although Spinoza seemed not to believe in heaven, he did say that people have at least a *limited* amount of free will. After all, we're made up of the same stuff that God is. We are free, said Spinoza, to accept what happens to us by understanding how we fit into the big picture of existence. In other words, we can decide to go along with what our substance is predetermined to do.

The Truth Will Set You Free

We can do this, said Spinoza, by looking past our passions. Spinoza's view of the passions is similar to that of Descartes': our passions are likely to mislead us into worrying too much about ourselves. Spinoza thought that our passions stand in the way of our ability to accept what we are and to see how we fit in with everything else.

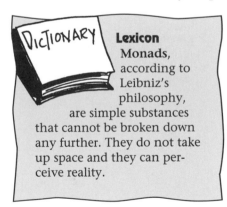

Wisdom at Work
Use Spinoza's idea that people's substance stays around forever as another reason for not littering. The substance contained in the trash you throw around may once have belonged to your great grandmother. Treat eternal substance with respect by disposing of it properly, or by recycling!

Accepting what we are, seeing ourselves as part of God, Nature, and the substance of reality, for Spinoza, is better than dying and going to heaven. He said that his belief in one substance was not only truer, but actually more hopeful and uplifting than religious belief in an afterlife. Seeing yourself this way, he said, is like seeing yourself as a part of eternity. *You* won't be around forever, but your substance will.

Spinoza wanted to be accepting of life and of other people. He said, "I have striven not to laugh at human actions, nor to weep at them, nor hate them, but to understand them."

A Man of Many Monads

Spinoza believed that people can exercise a limited amount of free will by choosing to go along with what happens and by understanding how what happens fits in with the big picture. This view is related to the way he sees people as only partially distinct from substance in general. You are made up of the same substance as everything else; the only difference is that you can decide how you feel about things and choose to act on your reason rather than your passion.

Lexicon
Monads, according to Leibniz's philosophy, are simple substances that cannot be broken down any further. They do not take up space and they can perceive reality.

Leibniz's philosophy, like Spinoza's, sees people as only partly distinct from everything else that exists. Everything, people included, is made up of monads. All monads have similar properties, but each monad is different. Like snowflakes, no two monads are exactly alike.

Different monads have greater or less ability to see what's going on around them. Those monads with the most ability to think and perceive are human souls. All monads, though, reflect the world. To better grasp this, think of each monad as a kind of point of view for seeing everything, and everything is actually made up of an infinite number of different points of view.

Many Views, One Picture

Leibniz believed the world has infinite variety. At the same time, everything is connected, not only in fact, but logically too, in that it all makes sense together. Leibniz said that if people (or monads) had infinite minds like God, we would be able to understand everything in its infinite variety just by looking at one individual thing.

The truth is, though, that people *don't* have infinite minds. We can only understand certain things about the world. Only God can see the big picture. This means that things that may seem accidental to us are still part of God's plan.

Philoso-Fact
Leibniz's idea that the world contains infinite variety encouraged speculation during his time that the universe may be infinite and that intelligent life may exist on other planets.

What Happens to You Is Part of You

What does this mean exactly? Well, think of Caesar crossing the Rubicon. Caesar crossed the Rubicon, but if he hadn't crossed the Rubicon, he wouldn't have been Caesar. Even before he crossed it, he was going to. The fact of his crossing the Rubicon is one of millions of facts that make up the completeness of Caesar. These facts, said Leibniz, are all a part of what Caesar is, so if you change any of them, you no longer have Caesar as he actually existed.

This way of looking at things means that there is no real difference between *innate* characteristics—characteristics that are internally part of something—and *acquired* characteristics—characteristics that happen to things somewhere along the way. What happens to you is just as much a part of you as what you already are.

The difference is in how people see things. Different things might happen to you in another possible world, but that world would not be as good as this one. Leibniz says that God chose to make the world be the way it is because this world is "the best of all possible worlds."

The World Is a Math Problem

According to Leibniz, a better world could not possibly have existed. Leibniz's ideas about what makes for the best possible world are based on mathematical ideas. As a mathematician, Leibniz looked for the simplest explanations that would account for the greatest number of numerical relationships. And as a philosopher, he believed God set up the world so that the simplest reasons would account for the most variety.

Reality Check

When Leibniz spoke of "the best of all possible worlds," he did not mean a world in which people are happy and don't have to pay taxes or clean the bathroom. He meant "best" from a logical standpoint: a tremendous variety of things can be explained with a few simple ideas.

God might have made other worlds, but they would not be as infinitely various or as logically organized. Still, we can imagine what these worlds would have been like. If fewer mathematical possibilities could be explained by each simple rule, then logically there would be less variety. Thus, in these other possible worlds lies a limited amount of freedom.

Like Spinoza, Leibniz did not leave much room in his world for free will. Leibniz believed that everything that happens is a result of what already exists. In turn, what exists depends on God. Because God might have caused things to be different, there is a certain amount of free play in Leibniz's system. The facts might have been different, but logically it must make the best sense for them to be the way they are.

A Man of Principles

Here are some logical rules that form the basis of Leibniz's philosophy:

> ➤ **The principle of non-contradiction:** Any contradictory relation is false.
>
> ➤ **The principle of sufficient reason:** There is a good, or "sufficient" reason for everything that is true, even if we don't know that it is.
>
> ➤ **The principle of predication:** Everything that happens to something (all of a thing's predicates) is a part of what that thing is, both logically and in fact.
>
> ➤ **The principle of the identity of indiscernibles:** No two things can be exactly alike (indiscernible) without being the same thing.
>
> ➤ **The principle of the best world:** God made this world the best of all possible worlds; it is logically the most various and the simplest to understand.

It's Only Logical

Both Spinoza and Leibniz were interested in math and logic and believed that the world reflects logical relationships. Logic, for these philosophers, is not just something your mind does, it is actually the basis of reality.

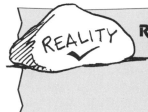

Reality Check

One big problem with basing reality on logic is that you have to start with some assumptions somewhere. If your initial assumptions aren't true, your whole system may be wrong.

These philosophical views are not based on observation and experience, but on what must logically be the case, given the ideas of God and substance. Like Descartes, then, Spinoza and Leibniz are rationalists, believing that knowledge is reliable when it is not based on observation, but reason.

Taking a Chance on Substance

For Cavendish, unlike Leibniz and Spinoza, reality, including the mind, is organized by chance. Cavendish's theory says that although everything is made up of the same substance, that substance is infinitely divisible. And although all the different parts can think, they don't necessarily agree on how to come together in order to form the world. As a result, the substance that makes up reality is often in conflict with itself.

Different substances may agree to come together to form a rock or a plant or a person. Later, the same substances may disagree and decide to come apart at the seams! It all depends on how well all the parts get along.

Philoso-Fact
Many people in Cavendish's time thought she was mad. And she didn't dispute this but played along to show how things—including not only the world but her own thoughts as well—tend to become disordered.

Pushing the Limits

Cavendish is one of a very few women philosophers to write prior to the 20th century. In fact, she saw herself as the first woman philosopher and was proud of being unusual. In her day, women were not expected to come up with their own philosophies, and as a result, Cavendish seems not to have expected people to take her seriously.

Rather than try to persuade men that she was as smart as they were, she looked at all ideas as equally irrational, including her own. To Cavendish, the point of an idea was not to be right, or true, but to reveal the richness and variety of nature. Ideas, for Cavendish, are natural things that work pretty much the way all natural things work.

Although Cavendish's philosophy drew on the new currents of empiricism and rationalism, her philosophy was based neither on logic nor on observation. Instead, Cavendish believed that the substance of nature was not limited by logical or empirical laws.

The Matter with Cavendish

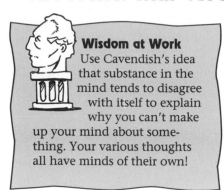

Wisdom at Work
Use Cavendish's idea that substance in the mind tends to disagree with itself to explain why you can't make up your mind about something. Your various thoughts all have minds of their own!

Cavendish called natural substance *only matter*. Only matter, unlike Leibniz's monads, is infinitely divisible. What's more, different portions of only matter do not exist in a "pre-established harmony" as they do in Leibniz's substance. Instead, different portions of substance can disagree.

When Cavendish's substance disagrees, things fall apart. A body dies and decomposes, for example, when the substance that forms it no longer wants to stay together in that body. Similarly, when substance disagrees in your head, you will be confused and have contradictory ideas.

It's All Mental

In fact, the substance inside Cavendish's head was frequently in a state of disagreement. She expressed this disagreement in her philosophical writings by talking about how her "thoughts" believed different things about the world. For example, some of her thoughts think that when the body dies and decays, its parts will reunite in a perfect world where they will always be happy. Other thoughts think that this idea is ridiculous and say that the body will never come back together once it has come apart.

Philoso-Fact
Although Cavendish was extremely shy about speaking in public, she liked to show off by designing her own fancy costumes and driving around London in her coach.

Cavendish often contradicts herself when she writes about issues that other philosophers argued about in her time. These issues include whether there is such a thing as immaterial substance, whether the universe was formed by random combinations of atoms, and whether women are the intellectual equals of men.

She does not always resolve her disagreements, but when she does, she often suggests that the solution is not found by logical reasoning, but by force. Thoughts are material things, and persuade other thoughts that they are "right" by overpowering them, threatening them, or promising to help them.

Thoughts, then, care first and foremost about themselves. In fact, Cavendish's own thoughts were important to her not so much because she thought they were true, but because she hoped that they would make themselves—and her—famous. She had them printed and bound in expensive leather bindings and sent them to other philosophers and to important universities in hopes of making a big splash!

Knowledge in Conflict

Thoughts, in other words, behave just like people do, pretending, arguing, threatening, sympathizing, forgiving, agreeing, and disagreeing. In fact, according to Cavendish, all material substance can think and forms itself into bodies just as people organize themselves into groups. Bodies come apart just as people disagree and argue.

As Cavendish saw it, people's ideas in general are prone to disagree with one another. Ideas behave the same way everything else does: by conflicting and by trying to do the best they can. And in fact, this kind of conflict was abundantly evident in the philosophical arguments that took place during Cavendish's time.

Because ideas are always in conflict just like everything else, Cavendish says a philosopher cannot simply "know" the truth of the way things are. Instead, the things a philosopher thinks simply reflect the way substance is coming together in his or her head.

Cavendish sees reality as made up of substance that is mostly in a state of conflict with itself. Conflicts may be temporarily or partially resolved so that living things can take shape.

Cavendish's view of conflict applies not only to mental and physical reality, but to society too. In fact, she developed her philosophical ideas during the English Civil War and wrote philosophical poetry comparing this war to the violent motions of atoms.

Imagining Philosophy

Cavendish's writing is philosophical not only because she wrote about philosophical ideas, but because she believed that writing was a natural activity of her mind. Her writing not only *explains* how the world works, it also *demonstrates* how it works by showing how her thoughts behave in the same contradictory way as the rest of reality.

Cavendish's thoughts take shape out of the substance of her mind, just as things in the world take shape out of the substance of reality. This means that she sees less of a clear distinction between reason and imagination than other philosophers of her time. As a result, her philosophical thinking is filled with imaginary concepts, and her imaginative writing is filled with philosophical ideas.

Philoso-Fact
One of Cavendish's imaginative philosophical ideas is that your brain is inhabited by fairies who do your thinking for you. She says that when you get a toothache, it's because the fairies are digging out the substance of your teeth to use as building materials for their city inside your brain.

Cavendish wrote numerous philosophical and imaginative descriptions of the brain and the brain's thoughts. In her stories, plays, and poems she compares the brain to things like a garden, a wilderness, a city, a university, and a church; she compares thoughts to flowers, trees, animals, people, and food.

In a literal sense, her own thoughts really do take the shape of the things she compares them to. A thought about an animal closely resembles the animal and may roam around in her mind just as a real animal moves through the forest.

The Least You Need to Know

➤ Spinoza, Leibniz, and Cavendish saw thought as an inherent aspect of substance.

➤ Spinoza and Leibniz were rationalists who saw logic woven into reality.

➤ Spinoza believed that God, Nature, and substance are the same thing.

➤ Leibniz believed that substance is made up of an infinite number of independent monads.

➤ Cavendish saw everything as taking shape out of conflict, including physical things, society, and the mind.

Chapter 16

Learning by Observing

In This Chapter

➤ How Locke explained human understanding

➤ The mind as a blank slate

➤ Locke's new ideas about government

➤ Why Berkeley said there is no substance

➤ How Hume tried to apply science to morality

By the end of the 17th century, science had scored it big in physics, biology, astronomy, and other areas. Impressed with these accomplishments, philosophers began to think that maybe science could be used to shed new light on moral philosophy as well—that maybe scientific techniques could be used to explain how we think, how we understand, and how we should live in society.

This scientific approach opened up new opportunities for philosophy because it provided a potential new source of knowledge about what people are like. It made philosophers hopeful that they could find better ways of thinking about religion, human rights, and human nature.

The Sun Never Sets on British Empiricism

Many of the important empirical philosophers of the 17th and 18th centuries were British. This might have been partly because of all the religious and political difficulties England was suffering at the time. Religion and government were often out of control, but at least empirical reality is almost always well organized!

Observant Brits

➤ **Sir Francis Bacon** (1561–1626) proposed a program for revising old knowledge and learning new knowledge based on observation.

➤ **Thomas Hobbes** (1588–1679) derived his philosophy of mind and government from mechanical principles. He rejected the notion of "immaterial spirit."

➤ **Sir Robert Boyle** (1627–1692) studied physics and chemistry and invented the barometer.

➤ **John Locke** (1632–1704) described human understanding in empirical terms, arguing that there are no innate ideas. He based his political views on the idea of "natural rights."

Philoso-Fact
Empiricism in Britain got a big boost from the British Royal Society, an organization of scientists and philosophers who met to share ideas and conduct experiments.

➤ **Sir Isaac Newton** (1642–1727) revolutionized physics with his formulas for matter and motion. He also helped develop calculus and made important discoveries in the field of optics.

➤ **David Hume** (1711–1776) developed a philosophy of human nature by describing the limitations of scientific reasoning.

➤ **George Berkeley** (1748–1832) argued against the existence of substance by saying that empiricism tells us only that our ideas exist.

A Locke on Understanding

Empiricism in Europe had been gathering steam for many decades before the British philosopher John Locke made it popular by using it to explain how people know things. According to Locke, empiricism isn't just a way of thinking for philosophers and scientists; it's the basis for how all people learn everything they know.

Empiricism, as you may remember from Chapter 3, is the idea that knowledge we get through observation and experience is more reliable than knowledge we get from just reason alone. Locke took this idea even further by saying that *all* knowledge comes from observation and experience. As he put it, there are no innate ideas.

An innate idea is an idea you are born with, and Locke said we are born with no ideas whatsoever. We get all our ideas through experience. This includes not only ideas of things that we have actually observed, like fire hydrants and chicken soup, but of abstract concepts too, like number, shape, and size.

Locke provides a detailed explanation of how we get all of our various and complicated ideas through experience in his famous work *An Essay Concerning the Human Understanding*. Here he says that the senses and the mind work together to turn experience into understanding.

Your understanding, he says, is made up of impressions, ideas, sensations, and reflections, all responding to experience and interacting to produce everything you think. Even imaginary ideas, like dragons and ghosts and winning the lottery are put together out of things that we've actually experienced.

Wisdom at Work
Use Locke's idea that everyone's understanding is based on experience to explain why you see things differently from everyone else. For instance, if you grew up getting criticized for arguing, you'll see things very differently from someone who was encouraged to argue.

Your Mind Was a Blank

When you're born, says Locke, your mind is like a blank slate (or *tabula rasa*, which means "blank slate" in Latin). As you see things, hear things, and touch things, you learn about them and remember them. Experience and observation are like the chalk that writes knowledge on your blank slate.

This view revised the older Aristotelian idea that the things we perceive are actually inside our minds when we perceive them. Instead, said Locke, we know of things only because our perceptions produce sensations of things from which we form ideas. These ideas may be very different from the things themselves.

Is Knowledge Accidental?

Locke's concept of *the understanding* as wholly based on experience, was controversial in his time. His strongest opponent, Gottfried Leibniz, complained that Locke didn't give logic and reason big enough parts in the understanding. Leibniz said that the mind has an idea of substance, of the self, and of God without ever having to experience them. To Leibniz, Locke's view of the understanding left too much to chance. We don't know things just by accident, but rather according to a natural design, a divine plan.

In spite of objections, Locke's thinking was popular and influential. People found it important because of what it says about knowledge: What we know is limited to our experience. Putting such limits on knowledge means that a lot of what people thought they knew had to go out the window. In fact, Locke devoted much of his time and energy to arguing against old political views.

Taking God out of Government

Locke didn't go so far as to say that there is no such thing as God. Even though we can't experience God, Locke said we can demonstrate his existence in much the same way that a geometric proof can be demonstrated. Although he left room for God, he argued against another "sacred" idea that many people held during his time: *the divine right of kings*.

Divine Right Bites the Dust

The divine right of kings had justified kingship for centuries. It was defended in Locke's day by a now-obscure political philosopher, Robert Filmer. Filmer said that all true kings are directly descended from Adam, the first man to be created by God.

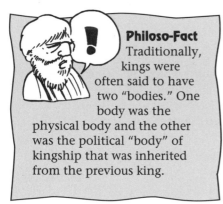

Philoso-Fact
Traditionally, kings were often said to have two "bodies." One body was the physical body and the other was the political "body" of kingship that was inherited from the previous king.

According to Filmer, when God granted Adam and his offspring dominion over the earth, (as it says in the Book of Genesis) he also implicitly granted a special right to kings to rule over other people. Kings loved Filmer and his idea because it helped secure people's loyalty to them. By the time Locke came along, though, the divine right of kings idea had pretty much run its course.

Locke had lived through some dramatic changes in the way England was governed. He saw two revolutions. The first involved a civil war and resulted in King Charles I getting his head cut off. The second one, known as the "bloodless revolution," involved replacing King James II with King George I from Germany.

With all these kings coming and going like bad TV shows, England needed a new way to think about government. Clearly, rule by divine right wasn't making it anymore.

In place of the divine right of kings, Locke proposed a government based on reason and natural rights.

Back to Nature

Locke said that people have natural rights even before they get together to form a society. These rights don't depend on any form of government or on any conventional agreements between people. This idea of a natural human society that exists without any laws or agreements draws on Thomas Hobbes' concept of *the state of nature*. Nature for Locke, though, is a much nicer place than it is for Hobbes. For Hobbes the only "natural" right people have is to beat up on one another.

For Locke, in contrast, people have the natural right to make free choices, to live without being injured by others, and to own property. What gives people the right to own property, says Locke, is the work they have done in order to get it or develop it.

Reality Check

The *state of nature* is only a theoretical idea. In fact, there are no human societies that exist without laws, conventions, or agreements for how to do things. Different societies make different rules, so it's hard to say which rules are more "natural" than others.

My Work, My Stuff

Someone who plows and plants a field and harvests the crops, for example, has a right to own the crops, since he or she labored to produce them. Locke said this rule makes natural sense and does not depend on a particular form of government.

This connection between labor and the right of ownership helped promote *capitalism*, the economic practice of making things and selling them to make a profit. Capitalism gradually replaced feudalism in Europe. *Feudalism* is the economic structure in which land is owned by the nobility and worked by the peasants; the peasants in turn gave allegiance to the nobility in exchange for protection. Locke would say that feudalism violated people's natural right to own property.

Lexicon
Capitalism is the economic practice of producing goods and services and selling them at a profit. Capitalism gradually replaced **feudalism**, the economic structure in which the nobility owns the land that is farmed by the serfs, or peasants, who support the nobles in exchange for protection.

149

Society's Dotted Line

Because everyone has natural rights, he said, government should be a matter of mutual consent among everyone involved. He called this mutual consent a *social compact* (or contract). People agree to come together as a group and be governed in order to have their rights protected.

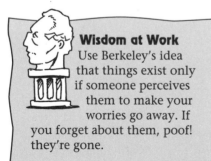

Philoso-Fact
Locke's ideas about government figured prominently in the thinking that took place during both the American and the French revolutions. Versions of Locke's natural rights were adopted into the *American Constitution* and the *Bill of Rights* in the U.S., as well as into the French *Declaration of the Rights of Man and the Citizen*.

Locke said this agreement did not have to be official; it could be implied. If you live under a government without complaining, you agree, in effect, to live by the rules of that government. If you don't like it, said Locke, you can always move somewhere else.

This was a far cry from the concept of the divine right of kings. Lots of people picked up on it, including the French philosopher Jean-Jacques Rousseau, and Americans like Thomas Jefferson and Thomas Paine.

Just as Locke's political ideas had a big influence on other political philosophers, his ideas about understanding influenced other empirical philosophers. Two philosophers in particular, Bishop George Berkeley (1685–1753) and David Hume (1711–1777), built on Locke's ideas, taking his thinking in very different directions.

A Better Idea

Although Locke's empiricism made sense to a lot of people, many noticed problems with it. One problem had to do with the idea of substance. Locke said that substance exists, even though all we can know about it are ideas that we get through our impressions; furthermore, these impressions don't tell us that what we are sensing actually *is* substance.

Wisdom at Work
Use Berkeley's idea that things exist only if someone perceives them to make your worries go away. If you forget about them, poof! they're gone.

Substance may cause our senses to send messages to our brain, but it is not the same thing as those messages. How, then, can Locke be sure that substance really exists?

Berkeley and Hume came up with different answers to this question. Hume said that we have to put up with not being sure about a lot of things, including substance, causality, and even the self. Berkeley's answer was even weirder: material substance doesn't exist. All that exists are ideas and the souls that perceive them. The only place that anything exists, says Berkeley, is in the mind, or soul. In order for something to exist, someone has to perceive it. If no one perceives it, it doesn't exist.

If a Tree Falls in the Forest...

Take this book for example; or a chair, or your fingernails. Berkeley would say these things have no material existence, but that they are only ideas. Some ideas are ideas we perceive, others are ideas we remember, and others we invent out of other ideas we once perceived. Understanding, according to Berkeley, works pretty much the way Locke said it did, only there's no material substance that's making it all happen.

It was after reading Berkeley that someone asked the famous philosophical question: "If a tree falls in the forest and no one is around to hear, does it make any sound?" Berkeley had an answer for this. He said that all things exist in the mind of God. God perceives everything that exists. As a result, things can continue to exist indefinitely and as they really are, even though they are only ideas. The falling tree, then, makes a sound because God is there to hear it.

We have some of the same ideas God has. On the other hand, when we have mistaken ideas, the whole world doesn't go out of whack, since God is there all along with the right ideas.

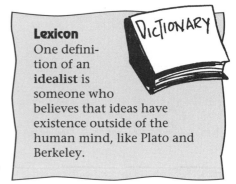

Lexicon
One definition of an **idealist** is someone who believes that ideas have existence outside of the human mind, like Plato and Berkeley.

Because he said that ideas exist in the mind of God independently of human minds, Berkeley is, like Plato, an *idealist*. Plato said that ideas are the cause of actual things and that they are perfect and unchanging. Berkeley, unlike Plato, made no distinction between ideas and material reality. For Berkeley, material reality isn't real at all.

Although Berkeley said that only ideas exist, he was, in a way, an empiricist too. Ideas, he said, are pretty much all we can experience. All that our experience and observation can really tell us is that we have ideas. It would be a mistake, therefore, said Berkeley, to assume that there is anything besides ideas and those people doing the perceiving.

Soul Exceptions

There are only two things, other than ideas, that exist according to Berkeley: God and souls. Although we cannot directly perceive souls or God, we can figure out they exist based on the way our ideas hold together.

Berkeley saw God and souls as the reality behind sense impressions in much the same way as Locke saw material substance. Our impressions add up to something that is more than just them, so even though they are all we have to think with, we can be sure that there is a real world. Locke and Berkeley simply disagreed about whether the real world consists of material substance or of God and souls.

Hume-an Nature

Both Locke and Berkeley focused on sense impressions as the basis of understanding and they tried to figure out what we can say for certain based on these. Another philosopher who did this was David Hume. Hume wanted to develop a science of the mind and of human nature that would be as coherent and reliable as the science of physics as practiced by Isaac Newton and some of his contemporaries.

Blinded with Science

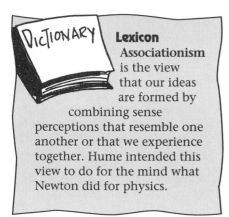

Lexicon
Associationism is the view that our ideas are formed by combining sense perceptions that resemble one another or that we experience together. Hume intended this view to do for the mind what Newton did for physics.

In his efforts to formulate a scientific view of the mind, Hume met with some serious obstacles—obstacles created by our own natural inability to think about the world scientifically. Hume comes close to using science against itself—using science, that is, to show science's limitations.

Hume tried to look at human understanding in much the same way that physicists were looking at matter, motion, gravity, and other natural forces. Based on an analogy he noticed between physical and mental processes, he proposed a new way of thinking about how sense impressions come together to form ideas. Just as masses in space are attracted to each other by the force of gravity, our impressions are attracted to one another too. Hume's view of how the mind works is known as *associationism*.

Ideas Associated

Sense impressions, says Hume, come together in our minds if they are similar to one another or if we experience them together. In other words, they come together in our minds through association.

For example, we may associate dogs with fleas because we often experience them together. This association contributes to our ideas of what dogs and fleas are. Our entire idea of dogs is formed by all the associations our minds have made in perceiving dogs, including drooling, biting, chasing squirrels, and smelling funny.

Hume's associationism is based on an empirical view of the understanding just as Locke's and Berkeley's ideas are. For Hume, though, associationism leads away from empirical knowledge. The stuff we know is put together out of resemblances and coincidences—connections that aren't as reliable as the scientific laws Newton formulated.

Hume's Fork

Part of the problem, said Hume, has to do with the difference between facts on the one hand and reason on the other. This split between facts and reason is known as *Hume's fork*. Facts are just facts. You can't use them to tell anything certain about other facts. What's more, facts aren't logically necessary. We have no way of knowing that what exists *has* to exist or whether something else might have existed just as easily.

On the other hand, there are logical connections that we can make among ideas. Even so, these connections tell us only about relationships, not about facts. This means that facts and relationships are split like the prongs of a fork. We may associate them in our minds, but they are really different things. Accidental facts and logical relations can't work together to tell us what reality is like for certain. All we can really do, said Hume, is make guesses.

Hume complained about philosophers who mistakenly make assumptions about reason based on facts and about facts based on reason in order to come up with metaphysical ideas about reality. These mistaken ideas include God, the self, and causality. We can't prove them, either by relating them to other ideas or through experiment.

Hume said that we tend to believe that things have causes, but we have no way of knowing what things in particular cause other things. Instead, we form beliefs about cause based on associations we have made. These associations do not tell us how things actually happen. Instead, they reflect the way our natural instincts, habits, and social conventions have formed our beliefs about the world.

Lexicon
Hume's fork represents the idea that facts do not exist in any necessary logical relationships, and relationships do not presuppose any particular facts. Hume used his "fork" to criticize metaphysical notions including causality.

A lot of how we think, in other words, does not depend on reason or on empiricism, but on human nature. Hume relied on this idea of human nature in order to defend our beliefs. They may not be exactly true, but we need them to think with, so we shouldn't reject them.

Inner Virtue

Hume applied his scientific view of human nature not only to our beliefs about matters of fact, but to our moral judgments as well. He compared ideas of virtue and vice (good and bad behavior) to experiments Newton had done with the colors of light.

Newton said that light doesn't really *have* color. Instead, light produces a sensation of color in our minds when we see it. Similarly, people's actions in and of themselves are neither good nor bad, but produce judgments of good and bad inside us.

Killing someone, for example, has no significance outside of the feelings of the people who are aware of the killing. It's just a fact. This fact, though, causes people to judge the killing as a bad thing. This tendency to judge things is part of human nature. It is in *us*

Wisdom at Work
Use Hume's concept of human nature to explain anything people do that seems to have no other explanation. Why do we buy so many things we'll never use? It must just be human nature.

rather than in the actual event that we respond to. In Hume's words, "Beauty in things exists in the mind which contemplates them."

Making judgments about the way things ought to be based on the way things are is not a purely logical way of thinking. Logically, facts and judgments of facts have no necessary relationship. Judgments, in other words, are not "true" in the sense that facts can be true.

People like to believe, though, that their actions and judgments are based on logical reasons. When we think this way, says Hume, we are only fooling ourselves. Our actions and, to a large extent, our beliefs, are determined by desire rather than reason.

Is, Isn't, Ought

The mistaken idea that we can say what ought to be true based on what is in fact true is known as the *naturalistic fallacy*, and was first described by Hume. The naturalistic fallacy is also known as *Hume's law*, which says "no is from an ought."

Lexicon
The **naturalistic fallacy** is the mistaken idea that we can say how things ought to be, based on a knowledge of how things are. It is also known as **Hume's law**.

The naturalistic fallacy is significant because it places the philosophy of ethics and morals on uncertain footing. Science and logic can tell us a lot about what the world is like. According to Hume, though, this information doesn't do a bit of good in telling us how we ought to act.

Hume said the best we can do is follow our instincts and conventions. These things tend to work and it is unreasonable to insist that they do not work just because we can't prove them to be scientifically reliable.

Even so, not everyone was satisfied with Hume's solution to the problems of uncertainty and morality. Philosophers who came after him continued to work on developing a philosophical basis for what we know and how we should act.

The Least You Need to Know

➤ Locke used empiricism to explain how human understanding works.

➤ All understanding is based on experience, according to Locke; there are no innate ideas.

➤ Locke proposed a new view of government based on the natural right to own property and on the social contract.

➤ Berkeley believed that only ideas ⬛⬛⬛⬛⬛ived by human souls and by God.

➤ Hume said that, even though exp⬛⬛⬛⬛⬛ur only source of knowledge, it can't tell us much about reality. As a result, most belief is based on habit, convention, and human nature.

154

Chapter 17

Light on the Subject

In This Chapter

➤ The French philosophes

➤ Montesquieu relates law to society

➤ Voltaire takes the dogma out of religion

➤ Rousseau criticizes civilization

The period known as the Enlightenment took place all over Europe, but in France it took place with special urgency and flare. There, even the philosophers had style. These "philosophes," as they were called, held their own in sophisticated society along with the "erudites," or people of learning, and the "beaux esprits," or free-spirited pleasure seekers.

The philosophes were excited about the new developments in rationalism and empirical science and were eager to try to put these ideas to work in changing the way people think and in restructuring French society. They were outspoken critics of the old ways, including church authority and aristocratic privilege. As a result, many of them spent time in jail, in exile, and fighting law suits.

In spite of the difficulty, the philosophes succeeded in transforming French society forever. In fact, the transformation, when it came, was sudden, drastic, and bloody. By the end of the 18th century, thanks to the French Revolution, France was no longer a monarchy—it was a republic.

French Lights

The *philosophes* were aware that big changes were brewing and wanted to be on top of them, pointing the way to what they saw as a truer, freer way to think and live. Here are some of the more famous philosophes.

Enlightened Luminaries

➤ **Charles-Louis, Baron de Montesquieu** (1689–1755)   His ideas about the separation of powers in government exerted a strong influence on the U.S. Constitution.

➤ **Francois Marie Arouet de Voltaire** (1694–1778)   A novelist and an outspoken social critic, he was a figurehead for the philosophes.

➤ **Jean-Jacques Rousseau** (1712–1778)   He argued that the best political system is one that reflects "the general will" of the people. Otherwise, he saw civilization as having a bad influence on the individual.

Lexicon
The **philosophes** were the philosophers of the French Enlightenment. They believed that philosophy was an important means of bringing about progress.

➤ **Denis Diderot** (1713–1784)   He came up with ideas about the importance of childhood in the development of the mind, anticipating Freud; and about the evolution of animals, anticipating Darwin. He also edited the massive *Encyclopedie*, a 17-volume dictionary of the sciences, arts, and trades that stands as a monument to Enlightenment thinking.

➤ **Paul Thiry, Baron D'Holbach** (1723–1789)   His *System of Nature* denied the existence of God and replaced religious belief with a faith in nature and free will.

A New Look at Laws

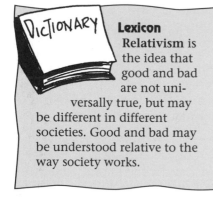

Lexicon
Relativism is the idea that good and bad are not universally true, but may be different in different societies. Good and bad may be understood relative to the way society works.

Although the Enlightenment in France covered a lot of philosophical territory, it had especially strong influence on law, politics, and government. These topics were important to many of the philosophes, and among the first of the French Enlightenment thinkers to deal with these issues thoroughly was Baron Montesquieu.

There are two related ideas that form the basis of Montesquieu's understanding of law. One is that people can develop laws that are reasonable if they have the freedom to do so. And the other is that reasonable laws for one society may be different from those of another society. Good laws depend on what the society is like.

The idea that what is good or bad depends on the way a particular society works is known as *relativism*. Montesquieu was one of the first thinkers to apply relativism to the law.

Building from the Bottom Up

Both these ideas suggest that law should be based on the way people live and think rather than on the desire of rulers to hold power over their subjects. Montesquieu was especially opposed to despotism, the arbitrary use of power by a king. While he recognized a variety of political and legal systems as reasonable and workable, he condemned the use of power for its own sake.

Philoso-Fact
Montesquieu's dislike of despotism stems from the excesses of France's King Louis XIV, who used his power to surround himself with luxury.

Montesquieu believed that laws and government should be set up to allow people as much freedom as possible. The best way to do this was for government to be moderate, not impose any laws too severely, and allow human nature and social custom to do most of the work in regulating people's behavior.

Taking Power Apart

He especially admired the way England was governed. In Montesquieu's day, England was ruled by three separate ruling bodies: the House of Commons, the House of Lords, and the King. These three bodies worked together while limiting the power of each individual body. Montesquieu believed this form of government encouraged personal freedom, trade, and religious toleration.

Montesquieu was among the first to recommend that a similar approach be adopted in France. This approach came to be known as "the separation of powers," and was written into the U.S. Constitution and later into the constitution of the French Republic.

The New God of Reason

While Montesquieu admired England for its government, Voltaire was one of many French philosophes who admired England for the advances it made in empirical philosophy. In fact, Voltaire ran off to England after he was beaten and imprisoned in France for criticizing an aristocrat. Voltaire saw the new empirical thinking as pointing toward new ideas in all areas, including religion.

Philoso-Fact
Voltaire, like Rousseau, was a novelist as well as a philosopher. Voltaire's novel, *Candide*, is a satire on Leibniz's view that the world is "the best of all possible worlds."

Keeping Freedom and Belief

One of the main interests of the French philosophes, along with politics, was religion. Religion was a touchy subject during the Enlightenment. There were a variety of attitudes, ranging from blind obedience to the established church to outright atheism. Those who did not wish to belong to the Catholic church had to be careful, since religious intolerance was widespread and heresy was harshly punished.

Voltaire was one of the more outspoken critics of religious intolerance. He objected most strongly to the practice of torturing those who did not belong to the church. Although Voltaire criticized excess in religious thinking, he was not an atheist. In fact, he criticized atheism.

It's Still Ticking!

Voltaire himself was a *deist*. A deist is someone who believes in God, but believes that God's will cannot be known and that God, having created the world, does little or nothing to influence its ongoing natural processes. Deism sees God as a kind of watch-maker with the world as his watch. God made the world and wound it up, and now he just lets the mechanism take care of itself.

Lexicon
Deism is the belief in an unknowable God who set the world in motion at the beginning of time but has done little to interfere with nature since then.

Voltaire's deism is based on his philosophical skepticism. He believed that we can't know about God one way or another, so we shouldn't make assumptions about how he should be worshipped. For this reason, Voltaire opposed organized religion; he believed that we should not assume that God doesn't exist just because organized religion gives a false impression of what God is.

Voltaire's deism envisions a god that allows people to exercise their reason rather than rely solely on faith. According to Voltaire, it isn't up to us to try to figure out what God wants. Instead, we should try to figure out how the world works and how people can best get along.

As a result, Voltaire objected to religious teachings, or dogma, as well as to the bureau-cracy of the church. He complained that men were given cushy positions within the church based on their connections, and he regarded the practice of celibacy—abstaining from sex—among the priesthood as a sin against nature.

The Enlightenment Speaks Volumes

During the Enlightenment there was considerable disagreement between the philosophes and the people they criticized—especially the political and religious conservatives who wanted to keep power in the hands of the king and the church. There was also disagreement among the philosophes themselves about philosophical, religious, and political ideas.

Voltaire, for example, criticized Baron D'Holback for his atheism and criticized Rousseau for putting down civilization. Even so, there was also general agreement about the potential for Enlightenment thinking to uncover the truth about the world and the importance of human thought and action within it. So much so, in fact, that the philosophes carried out a huge group project intended to establish the new thinking and make it available to everyone.

This was the 17-volume *Encyclopedia of Science, Art, and Trade*, edited by Diderot, including contributions from virtually all the major philosophers and scientists of France. Entries covered physics, art, morality, religion, politics, engineering, history, and commerce. Diderot wrote many of these entries himself.

> **Philoso-Fact**
> Because of his wide-ranging interests, Diderot was nicknamed "Pantophile," which means lover of everything.

The project was in danger of falling through a number of times, but luckily Diderot stepped in, took control, and brought it to completion. Although the project was huge in scope, the entries tended to adopt the Enlightenment point of view: Human reason was leading to a clearer understanding of the natural world and to more just and free political organizations.

A Feel for Philosophy

Jean-Jacques Rousseau stands out among Enlightenment thinkers as a philosopher who defended the value of the emotions along with reason. He said that the need to fit in with society makes people lose touch with their feelings.

> **Wisdom at Work**
> Use Rousseau's idea that people disguise their feelings in order to be liked by those with more power to explain why so many people act phony at work. No one wants the boss to think they have a bad attitude!

In contrast to most other Enlightenment thinkers, Rousseau did not believe that reason was the solution to social problems. Instead, he believed that problems sprang from denying the importance of the emotions. Many Enlightenment thinkers regarded the emotions as dangerous forces that needed to be reigned in by means of reason; but not Rousseau. He felt that we need to allow our emotions to surface.

Civilized People Are Apple Polishers

Rousseau believed that human nature is inherently good, but that society makes people corrupt. In order to fit into society, you have to deny your natural desires, and this makes people deceitful and greedy. In civilization, everyone has to go around disguising their feelings and desires in order to be liked by those with more power.

According to Rousseau, the only individual in a civilized society who is truly free is the king, because the king is the only one who isn't trying to get in good with someone above him. In Rousseau's famous words, "Man is born free but is everywhere in chains."

Rousseau viewed civilization as bad, but he idealized Indians and others that he saw as "uncivilized," by describing them as *noble savages*. The noble savage exemplifies the natural virtue of humanity uncorrupted by civilization. Such a being is free and honest because he doesn't try to fool people into liking him the way civilized people do.

Inventing Virtue and Vice

Like the English philosophers, Hobbes and Locke, Rousseau based much of his thinking on the idea of "the state of nature," the condition of humanity before laws had been invented. Rousseau's view of the state of nature differed from Hobbes and Locke's. According to Rousseau, humanity in the state of nature was not only without laws, it was also without ideas of good and bad, virtue and vice. Ideas about good and bad were invented along with the rest of civilization in order to help people get along. In the state of nature, said Rousseau, these ideas were unnecessary.

Ideas of vice and virtue, according to Rousseau, were invented by civilized society and work to the advantage of the rich. They tend, in other words, to tell poor people what they can and cannot do so they won't cause trouble. This idea anticipates Marx's concept of ideology, which sees ideas as tending to justify the control of the rich over the poor.

Learning to Be Natural

One major difference between Marx and Rousseau is that Marx focuses on the economic problems of the lower classes whereas Rousseau is mainly worried about emotional problems. Another difference is that Marx recommends collective, group action to overcome the social control of the wealthy. Rousseau, in contrast, said more attention should be paid to the education of the individual. Education should help promote individual freedom and equality as well as counteract the negative effects of society.

Philoso-Fact
Rousseau wrote a novel, *Emile*, about a boy who is educated according to "natural" principles that had a powerful impact on theories of teaching.

Although Rousseau tended to place importance on the individual, he suggested that the laws of the state should be made in accordance with what he called "the general will." The general will is what is good for society as a whole and works best when people freely agree to uphold it. It unites the ideas of collective good and individual freedom.

The Least You Need to Know

➤ The French Enlightenment thinkers saw reason as the way to a freer society with more equality.

➤ Deism is a religious philosophy that leaves space for reason as well as human nature.

➤ Rousseau, unlike other Enlightenment thinkers before his time, emphasized the importance of feelings over the dictates of civilization.

WE'RE NOT ALONE.

ALONE IS SUBJECTIVE.

Chapter 18

Wheeling and Idealing

In This Chapter

➤ The transcendent unity of the German idealists

➤ Kant's view of the relationship between understanding and experience

➤ Kant's categorical imperative

➤ Hegel's new view of history

➤ Schopenhauer's emphasis on will

Reacting to the British empiricists were a group of philosophers known as German idealists, philosophers who gave a special place to the power of the mind in their view of reality. They believed that awareness is not limited by experience; rather, people and reality are part of a transcendent unity.

They believed that both the mind and the nature of the human understanding structures reality. Kant, the first of the German idealists, called this view "transcendental idealism." This differs from the idealism of George Berkeley in that, where for Berkeley, order and consistency of our experience of reality depends on God, for Kant and the transcendental idealists, this order is provided by our understanding.

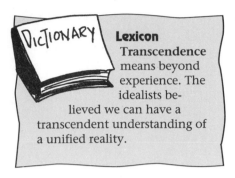

Lexicon
Transcendence means beyond experience. The idealists believed we can have a transcendent understanding of a unified reality.

While the idealists were reacting to the empiricists, though, they borrowed a number of empiricist ideas in developing their own philosophies. In particular, Hume's attempt to explain morality inspired the idealists to try to do the same, especially since Hume's conclusions made the idealists uncomfortable.

While Hume used empiricism to show the limitations of understanding, the idealists wanted to show that the understanding is not limited by experience. They developed a more optimistic view of reality, reason, human nature, and even history.

Big Idealists

Immanuel Kant (1724–1804) was the leading figure among the German idealists. Kant suggested that the mind and the rest of reality are part of the same unified picture. In doing so, he inspired a number of other German philosophers to look at things in terms of a *transcendent* unity.

Ideal-List

Here's a list of some of the key German idealists:

➤ **Immanuel Kant** (1724–1804) described categories of thought as concepts that enable us to understand the phenomenal world.

➤ **Johann Gottlieb Fichte** (1762–1814) described ultimate reality as a universal moral order.

➤ **Georg Wilhelm Friedrich Hegel** (1770–1831) described universal reason as a process that unfolds dialectically through history.

➤ **Friedrich Schelling** (1775–1854) described nature and consciousness as expressions of absolute reality.

➤ **Arthur Schopenhauer** (1788–1860) described will as an expression of absolute reality.

A Falling Out Over Unity

Although Kant's followers drew heavily on his ideas, Kant disagreed with much of what they believed. He felt that they were developing invalid conclusions about the way mind and world are related. In turn, Kant's followers felt he wasn't going far enough in unifying the various aspects of his philosophy—mind, nature, and morality.

Not Too Soft, Not Too Crunchy

Like Hume, Kant was interested in what our experience of reality can tell us about metaphysics—the area of knowledge that lies beyond physical reality. In fact, he says Hume made a big impression on him.

Before he read Hume, Kant was a follower of Leibniz's philosophy and accepted what Leibniz had to say about the way metaphysics can be derived from rational principles. That all changed, he says, after Hume woke him up from his "dogmatic slumbers." After that, Kant would not let sleeping dogma lie!

Kant went on to revise Leibniz's approach to metaphysics. At the same time, Kant believed Hume went too far in saying that we can't have any metaphysical knowledge of reality. (Hume said that even though we must depend upon our senses to gain knowledge, we can't trust them very far.) Hume, in other words, was too skeptical of the mind's abilities, while Leibniz was too confident in it.

Kant attempted to show that even though we can't trust our senses to tell us directly about reality, our senses do tell us a lot about how reality appears to us. And the appearance of reality isn't just guess-work as Hume suggested; it points beyond experience to a transcendent unity of the way the world seems and what the world actually is.

> **Philoso-Fact**
> Idealist philosophy is closely related to the movement in art and literature known as Romanticism. Like idealist philosophy, romantic art suggests that we are part of a unified reality that transcends our individual experiences.

Judging Reality by Its Cover

Kant distinguished between what the world actually is and the way it appears. The appearance of things he called *phenomena*. The actual world he called the *noumena*, or the "ding-an-sich," the "thing in itself." Kant said we cannot know the noumena directly, but we can apprehend it, based on the way we perceive the phenomenal world.

The Way the Cookie Crumbles

> **Lexicon**
> The **phenomenal** world is the world as it appears to our senses. The **noumenal** world is the world as it actually is. Although we cannot know the noumena, we know it's there, based on the way we understand the phenomenal world.

Hume said that nothing can be known without experience, and that we need to make judgments about our experience in order to make sense of it. These judgments, though, aren't reliable, since they don't come from experience, but from habit, convention, and human nature.

These judgments, in other words, depend on the position from which we see them. They are not true independently of who sees them and how they are seen. Hume suggests that even though we can't prove these ideas are true, we can't do without them.

There are limits, in other words, to empiricism's power to tell us what is true for certain. The empiricists said that knowledge has to conform to objects in the real world. Hume, albeit an empiricist, argued that the mind has to rely on connections it makes on its own that are not simply based on real objects.

Kant tried to solve this problem by reversing the empirical attitude toward knowledge. Rather than saying knowledge must conform to objects, he said objects (the noumenal world) must conform to knowledge (the phenomenal world). Objects, in other words, get organized by the mind.

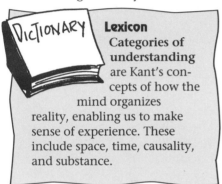

Lexicon
Categories of understanding are Kant's concepts of how the mind organizes reality, enabling us to make sense of experience. These include space, time, causality, and substance.

We might think of the noumenal world as cookie dough and the phenomena we experience as cookies. Kant would say we can't ever experience the cookie dough directly—no licking the bowl! All we can know directly are the cookies, which have been cut out by our understanding. The cookie-cutters of understanding are concepts including space, time, substance, and causality. Kant called these cookie-cutters *categories of understanding*.

We don't have any direct experience of these concepts. Instead, through them, we experience the things that we *say* have substance, exist in time, are caused, and so on.

Concepts Before Experience

Kant called these concepts *a priori concepts*. A priori is a Latin phrase meaning "what comes before." *A priori concepts*, says Kant, come before experience; they make experience possible. As a result, they are not concepts that people have made up; they existed before our existence, before we ever gave them any thought. But they are necessary in order for us to be able to understand things.

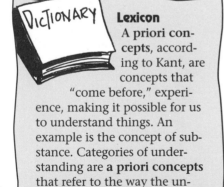

Lexicon
A priori concepts, according to Kant, are concepts that "come before," experience, making it possible for us to understand things. An example is the concept of substance. Categories of understanding are **a priori concepts** that refer to the way the understanding makes judgments about such things as quality, quantity, time, and space.

A New Copernicus

Kant compared his approach to the relationship between experience and understanding to Copernicus's explanation of the relationship between the earth and the sun and stars. In Copernicus' day, people were having trouble explaining the motions of the stars circling the earth, since the circles are irregular. Copernicus figured out that the stars only seem to circle the earth. What is actually happening is that the earth is turning on its axis and circling around the sun.

Similarly, people in Kant's time were having trouble explaining how we get knowledge from experience, since that knowledge seems unreliable. Kant said that what actually happens is that we get experience from knowledge. That is, our ability to know makes it possible for us to have and to understand our experience. In this way, like Copernicus, Kant started looking at things from a whole new perspective.

Kant's philosophy did not end with his ideas about the understanding and its relationship to the noumenal and phenomenal worlds. He went on to think about ethical questions—issues having to do with morality—and tried to find an objective basis for moral ideas.

REALITY ✓

Reality Check

Philosophers continue to debate not only whether there can be an objective basis for morality, but also whether objectivity is possible at all. Many believe morality—like everything else—depends on your perspective.

We're All in This Together

Kant picked up on the distinction made by Hume between ideas about what exists and ideas about what ought to be. Hume said that we can't draw conclusions about what ought to be, based on our knowledge of what exists.

To deal with this problem, Kant came up with the view that there are objective categories of moral thought. He referred to moral thinking as *practical reason*, or reasoning about how we *should* act. He contrasted practical reason to *pure reason*, or reasoning about what exists.

In his study of practical reason, Kant said we can come up with ideas about what we should do called *imperatives* that hold true for everyone.

In particular, Kant described the *categorical imperative*, which, he said, makes practical judgment possible just as the categories of substance, quality, etc., make understanding possible. The categorical imperative, he said, is an *a priori concept*. We can see that it holds true prior to experience.

Kant described the categorical imperative as a universal moral law. We can tell our actions are in keeping with this law if they would be right, would be moral, for everybody.

Lexicon
The **categorical imperative** is a moral law which, according to Kant, holds true for everybody and forms the basis of our **practical reason**, or moral understanding. It refers not only to how we should act, but actually enables us to behave as moral beings.

Hegel Can Do What Immanuel Kant

Kant provided a lot of inspiration for the other German idealists. His work suggested that there is a unified reality based on categories of human understanding, and that this human understanding is something that is built into reality itself.

The human mind, in other words, has a lot to do with the way reality takes shape.

While the younger German idealists liked these aspects of Kant's thinking, they felt he didn't go far enough in unifying mind and reality. They felt he left gaps between the noumenal and phenomenal worlds, between subjectivity and objectivity, and between moral action and rational understanding. Kant claimed that reality was unified, but his philosophy suggested otherwise.

One of the main ways Kant's followers tried to unify his system was by placing even more importance on the understanding as an actual part of reality. They talked about understanding as a spirit that made things what they are.

Kant himself did not like this conception of reality, but it had the advantage of closing gaps between what people think and the way the world actually is. The idealists after Kant tended to see mind and world as one and the same.

Philosophy Goes Down in History

Philoso-Fact
Kant and the German idealists were all teachers as well as philosophers. As a result, their writings tend to have an academic style that is difficult to understand. This is especially true of Hegel.

Lexicon
Dialectic is Hegel's term for the historical process through which ideas are developed in relation to their opposites. An idea, or **thesis**, takes shape in relation to its opposite, or **antithesis**. Eventually, the interaction of the thesis and antithesis leads to a resolution, known as the **synthesis**.

The most important of Kant's immediate followers was Georg Wilhelm Friedrich Hegel (1770–1831), who applied Kant's ideas about the unity of action, understanding, and phenomenal reality in developing a new view of history.

Hegel drew on Kant's conception of categories of understanding that give shape to reality. For Hegel though, unlike Kant, the categories keep changing and tend to conflict with one another.

For Hegel, these categories work themselves out through time. They are constantly developing and are constantly in a state of flux with their opposites. Hegel refers to this process as *dialectic*. He borrowed the idea of dialectic from Plato who used it to describe the Socratic technique of reasoning through question and answer. Hegel used the term to refer to the back-and-forth process of ideas getting worked out through history.

This process occurs when an idea, known as the *thesis*, comes into conflict with its opposite, known as the *antithesis*. Eventually, conflict between thesis and antithesis is resolved, resulting in a *synthesis*.

Pretty abstract, huh? That's Hegel. He's talking about how reality unfolds through time, and how we need to think of reality as a big mind trying to figure itself out. The point of reality is to realize itself—to see what it is and to become that thing it sees.

Hegel gives an example—although, still a pretty abstract one—that shows how his dialectic works. He gives "being" as an example of a thesis. Being's antithesis is "nothing." As being and nothing work out their differences, they resolve into the synthesis, "becoming."

We see this process taking place, says Hegel, in the history of human thinking. Hegel saw the history of thinking as the process through which people try to figure out just what their problem is. They have made gradual progress through the centuries, but they still hadn't got it quite right; at least not until Hegel came along!

Alien Life Forms

This process is directed toward a universal experience of self-recognition in which reality figures itself out and becomes free. Until then, people will experience suffering and *alienation*. Alienation, says Hegel is what happens when ideas become fragmented and distance themselves from other ideas. When an idea doesn't see itself as part of the big picture, but becomes cut off from the rest of idealized reality, that idea is alienated.

One example of Hegel's alienation is the idea that God is unknowable and separate from humanity. Because they believe in a god that is separate from them, people feel cut off from reality, rather than an integral part of it.

> **Lexicon**
> **Alienation** is Hegel's word for what happens when people and ideas get cut off from unified reality. Alienation takes place when thinking conflicts and doesn't get resolved. Years later, Karl Marx adapted this concept to refer to the problem of workers who don't have a direct stake in their own labor. Alienated labor is thus the problem of working for someone else.

Slaves to Recognition

As another example of the problem of alienation, Hegel tells the famous story of the master and the slave.

According to Hegel, before we have true universal self-consciousness, all we have is desire. Desiring consciousness doesn't know anything; it just wants to be what it is. And as it tries to be what it is, it encounters opposition from other desiring consciousnesses.

When two desiring consciousnesses meet each other, they engage in a battle of wills to achieve mutual self-recognition. One wins and becomes the master; the other loses and becomes the slave. The good thing is that they have learned to recognize themselves and each other. The bad thing, though, is that neither one is happy about it.

The master and the slave, says Hegel, each have half a true self-consciousness. The master has the power to realize its will, but doesn't actually do anything, since the slave does the work. The slave is learning to recognize itself in the things it actually does, but doesn't get to do things for itself, only for the master.

The solution, according to Hegel, is for both master and slave to recognize the will of the other. Recognizing another's will is the first step in participating in the universal will of reality.

Different Slants on Hegel

Hegel presented his philosophy in metaphysical terms, looking at knowledge and moral action as aspects of how reality is structured. Many readers have found this approach to philosophy inspiring, while others have rejected it as unconvincing.

Philoso-Fact
Hegel wrote his philosophy during the time known as the Industrial Revolution, when workers had almost no legal rights. As a result, Hegel's master-slave story has been interpreted by Karl Marx and others as a parable about labor relations.

Philoso-Fact
In spite of the fact that there are important similarities between Schopenhauer's and Hegel's philosophy, Schopenhauer called Hegel's work "stupid and inept."

Hegel's detractors object to his view of logic as something that changes over time, and to his murky, convoluted style of writing. Hegel's writing is notoriously hard to figure out and this has caused all kinds of disagreements about its meaning and significance.

In spite of metaphysical, logical, and stylistic problems, Hegel's philosophy has been influential in accounting for social interaction and the human predicament. The so-called "young Hegelians," including Karl Marx, drew most heavily on this aspect of Hegel's work.

In place of Hegel's idealism, the young Hegelians saw social reality in materialistic terms. They, like Hegel, viewed social forces as changing dialectically. But unlike Hegel, they believed that these social forces are determined not by reason and understanding, but by material forces including money, resources, and labor.

The young Hegelians, and Marx in particular, gave rise to an important new way of looking at the world—looking at it in terms of material human struggle instead of abstract metaphysical conflict.

Not all those who drew on Hegel's work, though, rejected his idea of a unifying metaphysical principle like the young Hegelians did. Arthur Schopenhauer (1788–1860) accepted Hegel's thinking, but modified it. Where Hegel saw reality unified by reason, Schopenhauer saw reality unified by will.

Will Is the Way

Like Hegel, Schopenhauer placed importance on the idea of will. Will is the driving force that makes things happen for both the natural world and for people. Will is the great unifier for Schopenhauer; it is at work in everything. Observable reality is an expression of will, a strong desire to exist that takes on physical shape.

Schopenhauer's distinction between will and observable reality corresponds to Kant's distinction between the phenomenal and noumenal worlds. Will is what actually exists (the noumena) but observable reality (phenomena) is what appears to us.

Just as observable reality is the physical expression of will, each individual person is the expression of his or her own individual will. Will gives shape to people and to natural reality.

Schopenhauer saw will differently than Hegel did. For Hegel will was an aspect of reason, something that is part of, and leads to, universal self-recognition. But for Schopenhauer, will doesn't have reason behind it. It's there, but it isn't rational. It doesn't know what it's doing. Will is blind.

A Will to Know

People, unlike the rest of reality, can know what's going on. They are capable of understanding that will makes things the way they are, and they can recognize their own will causing them to be who they are. In fact, knowledge is simply one aspect of will. We know things because our will makes us know.

In seeing things this way, Schopenhauer switched the way most people understood the relationship between will and knowledge. Hegel believed, for example, that it is knowledge that gives shape to the will. For Schopenhauer, it's just the opposite. This view of will later influenced Sigmund Freud's idea of the subconscious. You don't control it, it controls you!

As a result, Schopenhauer saw people as being obsessed with their own ways of seeing and doing things and as basically unaware of the big picture. This is not "alienation" the way Hegel would see it, but just the normal state of things. People are capable of seeing past their own wills to the big picture, but few people actually do this.

Wisdom at Work
Use Schopenhauer's concept of blind will to explain why you always have to get up and rearrange the furniture every time you sit down to balance your checkbook. Your will takes the form of furniture rearranging rather than of checkbook balancing.

Not a Pretty Picture

Although will is the driving force behind everything, it's more of a problem than a solution. Everything is always full of desire and never fully satisfied. There's a sense of futility in the way our will keeps trying to have its way, only to find that it can't, or to find that what it thought it wanted wasn't really what it wanted after all.

The will, for Schopenhauer is not free. It is determined by laws of causality just as motion in the physical world is determined by mechanical laws. We can't choose what to will; our will chooses for us. The result is a lot of conflict, suffering and futility.

Schopenhauer's concept of will as something that is not free and never satisfied, re-sembles traditional Indian philosophy, with its connection between desire and suffering. (See Chapter 11.) In fact, Schopenhauer was inspired by Eastern thought in his work.

Just as Indian philosophy recognizes the concept of *moksa*, or release from suffering, Schopenhauer believed it is possible to transcend will by laying aside personal desire.

One way to do this is with the help of philosophy. We can know things independently of will, said Schopenhauer, by contemplating platonic ideas. Thus Schopenhauer looked back to Plato for a way of transcending the suffering caused by will. Knowledge of pla-tonic ideas is what's left of knowledge after it has been purged of will. At this level, knowledge is objective.

This platonic knowledge is not a knowledge of particular things, but of universal forms. The universality of these forms helps keep them separate from individual acts of will.

Another way of transcending will is through art. Contemplating a work of art can help you see past your own particular predicament and get a more generalized view of reality.

The Least You Need to Know

➤ The German idealists were followers of Immanuel Kant and were interested in the idea of transcendent unity.

➤ Kant reversed the relationship between experience and understanding as it was described by Hume. For Hume, experience precedes understanding; for Kant, understanding comes first.

➤ Kant tried to develop objective categories of understanding and of morality. His famous moral principle is the *categorical imperative*, which says that ideas of good behavior apply to everybody.

➤ Hegel modified Kant's idealism by taking history into account in trying to describe ideal (rational) reality.

➤ Schopenhauer modified idealism by saying that will is the unifying force behind everything.

IT SAYS WE'RE IN DEEP TROUBLE.

FAT CATS

Chapter 19

Ideas of Freedom

In This Chapter

➤ Determinism vs. freedom

➤ Utilitarianism and happiness

➤ Marxism's problem with money

➤ Kierkegaard and the leap of faith

➤ Nietzsche and the superman

Freedom has been a big topic in philosophy. It goes back at least as far as the ancient Greeks, when they began to wonder about fate and whether or not it is inescapable. Freedom is important in terms of politics, of course. Do people have a right to control other people? But it's also important in terms of metaphysics. Are you actually in control of your own life or are your actions determined by forces—human, natural, or historical— that you cannot control?

Ever since Newton found formulas for explaining the physics of motion in mechanical terms, philosophers have been thinking about whether people's minds, desires, and actions are also somehow mechanical. Maybe we only *think* we make choices; maybe in reality our "choices" actually have physical causes.

The German idealists refuted this view by saying that there is a kind of spiritual reason woven into the fabric of reality, so the world is not just one big cause-and-effect mechanism. But even though the idealists rejected a mechanical world view, they didn't leave much room for individual freedom within the grand, impersonal conceptions of reality they came up with. Hegel, for example, saw things as pretty much caused by history working itself out. For Schopenhauer, everything came down to will. In both cases, individuals were not seen as having much control over their lives.

During the mid- and late-19th century, philosophers began placing more emphasis on freedom, both individual and group freedom. According to some of these philosophers, we can have control over our own lives, and our freedom is crucially important. This is a common thread that unites some very different philosophical views including those of the British philosopher John Stuart Mill, the German philosopher Karl Marx, the Danish philosopher Søren Kierkegaard, and the German Friedrich Nietzsche.

Determine One, Get One Free

Mill, Marx, Kierkegaard, and Nietzsche, have different takes on *determinism*. This is the idea that things, including people's actions, have to happen the way they do.

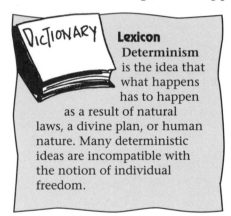

Lexicon
Determinism is the idea that what happens has to happen as a result of natural laws, a divine plan, or human nature. Many deterministic ideas are incompatible with the notion of individual freedom.

One view of determinism is *mechanical determinism*, which says that everything is caused by something. The empiricists, whose philosophy gave rise to mechanical determinism, did not argue that people's thoughts and actions are mechanically determined, but they had to go out of their way to explain how people's actions can be free and still have causes that make them what they are.

Another kind of determinism is *historical determinism*, in which social or intellectual forces govern human actions. The philosophies of Hegel and Marx can be seen as advancing this idea. Schopenhauer's concept of will is another view that can be interpreted as deterministic. These philosophies don't see individuals as having much control over their lives in the present, although Marx and Hegel see people becoming increasingly free through the course of history.

Freedom Goes Through the Mill

One objection to determinism was put forward by John Stuart Mill (1806–1873). Although Mill believed that all things have causes, he said that human beings have free will. Human actions are not inevitable.

Mill is the most important of the utilitarian philosophers. *Utilitarianism* is the view that any action is good if it leads to human happiness, and bad if it stands in the way of happiness. Utilitarianism started with the British philosopher Jeremy Bentham, together with J. S. Mill's father, James Mill. J. S. Mill developed their ideas, worked out some of the bugs, and defended utilitarianism against criticism.

It All Comes Down to Happiness

Mill believed that the more freedom people have, the happier they will be. Mill said we should all be free to go after our own happiness as long as our attempts to be happy don't interfere with the happiness of others.

Mill and the utilitarians faced a lot of criticism for their ideas. Their critics objected to the notion that happiness is the best thing people can hope for. They argued that justice is more important, and that if everyone tries to make themselves happy, the problem of justice will be shortchanged.

> **Philoso-Fact**
> Mill had a rigorous education that started when he was very young and resulted in a nervous breakdown early in his adult life. He attributed the problem to not paying enough attention to his emotions.

Mill countered that the idea of justice depends on happiness, so happiness is ultimately more important than justice. What's more, happiness doesn't get in the way of justice—it helps make the idea of justice possible.

Poetry vs. Pushpin

Another objection to utilitarianism was that it didn't distinguish between kinds of happiness, or concern itself with how people make themselves happy. Bentham's suggestion that "pushpin was as good as poetry"—that a child's game was as good as a cultivated art form—didn't sit well with everyone, including J. S. Mill.

Mill made a distinction between what he called "higher" and "lower" pleasures and said that people will inevitably learn to appreciate higher pleasures once they have experienced them. This means that people will naturally pursue cultural activities for the sake of enjoyment.

> **Reality Check**
> Mill's distinction between "higher" and "lower" pleasures may reflect snobbery on his part. This kind of snobbery could lead to the mistaken idea that people who prefer the so-called "lower pleasures" are less capable—and less deserving—of happiness than others.

Freedom for Women

Mill, most famous for his defense of utilitarianism, also wrote about logic and the rights of women. His book called *The Subjugation of Women* argues for women's equality. In it he writes that denying women social equality is morally wrong; it is bad for men as well as women, in utilitarian terms. Mill believed that marriage works best when men and women have an equal say in how the marriage works. Equality promotes the greatest happiness for both partners.

Determined to Be Free

Another very different attitude toward freedom and determination is put forth in the philosophy of Karl Marx (1818–1883). Marx picked up on Hegel's view of history as a process that leads to increased freedom as time goes on. But where Hegel was thinking about intellectual freedom, Marx was thinking about political and economic freedom.

Karl Marx

Like Hegel, Marx was a determinist to some extent. He believed that the way people live is determined by the "relations of production." In other words, people's lives are determined by the way they make, distribute, and use material goods.

174

The Rat Race

Marx said that the current way of life was determined by capitalism, the system in which people with money hire people without money to make things. People with money sell, for a profit, the things people without money make, and in turn use this money to hire more people (for as little as possible) to make *more* things to sell for *more* money.

Marx believed capitalism would eventually burn itself out and lead to a revolution resulting in "the workers' paradise"—a communist form of government that would ensure freedom for everybody.

> **Philoso-Fact**
> Although Marx is a famous materialist, he started off as a romantic poet.

We Can't Go on Like This

According to Marx, the days of capitalism are numbered because it leads to more and more money for fewer and fewer people. Eventually, there will be so many people without money that they will overthrow the system and replace it with a system in which money is insignificant. This new system is called *communism*. Under communism, everyone will be free to work for themselves and for the common good.

Freedom for Marx is being able to take pride in your work, not in the worth and amount of your possessions. This doesn't happen under capitalism, says Marx, because the work people do is always for someone else. And this leads to unhappiness and discontent because people are not inherently happy working for others, no matter how much money they make. Marx called working for others "alienated labor."

As you probably know, many countries have tried to put Marx's ideas into practice by instituting a communist form of government. The results have been mixed at best, and it is questionable how closely these countries—like China, Cuba, and the old Soviet Union—have actually adhered to Marx's form of communism. In any case, things so far haven't worked out the way Marx said they would. And the people who have instigated communist revolutions generally have not been workers, but political activists.

> **Philoso-Fact**
> Marx worked as a journalist and struggled in his career because his views were so controversial; many newspapers were opposed to his views. As a result, he and his family were quite poor.

Factory-Sealed Thinking

When you think of Marx, you probably think about him in terms of the tremendous impact he had on economics and politics. But Marx has also been extremely influential in analyzing how ideology affects people's thinking and actions.

Marx says that people's beliefs, along with the other aspects of their behavior, are determined by the relations of production. Religion, philosophy, and popular belief reflect a society's power structure and at the same time compel people to fit in with that structure.

There are many examples supporting Marx's observation. A notable one is that, in capitalist society, commercial free enterprise and the values of individualism that go along with it are generally seen as good things, whereas under a feudal society, commercial freedom was often seen as depraved and a threat to the social order.

Freedom Is in Meaning

Philoso-Fact
Kierkegaard's father was racked with guilt for being sexually unfaithful to his wife. When his wife and some of his children died, he believed he was being punished for his misdeeds. Being raised under these circumstances prompted Kierkegaard to rethink the significance of religion.

In a very different response to deterministic thinking, the Danish philosopher Søren Kierkegaard (1813–1855) developed a philosophy based on the importance of the individual and individual choice.

Kierkegaard objected to the philosophy of Hegel in particular, because it is so impersonal. To Kierkegaard, Hegel's thinking was so abstract that it ignored actual people and the significance of the way they experience their lives.

Kierkegaard said that it is especially important for people to have a meaningful existence. And meaning, he said, comes from whether or not people sense that their lives have a permanent significance. The problem is, though, that most people believe that their lives have importance only temporarily.

Trapped in Time

Kierkegaard described this problem by identifying three stages of personal development: the aesthetic (artistic), the ethical (dutiful), and the religious stages. These stages correspond to periods Kierkegaard actually went through in his own life. The religious stage, said Kierkegaard, is the only one that gives life permanent significance.

The problem, says Kierkegaard, with a life devoted to pleasure and enjoyment (the aesthetic stage) is that these concerns are temporary. The artists of his time lived carefree lives, avoiding responsibility and living for the moment and for the enjoyment they received from artistic creations. Kierkegaard did not see art the way Hegel and Schopenhauer did, as connecting people with a sense of permanence.

He said that if you are aware of the importance of your existence, you will eventually feel dissatisfied with a life devoted to art and pleasure; then your own impermanence and insignificance will fill you with despair. At this point, you can either try to go on living in despair or you can try to lead a more ethical, responsible existence.

When you begin to take on ethical responsibility, says Kierkegaard, you begin to introduce a sense of permanence to your life. This sense of permanence, though, is only partial and creates conflict that leads to despair again.

Kierkegaard described this conflict as dialectical, taking place between an inner sense of temporality and a desire for permanence. It can compel you to take a leap of faith into the third stage of personal development, into a religious existence. For Hegel, dialectic is a historical process—a change that takes place through history. But for Kierkegaard, it is a very personal process, leading to a religious commitment.

> **Philoso-Fact**
> Although most of Kierkegaard's philosophy supports Christianity, he was critical of the sort of Christians he knew, saying they were too comfortable and satisfied with themselves.

Just Do It

Kierkegaard said that you can only reach this third stage through a leap of faith because there aren't any rational reasons for making this move. You have to make it without any philosophical or conventional religious excuses.

This, says Kierkegaard, is because what is most important is the truth of your own situation, and this is a subjective truth that only you can know. It can't be influenced by philosophical systems such as Hegel's, or even by religious institutions such as the church.

Kierkegaard calls for a personal commitment to religion. The decision to make this commitment involves both freedom and responsibility. You have to live with the consequences of deciding to live a religious existence, but the choice is yours to make; it's not determined by anyone but you.

Making this leap of faith is the way out of despair and it gives you a sense of the permanent significance of your life. But deciding to commit yourself to the idea of religious eternity does not provide a permanent solution to your problems in and of itself. You have to renew this decision periodically.

Kierkegaard was extremely influential in placing emphasis on the importance of personal meaning in the life of the individual. His work gave rise to the major trend in 20th-century philosophy known as *existentialism*, a philosophy that focuses on the meaning of existence for the individual.

It's a Poet! It's a Philosopher! No, It's Superman!

Another philosopher who influenced the existentialists of the 20th century was Friedrich Nietzsche (1844–1900). Like Kierkegaard, Nietzsche believed that the individual is especially important. He believed, however, that individuality should not be definable, since any attempt at definition would place limits on it.

It was Nietzsche's conviction that the individual is capable of developing into something better than what we now think of as the individual. He referred to this superior individual as the "superman" (*ubermensche*). Much as Kierkegaard said that we can't be objective about making a leap of faith that commits us to religion, Nietzsche explained that we can't be objective about paving the way toward the superman.

Me and My Error

Philoso-Fact
Nietzsche became physically disabled and insane as a result of illnesses stemming from venereal disease. This helps explain why he kept aloof from others.

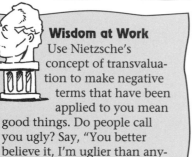

Wisdom at Work
Use Nietzsche's concept of transvaluation to make negative terms that have been applied to you mean good things. Do people call you ugly? Say, "You better believe it, I'm uglier than anybody and don't you forget it!"

Before Nietzsche came along, most philosophers saw mistaken ideas—anything that is not "true"—as bad. Nietzsche agreed to a point, but he also said that we need mistaken ideas. We need to think things that aren't true in order to make sense of what is actually a chaotic reality.

Our species has evolved because we've had the need to generate ideas to help us organize our lives, our minds, and our society. The whole purpose of thinking, according to Nietzsche, is to get along in the world, rather than to discover the "truth," as much of Western philosophy has said.

Nietzsche said that there is no objectivity, only subjectivity; "there are no facts, only interpretations." Given this, he suggested new interpretations for the way things are, with a special emphasis on survival. The idea of the superman is one of these. Nietzsche refers to the process of finding new interpretations as *transvaluation*. Transvaluation happens when you give an old idea new significance. For an example of transvaluation, think of how minorities or persons with alternative lifestyles sometimes co-opt prejudicial epithets used against them, inverting their meaning to make them badges of honor.

You Ain't Herd Nothing Yet

Nietzsche contrasted the superman with what he called "the herd"—all those average people who like to stick together and think and act alike. They do this to feel safe, but, said Nietzsche, this herd mentality limits one's possibilities in life. The herd prevents people from creating new ways of thinking and acting.

By resisting herd mentality, Nietzsche hoped that he was helping to pave the way for the superman—helping to bring about new possibilities for living. At the same time, he recognized that resisting the herd means taking risks, like rejecting the old ideas of good and evil.

One thing that Nietzsche has been widely criticized for is his attitude toward morality. Nietzsche felt that rigid ideas about good and evil are just herdlike ideas that lead to a safe, quiet, and boring existence. Emotions like pity and remorse are stupid and detract from leading an exciting, fulfilling life.

Reality Check

Nietzsche is sometimes blamed for fueling the kind of German nationalism that helped the Nazi party come to power.

Nietzsche says we need to look "beyond good and evil" if we want to realize our potential for living. We need to make our own values and disregard the feelings of the herd. As an individual, you should live for yourself, on your own terms. You should avoid being categorized by others and living according to other people's expectations.

The way to live for yourself is by exerting control over situations and succeeding in them so that you make yourself happy. The things that make you happy are not determined by what other people think, but solely by you.

Nietzsche's view of the nature of the individual is similar to Schopenhauer's in some respects. Both see the individual as obeying a distinctive will that characterizes that person and sets him or her apart from everyone else. There is an important difference, though, between Nietzsche and Schopenhauer.

Whereas Schopenhauer saw the will as a bad thing, as something that cannot be satisfied and only leads to trouble, Nietzsche saw will as something positive. Obeying your will is good; it's the most fulfilling way you can live your life.

Deja Vu All Over Again

If you obey your will, you will be happy with what you do and with your life in general. You will have no regrets and you would be satisfied living the same life again and again. Nietzsche called this idea of living your life over and over "eternal recurrence."

Some of Nietzsche's writing suggests that eternal recurrence is a guide for how we should live our lives. In other writings, he says that we actually *do* live the same lives over and over again. This uncertainty about Nietzsche's meaning of eternal recurrence may be an example of his conviction that there is no truth, only interpretation, only ideas about what reality is like. Nietzsche is almost never interpreted the same way twice. It can be hard to tell what he really believes as opposed to what he just wanted to think.

Nietzsche is often assertive, making definitive claims about his way of seeing things. But ironically, he frequently asserted that one can't know anything!

The Least You Need to Know

➤ Determinism says that events, including human actions, are necessarily caused by external forces.

➤ Utilitarianism says that any action that leads to human happiness is good.

➤ John Stuart Mill believed happiness was linked to freedom.

➤ Marx believed that people's thinking and actions are determined by material forces, namely the "relations of production."

➤ Marx also said capitalism would eventually collapse under its own weight, leading to "the workers' paradise."

➤ Kierkegaard believed that subjective meaning is the most important thing in life, and that a "leap of faith" into a religious commitment is the only way to avoid despair.

➤ Nietzsche believed that we should obey our will to live through the ideas of the "superman" and "eternal recurrence."

Part 5
Modern Philosophy

Beginning late in the 19th century, philosophy branched off into a number of specialized approaches that focused on different subjects. These specialized branches were partly due to the fact that philosophy became more institutionalized as a group of academic subjects, and partly due to the fact that different issues seemed most important to different thinkers.

Different branches of philosophy that got started at this time are Freudian psychology, sociology, anthropology, analytic philosophy, existentialism, and structural linguistics.

Common to all these approaches is a keen interest in meaning. What is it? What makes it possible? How does it work? Some felt that studying psychological drives provided the best way to explain how meaning works. For others, it was society, or culture, or language, or logic, or consciousness. Several different approaches started developing their own terms and techniques for looking at meaning.

Chapter 20

New Fields of Thought: Psych, Sosh, and Anthro

In This Chapter

➤ Freud's theory of the unconscious

➤ The Oedipus complex

➤ Jung and the collective unconscious

➤ Weber and the Protestant work ethic

➤ Durkheim and purposeful culture

Philosophy, like pretty much everything else, gets more and more complex as it heads into the 20th century. It wasn't just a matter of figuring out the relationship between faith and reason any more as it was in the Middle Ages.

Now there were issues like the mind, society, language, logic, and culture. These topics became so complex they were no longer considered simply aspects of philosophy, but rather whole fields unto themselves, each field having its own way of thinking about and doing things.

In particular, three new fields of study emerged at about the same time late in the 19th and early 20th centuries: psychology, sociology, and anthropology. You probably wouldn't study these fields in a philosophy course today, but they emerged out of philosophical thinking, drawing on the ideas of the philosophers who got the ball rolling.

Socializing Science

The beginnings of psychology, sociology, and anthropology are associated with the Austrian psychologist Sigmund Freud (1856–1939); the German sociologist Max Weber (1864–1920); and France's sociologist and anthropologist Emile Durkheim (1858–1917). These figures are often said to be the "fathers" of their respective fields.

> **Reality Check**
>
> These different fields have a lot of ideas in common. In fact, both Freud and Marx have had a big impact on a number of fields: psychology, sociology, anthropology, and political science.

Together with Marx (see Chapter 19), these thinkers helped to formulate the main principles behind the idea of "social science"—the attempt to study human behavior and society by forming and testing hypotheses. In addition to doing the philosophical work of thinking, social scientists also do experiments and research in order to develop their ideas.

These early social scientists began the move toward studying people in relation to society, and they realized that both people and society can be shaped in different ways.

Here's what these different thinkers emphasize in their attempts to explain people and society:

➤ Marx argues that economic forces influence thinking and social organization.

➤ Freud says that psychological drives influence personality formation.

➤ Weber believes cultural belief influences economic organization.

➤ Durkheim says culture is its own system, including psychological and economic aspects.

A New Way of Thinking

Sigmund Freud revolutionized the way people think about the mind with his theory of the *unconscious*. The unconscious is that aspect of your psyche that thinks and feels without your awareness of those thoughts and feelings. You can tell it's there, though, because it sometimes does funny things, like make you have recurring dreams about running around naked with important political leaders! According to Freud, dreams are coded messages about what's on your unconscious mind.

Secret Desires

You have an unconscious, says Freud, because you desire things that you think you shouldn't. You can't admit—even to yourself—that you want certain things, because you have learned at some point (usually in infancy) that those things you want are bad. As a result, you *repress* those desires. You ignore them and even deny them, but they don't go away. They hang around in your unconscious, waiting for a chance to surface.

In general, repressed desires are sexual. For Freud, sexuality is extremely important. In fact, says Freud, we are all sexually motivated from birth, and our sexuality develops in stages. You go through an oral stage—when you are especially excited by putting things in your mouth—an anal stage, and finally, by the time you reach adulthood, a genital stage.

Lexicon
The unconscious is the aspect of the mind that contains wishes and desires that are not consciously recognized. These wishes have been **repressed**, or denied, by the conscious mind because they are not socially acceptable.

Rain on the Parade

These stages develop in response to the interplay of two principles that most strongly influence our psyches: the *pleasure principle* and the *reality principle*. The pleasure principle says that we pursue pleasure from the moment we are born in the form of physical gratification. The reality principle states that we can't always get what we want and that even when we can have what we want, we have to behave appropriately to get it.

It is the fact that we want pleasure, combined with the fact that we have to adjust both to find it and possibly to do without it, that determines our development from birth. These influences shape our personalities and result in at least a certain amount of repression.

Lexicon
The **pleasure principle** says that all people from birth pursue pleasurable experience in the form of physical and emotional gratification. The **reality principle** claims that our desires are often frustrated by our circumstances.

Even though we don't think about them, repressed desires, says Freud, have ways of letting us know they are there. Dreams are only one way; jokes are another. Sometimes if your desires are especially strong or have been really severely repressed, perhaps because of some traumatic experience in your youth, your repressed desires will return in the form of strange behavior like compulsions, obsessions, and hysterical fits.

Tragic Beginnings

Although some people's repressed desires give them more trouble than others', we all have them, according to Freud. In fact, Freud identified an entire complex of repressed desires that, he says, virtually all men have to deal with as part of being male human beings. He called this the *Oedipus complex* after the ancient Greek king, Oedipus, who unknowingly killed his father and married his mother.

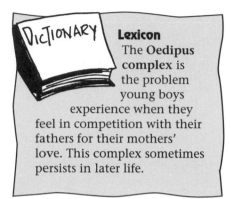

Lexicon
The **Oedipus complex** is the problem young boys experience when they feel in competition with their fathers for their mothers' love. This complex sometimes persists in later life.

Male children develop an Oedipus complex, says Freud, as a result of having to compete with their fathers for their mothers' affection. During this time, they are still dependent on their mothers and they haven't learned to accept their fathers' authority. According to Freud, this is a stage boys in general have to go through as part of developing into emotionally and sexually mature adults.

Many men, though, have difficulty getting through this stage. They never achieve independence from their mothers and never learn to deal with authority. Dealing with authority, says Freud, is the price we pay for living in a civilization. It isn't pleasant, but it has to be done in spite of the stress it exerts on our psyches.

Your Problem Is Obvious

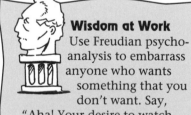

Wisdom at Work
Use Freudian psycho-analysis to embarrass anyone who wants something that you don't want. Say, "Aha! Your desire to watch soap operas rather than the baseball game stems from your repressed infantile fantasies that lead you to crave melodrama!"

The Oedipus complex is just one example of how Freud interprets things—in this case, the Oedipus story—in terms of what they say about sexuality. He also interpreted dreams, jokes, myths, and other stories in this way. Freud's way of reading things gave rise to the practice of psychoanalysis—interpreting what people say and do in order to figure out what their problems are.

In fact, pretty much anything people do can be interpreted as a weird act that somehow expresses repressed infantile fantasies, from model train collecting to bungee jumping. Many of Freud's ideas suggest that there is no reliable distinction between "perverse" and "normal" behavior. As a result, amateur psychoanalysis has become a favorite pastime.

Jung at Heart

Freud's ideas were controversial, especially since he suggested that everything comes down to sexual problems and infantile cravings. One of those who objected to the emphasis Freud placed on sex and on emotional trauma was the psychologist Carl Jung (1875–1961). Jung worked with Freud before falling out with him and developing his own psychological theories.

Instead of emphasizing the traumas that mark people's characters, Jung modified Freud's idea of the unconscious by saying there are unconscious ideas everyone has in common. These ideas are part of what Jung called the *collective unconscious*.

Jung believed that the unconscious is shaped not only by things that happen to you while you develop, but also by instinctual ideas that everyone inherits from early humans. Jung said that mythic and religious ideas are filled with symbolism from the collective unconscious.

Included in the collective unconscious are what Jung called *archetypes*—recurring images in stories and dreams that stem back to ancient myths. Sometimes there are patterns in archetypes that subtly influence people's behavior.

For example, one of the archetypes Jung identifies is "the Trickster." The Trickster, says Jung, has been around for centuries and is in the collective unconscious to this day. Sometimes people tap into the collective unconscious and act in strange and inappropriate ways characteristic of the Trickster, without realizing it.

Some other archetypal figures are the Hero, the Orphan, and the Wanderer. Jung identified these archetypes by noticing common ideas in the dreams of his patients that can be found in old myths and legends.

Lexicon
The **collective unconscious** is the body of symbolism and mythic images inherited from early humans that people have imbedded in their unconscious minds. Included in the collective unconscious are **archetypes**, patterns of images for different approaches to life.

Philoso-Fact
In his early days, Weber favored German imperialism, the push to extend Germany's national boundaries. He revised his views later and opposed the rise of the imperialistic Nazi regime.

Why We All Work Too Hard

While Freud and Jung were getting psychology established as a field of its own, Max Weber was helping to develop the field of sociology. Whereas Freud said civilization was a problem in general, Weber looked at particular historical developments that have caused trouble in Western civilization.

Mind over Money

Lexicon
The **infra-structure** is made up of those aspects of society that have to do with economy and what Marx called "the relations of production," centered around money, labor, and material goods. The **superstructure** includes the aspects of society that express beliefs, including religion and the arts.

One of the most striking features of Western civilization, as Weber noticed, is capitalism, which has a tremendous influence on what people think and do. Weber saw a strong connection between the rise of capitalism and Protestant religious thinking. While Marx believed that society's economic structure determines the way people think, Weber believed just the opposite: People's beliefs influence the way they set up their economy.

Marx called those aspects of society's economy—what he called the relations of production (see Chapter 19)—the *infrastructure*. Those aspects of society that deal with beliefs, including religion and the arts, Marx called the *superstructure*. And according to Marx, the infrastructure determines the superstructure. Weber, on the other hand, believed that the superstructure determines the infrastructure.

God and Money

Weber was especially interested in one of the key ideas of Protestantism known as *predestination*, advanced by the French theologian, John Calvin, way back in the 16th century. Predestination says that our destinies are predetermined: God knows ahead of time who is going to heaven and who is going to hell, and there is nothing anyone can do about it. Although God knows who's going where, we don't. All we can do is hope and worry.

Lexicon
Predestina-tion is the Calvinist belief that God has determined ahead of time whether you will go to heaven or hell. Weber saw this as a contributing factor to the **Protestant work ethic**, the tendency, especially among Protestants, to work hard and lead thrifty lives. This work ethic fostered the development of capitalism.

Although Protestants don't know if they're going to heaven, they figure the deciding factors are going to be who they are and how they've lived their lives. As a result, their hoping and worrying gets them to live as they think God would want them to—working hard and being frugal.

This *Protestant work ethic*, as Webster called it, suggests that the point of working isn't just to get things done that need to be done, but to reassure yourself that you're the sort of person God wants in heaven. As a result of this work ethic, says Weber, people get carried away with working.

In addition to working hard, people with the Protestant work ethic are careful not to waste money. Instead, they save it, or invest it so that it makes more money. Economic prosperity reassured people that they were favored by God.

It's All Culture

The problem of how beliefs, social practices, and economic factors are related to one another has been a central focus of sociological discussion ever since Marx picked up on Hegel's ideas and made a big deal of the issue. The French sociologist and anthropologist Emile Durkheim concluded that they're all connected because they're all part of culture—and everything, basically, is culture.

Culture doesn't need to be explained in terms of economic forces or psychological drives. It makes up a system of its own that can be studied independently.

Society's Big Mind

According to Durkheim, the important ideas are those that are shared by an entire society. These ideas make communication possible. He lumped them all together and called them the *consciousness collective*.

The consciousness collective is, in effect, the mind of a society. Durkheim said we can study this mind by analyzing ideas, things, and practices as *social facts*. A social fact exists in its own right in relation to all other social facts, independently of non-social factors.

Durkheim's view of culture initiated an important change in the way philosophers thought about society. Prior to Durkheim, philosophers emphasized either individuals, or impersonal, abstract forces as influences on the development of society. Durkheim's work suggests we don't need to go outside society to think about how society works.

Locke, for example, with his view of the social contract, regarded society as a kind of fiction, having no real existence unto itself; it only existed in people's heads. Durkheim revised this view by saying that culture is a system that assigns things meaning within that culture. The meaning isn't just in the minds of individual people, but is part of the whole cultural system, allowing people to live as members of society.

> **Lexicon**
> The **consciousness collective** is the set of ideas that's shared by an entire society, making it possible for individuals to communicate and do all the things they do as members of the society. **Social facts** are things and events that pertain to social existence, such as the way people say hello and whether it's polite to scratch in public. As such, they don't need to be explained in terms of non-social influences.

Patterns and Purposes

Durkheim's work suggests that society is something like a living creature. All the things that happen within it are its parts, and the parts work together to form the whole. We can study the parts of society—the social facts—by looking at how they work as part of the whole society.

Durkheim's ideas paved the way for a major current in anthropology known as *functionalism*. Functionalism is the view that all features of society serve a social purpose or purposes. In some societies, for example, market day may not just be a time for buying and selling things, but can also be an occasion to spread news and gossip and meet friends and lovers.

Lexicon
Functionalism is the anthropological theory that all the various aspects of a culture serve a social purpose. **Structuralism** is the anthropological theory that different aspects of thinking, language, and culture are related to one another in a logical pattern.

Functionalism is just one of the anthropological theories Durkheim helped to start. Another is *structuralism*—the theory that thought, language, and culture take a recognizable shape when all the different elements are seen in relation to one another.

According to structuralism, the structure of a society not only reveals how people organize their world socially, it also reflects how the human mind is structured. This idea was put forward by one of Durkheim's followers, Claude Levi-Strauss, who said that kinship patterns and variations of tribal myths are logically organized in a way that shows what the mind is like.

Both structuralism and functionalism are theories that grew partly from Durkheim's interpretation of culture as a distinct area of study that's not dependent upon other areas. The difference between structuralism and functionalism is that functionalism focuses on the social purpose of social facts, whereas structuralism focuses on logical relationships among them. Or, to put it simply, functionalism looks at what the parts do, structuralism looks at how the parts are all related.

The Least You Need to Know

➤ Freud, Weber, Durkheim, and Marx are leading figures in the rise of the social sciences.

➤ Freud says the unconscious is the home of repressed desires.

➤ The Oedipus complex occurs when a young boy feels he is competing with his father for his mother's love.

➤ Jung modified Freud's views saying we all share aspects of a "collective unconscious."

➤ Weber said that capitalism developed as a result of the Protestant work ethic.

➤ Durkheim believed that culture can be studied on its own terms and doesn't need to be explained in terms of outside factors like psychological drives or economic forces.

Chapter 21

The New Logic

In This Chapter

➤ Analytic versus continental philosophy

➤ Frege's application of logic to math and language

➤ Propositions and symbolic logic

➤ Wittgenstein's attempt to find the structure of reality

➤ Wittgenstein's shift to seeing language as a game

➤ Pragmatic philosophy

At around the time when the social sciences were coming into their own as fields independent of philosophy, a serious split began to form between two completely different ways of thinking about philosophy's task.

One side of the argument is sometimes referred to as continental philosophy, because it is rooted in thinking from France and Germany. The other side is sometimes called analytic philosophy; it focuses heavily on logic and includes the movements known as logical positivism and pragmatism.

Analytic philosophers developed new ways of using logic to think about language and in the process factored out a number of issues, including psychology and sociology, that continental philosophers were all hopped up about. In eliminating these things from their philosophical investigations, the analytic philosophers saw themselves as clarifying a confused situation.

Philosophy Chooses Up Sides

Analytic philosophers criticize continental philosophy because it focuses on all the things that make it hard to say for certain, once and for all, what anything means, including political struggle and the unconscious. According to continental philosophy, on the other hand, social and psychological uncertainty are problems we need to understand.

> **Reality Check**
>
> The terms **analytic** and **continental philosophy** can be somewhat misleading. All philosophers analyze things; "analytic" philosophers just have particular methods for their analyzing. And "continental" philosophy is not the only philosophy that has its roots on the "Continent" (of Europe).

In contrast, analytic philosophy tries to look at what we can say for certain once social and psychological difficulties are left out of the discussion. Analytic philosophers believe they can avoid social and psychological problems by thinking about language in logical terms.

This split in philosophy began late in the 19th century and continues today.

It's All in How You Say It

The analytic philosophers say that the continental philosophers aren't being careful enough with language. As a result, they don't make sense.

In fact, the analytic philosophers tend to look at the history of philosophy as a series of attempts to find the best language for talking about reality. The philosophers of the past went wrong, they say, because they used words that didn't have real meaning. And because they used confusing words, their ideas can't be verified.

Philoso-Fact Calling words that don't directly relate to observable reality "nonsense" has been part of the empiricist tradition since Hobbes and Hume.

According to many analytic philosophers, we can only tell what a word means if it refers to something that we know actually exists. This is called the *principle of verification*. For words to mean anything, we have to be able to check to see whether what they say is true. This view sees words like "beauty," "goodness," and "the big pie in the sky" as meaningless because they *could* mean almost anything, but refer to nothing that anyone has ever seen.

You Can't Reason Your Way Out of This

In turn, the continental philosophers say that analytic philosophy is, at best, empty. It has nothing to do with anything that matters—like all of the problems that actually influence people's lives and make the world what it is—and, at worst, deceptively hides the ways it analyzes unavoidable social and psychological problems.

This disagreement has not slowed down either side. The continental thinkers keep talking about social and psychological problems while the analytic philosophers keep trying to avoid these problems and analyze with logic.

Eminently Logical

Logic re-emerged as an important branch of philosophy in the late 19th and early 20th centuries and has remained a major current ever since. One of the key figures in the revival of logic was the German philosopher Gottlob Frege (1848–1925). Frege revolutionized the study of logic, which for the past 23 centuries had been based on the work of Aristotle.

Math's Deeper Meaning

Frege discovered that logic has common applications to math as well as to language, and by thinking of math as a kind of language, he was able to explain math in terms of logical operations.

But Frege was not entirely successful in his efforts to develop a logical explanation for math. As one of his contemporaries, Bertrand Russell, discovered, there are places where Frege's logical explanations involve contradictions.

Most importantly, Frege's concept of class, or set, was contradictory. A class or set is any group of things that fall under a category, such as "pigs" and "names beginning with the letter K." For math and logic to work together, each set has to be consistent with itself.

Russell pointed out, however, that there are sets that are contradictory. Russell's example was the set of "sets that are not members of themselves." Is this set a member of itself or not? If it is not a member of itself, then by definition, it must be a member of itself. Conversely, if it is a member of itself, it cannot be a member of itself. This is known as *Russell's paradox*. It provides devastating evidence that logic cannot fully be squared with math.

Philoso-Fact
Gottlob Frege, Bertrand Russell, and Ludwig Wittgenstein all played a major role in developing analytic philosophy. Frege worked out the new logic, Russell noticed its importance and provided feedback, and Wittgenstein developed new theoretical applications for it.

Even so, Frege's use of logic turned out to be tremendously influential, encouraging a number of other philosophers to apply logic to math and language.

Frege's work suggested to many the possibility of developing a more reliable use of language that would make it easier to see just what a sentence is actually trying to say. Looking at language logically helps get the bugs out of it. It helps you see where a single word can mean more than one thing or where two different words are used to mean the same thing, as well as where words don't really mean anything at all.

Math Spoken Here

Frege made a number of points that make it easier to see common ground between math and language. One of these points is that you shouldn't think of numbers as things in themselves, but rather as concepts that describe things.

Say you have a term called "x." One of the many things that might be true about "x" is the number of "x's" there are. Saying how many somethings exist is logically similar to saying that it is blue or it goes fishing on weekends. Numbers, to Frege, don't have a special existence of their own; they are only ways of describing things.

Concepts, including numbers, are not objects themselves, but are used to describe objects. Just as, in language, concepts can be put together to make sentences, numbers in math can be put together to make *propositions*.

Propositions are to math what sentences are to language. In fact, Frege made a distinction between *reference* and *sense* that applies, logically, both to language and to math. Reference has to do with the objects named by the concepts in a proposition—the things the proposition is about. Sense is the way in which the various terms of a proposition relate to one another.

Lexicon
Propositions are statements, in the form of language or math, that may be asserted, whether or not they are actually asserted and whether or not they are true. **Reference** is what a proposition has to do with the objects that it represents. **Sense** is the effect of the way the terms of a proposition relate to one another.

This distinction is important because propositions may have different senses, but the same reference. A famous example is the fact that "the morning star" and "the evening star" are actually the same thing, the planet Venus. Venus is the reference of both propositions, even though they have opposing senses.

Frege contends that we can think about what language and math do without worrying about their content. What's important to him is not what propositions refer to, but how they hold together. In other words, we don't need to refer to things in order to make sense. All we need are the right symbols to show what's going, in place of, or in addition to, the words and numbers that refer to objects. Frege developed a whole set of symbols to represent functions of propositions.

In fact, Frege is a leading figure in the development of what is known as *symbolic logic*. Symbolic logic is a language of symbols that describes the operations going on in a proposition or in a sentence. It allows for analysis of propositions in a way that is more clear and accurate than Aristotle's logic.

Frege came up with ways to use symbols in order to designate all the various operations that take place in mathematical and verbal propositions. These symbols include letters, dashes, parentheses, and other marks and characters. Since Frege's time, philosophers have been improving on his system to make symbolic logic even more clear and comprehensive—at least to those who know what the symbols mean!

A Proposition You Can't Refuse

Symbolic logic allows propositions to be accurately described so that they can be understood and worked with more easily. In effect, symbolic logic shows how propositions work. Understanding propositions means that you are less likely to get fooled by ambiguous language, since logical symbolism is unambiguous.

For example, symbolic logic helps you see what the word "the" does to a proposition, as opposed to the word "a." It also helps you see whether the word "is" says that something exists, might exist, or will exist.

Where Does Reality Fit In?

One of the important philosophers to be inspired by Frege's work with math, language, and logic was the Austrian Ludwig Wittgenstein (1889–1951). Wittgenstein attempted to show that logic reflects the structure of reality, which in turn provides the basis for the structure of language.

After writing an influential book that helped give rise to the logical positivism of the famous "Vienna Circle," Wittgenstein decided he was wrong and rejected the idea that logic is somehow rooted in the structure of reality. At this point, he advanced a whole new theory of language that sees all language as a kind of game with no necessary connection to any specific "reality."

Philoso-Fact
Wittgenstein served in the Austrian army during World War I. He wrote notebooks that formed the basis of much of his philosophical work while he was a prisoner of war in Italy.

Logic Gets Real

Before he revised his idea that logic reflects the structure of reality, Wittgenstein was critical of any use of language that was not based in logic but that attempted to make assertions about things that have no provable existence. This includes all statements about art, ethics, metaphysics, and religion.

Wittgenstein said that philosophical language should only be used to refer to observable things. When limited in this way, Wittgenstein believed that language could be reliably used to make truthful statements about the way the world works. In other words, meaning is only in a statement if the statement refers in a demonstrable way to actual things in the world.

Logic Spaces Out

At the same time, though, Wittgenstein saw logic as its own "space," made up of the world of logical possibility. Drawing on the work of Bertrand Russell, Wittgenstein identified logical units that are analogous to atoms in physics. Logical "atoms" are facts that are not dependent on other facts or propositions for their meaning—"a square has four sides" is true regardless of other facts. What's more, logical atoms cannot be divided into smaller independent facts.

Wittgenstein envisioned a perfectly reliable language made up of logical atoms coming together to form all the complex ways of saying everything that people can know and say for certain.

We Make the Rules

Wittgenstein's early work was extremely influential. Even so, he changed his mind about it and decided that the important thing about language is not the way it refers to the actual world of facts, but how all the things that it says relate to all the other things that it says. To use Frege's terms, Wittgenstein shifted from focusing on reference to focusing on sense. He came to believe that meaning in language depends not on what the words refer to, but on the way words relate to one another.

Wittgenstein came to see that the rules of language do not reflect an ideal logic, but are part of the way language works. They do not exist outside of language. In fact, Wittgenstein said that we can't know *anything* outside language. Language is all we have to think with.

What's more, he said that language does not depend on ideal rules of logic but simply on what people agree language means.

Wisdom at Work
Use Wittgenstein's idea that language is all you have to think with to explain why your intelligence seems to evaporate whenever you are surrounded by people who are speaking a language you don't know, especially when you are visiting a foreign country.

Wittgenstein came to see the idea of "truth" as a kind of game played with language. A proposition is verifiable not through the objective facts in the world that it refers to, but through the way it relates to other propositions.

What's more, the "game" of language has no out-of-bounds. We can't get outside of language in order to say what the truth really is. Any attempt to think about reality apart from language has to be done with language, so we can never get to that "reality."

To show how "truth" depends on people's ability to agree rather than on rules of logic, Wittgenstein made the point that all language is shared by at least two people. There's no such thing as one's own language.

Meaning Is Everybody's Business

Even your own innermost feelings, says Wittgenstein, can only be understood in terms of words everyone uses. These feelings don't have any meaning until you attach words to them, making them mean things that others can recognize. In this way, people's ability to agree about meaning make meaning possible.

Therefore, knowledge of truth does not depend on the individual mind looking at reality and finding the best terms to use to talk about reality. Instead, "truth" is something people agree to by accepting a particular set of standards for what truth involves. These standards may vary depending on the language being used and the people who decide what it means.

Philosophy Gets Practical

Meanwhile in America, around the turn of the 20th century, another philosophy based on logic was developing—*pragmatism*. Pragmatism is based on the thinking of Charles Sanders Pierce (1839–1914) and was developed further by William James (1842–1910).

Philoso-Fact
William James is the older brother of Henry James, the famous novelist who wrote *The Turn of the Screw*.

Like the analytic philosophers of England and Austria, the pragmatists looked at the meanings of propositions in logical terms. But whereas Frege and Wittgenstein thought about the reference and the sense of propositions, the pragmatists thought about their practical results.

For the pragmatists, the only important difference between two propositions is the difference in the results. Meaning is significant in the practical terms of what people and things do. If an idea isn't useful in solving a problem or bringing about a desirable result, it doesn't have any significance.

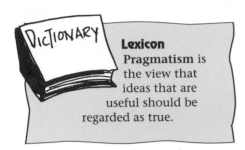

James took this way of thinking even further by saying that an idea is true if it does what you want it to do. This working of an idea is its "practical cash value," as he put it, and doesn't depend on what anyone may actually think about the idea, except insofar as people's attitudes come into play in influencing results.

Pragmatism, with its roots in empiricism, applies logic to language in order to think about how language relates to empirical events. From the pragmatic perspective, language should describe things that actually happen or that might happen. Language's description is not absolutely correct, but it is true insofar as it helps people see how things are and deal with what goes on around them.

Pragmatism triggered some intense debates because of its association of truth with practicality. Opponents of pragmatism felt that it placed severe and unnecessary limits on human behavior and understanding by suggesting that we all should live and think according to practical purposes.

In spite of pragmatism's opponents, it was a timely philosophy for many Americans who were interested in capping off their independence with financial success. In fact, pragmatism can be associated with the anything-goes approach to business that was popular in early 20th-century America.

The Least You Need to Know

➤ Continental philosophy focuses on social and psychological problems.

➤ Analytic philosophy avoids psychological and social problems and concentrates on logic.

➤ Frege helped get analytic philosophy started by applying logic to math and language.

➤ Frege helped develop a more flexible notation for logic called symbolic logic.

➤ Wittgenstein tried, at first, to show that logic reflects the structure of reality, but then changed his mind and claimed that language is a kind of game with no limits.

➤ Pragmatism is a philosophy that associates truth with practical results.

To Be or Not To Be

In This Chapter

➤ Phenomenology and consciousness

➤ Husserl's "bracketing" of science

➤ Existentialism and the meaning of being

➤ Heidegger and authenticity

➤ Sartre and absurdity

By the time the 20th century rolled around, two main currents of Western philosophy had established themselves: empiricism, with its interest in objectivity, and rationalism, with its idealistic view of subjectivity. In spite of repeated attempts to reconcile these two ways of thinking about things, they remained in opposition.

On the one hand, empiricism made the world seem like an impersonal machine, unaffected by the way people live and think. And on the other, rational idealism tended to factor out the world, leaving only brooding, self-absorbed thought.

The philosophy known as phenomenology was an attempt to reconcile and combine these opposing perspectives. Although it originally responded to problems in scientific thinking, it came to be useful in helping people deal with the problem of meaninglessness in their lives.

A more popular version of phenomenology, known as existentialism, became one of the most important branches of 20th century thought. It offered people a way of facing the cold realities of life without despairing, by saying "take responsibility for your world and work to realize the potential of your existence in your own terms."

Philoso-Fact
Phenom-enology is an approach to psychology as well as to philosophy. As a psychology, it differs from the ideas put forward by Sigmund Freud by focusing on consciousness, rather than the unconscious.

A Phenomenal Philosophy

Phenomenology was developed into a full-fledged philosophy by the German Jewish philosopher and psychologist, Edmund Husserl (1859-1938). It looks at the relation between the world on one hand, and the senses that experience the world on the other. The world as we experience it, as Immanuel Kant had said 150 years previously, is the phenomenal world.

Reality Meets Awareness

Husserl's phenomenology is unique because it sees the physical world and individual human consciousness as interconnected parts of a single relationship. You can't be aware without being aware *of* something—and you can't have reality without already being aware of reality on some level.

In fact, according to the phenomenologists, the tendency to see awareness and reality as separate things has led people to lose sight of their own experience of reality. As a result they see reality from an artificial point of view, in which their own lives and experiences are unimportant.

In response to this attitude, phenomenology says we should pay closer attention to our experience of phenomenal reality and be prepared to think about it in new and different ways.

Intent on Thinking

Husserl based his thinking on the ideas of the German philosopher and Catholic priest Franz Brentano (1838-1917) who studied how the mind works. Brentano said that whenever we think, we are always thinking *about* something. The things we think about may or may not exist, but, in either case, our thinking about them helps make our ideas what they are.

Brentano called this aspect of thinking *intentionality*. Intentionality has to do with the way ideas involve both what we think and how we think about them. If a red traffic light makes you feel impatient, Brentano would have said that feeling of impatience is part of how you experience the light, not a separate thing from it.

This is true regardless of what the actual red light is doing. Say, for example, that you're so impatient that you start banging your head on the steering wheel. Meanwhile, the light turns green without your realizing it. Even though the red light is gone, you still have the idea of a red light in your mind, making you bang your head on the steering wheel. The intentionality of your idea does this, not the light itself. In fact, according to Brentano, all ideas have intentionality.

The Intentions of Science

This means that ideas are not simply objective, but have significance according to how we feel about them. Husserl picked up on Brentano's concept of intentionality and developed it into his philosophy of phenomenology. He said that even science, which claims to be objective, has intentionality; it brings its own attitude with it toward the things that it studies.

Husserl says that science, in trying to be objective, imposes its attitude of objectivity on the world. The result is an "objective" reality that has the human significance stripped away from it.

Bring on the Brackets

To set things straight, Husserl says we should *bracket* all the assumptions we have about the world when we experience things, so we'll be able to see past all the layers of meaning that have built up around them. In other words, we need to set these assumptions to one side in order to try out other assumptions. In doing this, we'll be able to appreciate new possibilities.

We should try to see reality and our consciousness as the same thing. Husserl called this process *reduction*— the act of getting in touch with our own intentionality before scientific attitudes have had a chance to crowd it out.

Painting with Your Brain

Lexicon
The **intentionality** of a thought is both the attitude you bring with you whenever you think about something, and what it is you are thinking about. In other words, it's the relation between the thing you're thinking of and the manner in which you are thinking.

Lexicon
Bracketing is Husserl's process of setting aside assumptions about things that stem from scientific thinking. The point is to look at things with fresh eyes. **Reduction** is the act of identifying your own intentionality in the way you see things after you have bracketed out the intentionality of science.

Once you recognize the importance of intentionality, says Husserl, you can be more creative in the way you experience and think about things. In fact, Husserl's philosophy suggests that there is an element of art and fiction in the very act of looking, hearing, touching, smelling, etc. Husserl even regarded modern art as helpful to his phenomenological project, because it can help get people to perceive differently.

He said, for example, that when you look at a table, you should try to see the table as it really appears to you, and try to notice how your perceptions do funny things, thereby allowing yourself to see it in different ways. Even though you may think of it as being a certain color and having a certain shape, you can see, if you look carefully and without assumptions, that it seems to have many different shades and shapes.

Husserl said you should try these shapes and shades on for size, noticing them while resisting the tendency to say, "that's a table, it's brown, square, and flat and has four legs." This is a start to reclaiming your consciousness back from assumptions imposed on it by other people. The next step is to do the same with all the meanings in your life.

An Anti-Social Philosophy?

Phenomenology has been criticized for focusing on the picayune details of how we perceive things while ignoring important influences on behavior like social factors. In response to this kind of criticism, Husserl developed the idea of the *life-world*.

> **REALITY** ✓
>
> **Reality Check**
>
> It is not only phenomenology, but also existentialism that minimizes the importance of social influences on people's actions. Is meaning really up to the individual, or does it result from the ways people relate to one another?

According to Husserl, we are disposed to understand our experiences in terms of the way we relate to reality. And our relationship with reality is strongly influenced by our relationships with other people. Our life-world—how we think about things—grows from our social connections.

In coming up with the idea of the life-world, Husserl tried to square his phenomenology (which focused on individual consciousness) with other philosophies that emphasized social influences like Marxism.

Husserl's attempt to see the world with fresh eyes provided a starting point for the existentialists, who said that we need to rethink, or bracket, not only what science says about the world, but also what religion and even philosophy say. The existentialists contend that all religious, scientific, and philosophical interpretations are no truer nor any better than any other way of seeing things.

Let It Be

Existentialism is one of the most important philosophical views of the 20th century. And it is no coincidence that a student of Husserl's, Martin Heidegger (1889-1976), was one of the first existentialist philosophers. Heidegger built on Husserl's thinking by shifting from consciousness to "being." What was important for Heidegger was not so much our experience of reality but our existence itself.

Just as Husserl said that artificial attitudes interfere with our ability to appreciate our consciousness, Heidegger believed that the whole tradition of ideas about "being" actually interferes with our ability to appreciate our being. For Heidegger, the fact that things, including ourselves, exist is amazing and inexplicable, in spite of centuries of philosophical attempts to explain it. We need to see through these past explanations, says Heidegger, in order to see being for what it is.

His word for "being," is *da-sein*, or "being there." *Da-sein* is open to the possibility that you may need to create your own meanings for life, in order to achieve an "authentic" existence. *Da-sein* also recognizes that existence is only temporary.

Time Traveling

Existence for Heidegger is everything. Nothing lies outside, before, or beyond being, and being takes place in time. The fact that we exist in time means that we are always changing. We are no longer what we used to be.

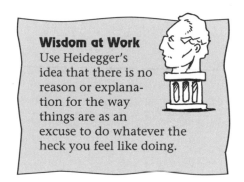

Wisdom at Work
Use Heidegger's idea that there is no reason or explanation for the way things are as an excuse to do whatever the heck you feel like doing.

Because things change, we are constantly presented with new possibilities, and it is up to us to make the most of them. We need to work with these changes, not resist them, by changing our attitude toward our old selves as we continue to exist in time.

There's no reason or explanation for life until we decide individually what reasons and explanations we believe in. It's totally up to each one of us to figure out what we should do about our lives, and we should always be trying out new possibilities.

Being aware of the possibilities, though, also involves an awareness of the limitations. The most important limitation is that we won't be here forever. This means that we have to take responsibility for our lives now.

Knowing What's What

Part of what Heidegger took from phenomenology and applied to existentialism was the idea that you can't separate knowledge from experience; they're both part of the same reality. You can't have an experience without in some sense knowing about it, and you can't have knowledge without experiencing the knowledge.

In fact, says Heidegger, we can "know" before we even realize it. In other words, we develop attitudes and assumptions toward things in our lives without necessarily thinking about them. For example, some people tend to be fearful, worried, angry, or hopeless about their lives. Thinking about their existence in phenomenological terms can help these people recognize the harmful ways they see the world and show them that there are other, more positive ways of seeing it.

The Real McCoy

Another problem phenomenological existentialism can help you avoid is living a phony life that comes as a result of trying to live up to other people's expectations. Accepting other people's view of reality can prevent you from living an *authentic* existence. Authenticity, for Heidegger, is refusing to take things for granted, refusing to act as if things are already figured out and understood.

Lexicon
Authenticity means leading your life on your own terms, refusing to accept the assumptions others make about the meaning of things.

Authenticity says, "It's my life and I'm going to do the best I can with it, regardless of what people think. Others may think they have things figured out, but I'm going to experience reality for myself and come up with my own sense of its importance."

Being Absurd

The French philosopher, Jean-Paul Sartre (1905-1980) pointed Heidegger's and Husserl's ideas in a new direction. He used them to show that reality is inherently absurd. The problem, according to Sartre, is that we would all like just to exist independent of a made-up meaning, but we can't; it's impossible.

Jean-Paul Sartre.

Too Free for Our Own Good

Sartre says that in addition to being what we are, we are also conscious of being. This is a problem because we can't simply be conscious of ourselves *being* without bringing some kind of meaning along with our consciousness. Whatever meaning we add isn't necessarily better than any other meaning we could have added instead. As a result, we get lost in our own freedom to come up with any of several possible meanings. In Sartre's words, "We are condemned to be free."

Philoso-Fact
Sartre's ideas made such a big splash that he was offered a Nobel prize, which he refused.

If we could just be without any meaning at all, like a stone or some other inert object, we might feel better about things, but we can't. Or, if there were some meaning that pre-supposed our being that we could hold onto as a necessary truth, that would be okay too, but there isn't. We can't do without meaning, but there is no single right meaning or even a way of figuring out the best meaning.

As a result, there's no purpose behind reality; nevertheless, we still need to decide what to do with our lives. Sartre called this predicament absurd.

Heroic Existers

All kinds of stories have been written in the 20th century with existentialist heroes. There's Batman and Spiderman and Philip Marlow—all dark, misunderstood individuals. They are unhappy and struggle with themselves. But they are true to themselves and always do the right thing, even though their authenticity isn't appreciated by the rest of the world.

Philoso-Fact
Sartre's view of life as absurd inspired many novels and stories. He himself was a best-selling novelist.

You Are What You Do

Sartre said that you not only choose *what to do* but, in choosing, you choose *who you are*. What's more, you choose out of nothing. Whatever reasons you have for the choices you make aren't enough grounds for making that choice. As a result, you have to make a lot of your choices just for the heck of it.

Even though you don't have reasons that determine your choices for you, you still have to make them. Not only that, but the choices you make greatly influence how you live your life. The hard thing about being human, then, is having to make important decisions without good reasons.

In many respects, Sartre's thinking resembles the thinking of the Danish philosopher, Sören Kierkegaard, whose ideas anticipated existentialism (see Chapter 19). Kierkegaard spoke of a "leap of faith," in which you have to commit yourself without knowing why. There is one obvious difference, though, between Kierkegaard's "leap of faith" and Sartre's "choosing": Kierkegaard was a devoted Christian, and Sartre was a self-proclaimed atheist.

The Least You Need to Know

➤ Phenomenology says our consciousness is always colored by our attitudes, or *intentionality*.

➤ Husserl says we should *bracket*, or set aside, scientific attitudes so that they don't unduly shade our own experience.

➤ Existentialism focuses on "being" and the possibilities of being for its own sake.

➤ Heidegger says authenticity involves refusing to take things for granted or accept other people's assessments.

➤ Sartre contends that the human predicament is absurd because we have to make choices without having adequate reasons for making them.

I CAN SEE MY
OWN MORTALITY.

CHILL.

Chapter 23

Structuring New Ideas

In This Chapter

➤ The structure of language

➤ The arbitrariness of signifiers

➤ How structuralism deals with historical change

➤ Culture as structure

➤ The unconscious as structure

One of many influential philosophies that took shape near the beginning of the 20th century is structuralism. And the first structuralist was a Swiss philosopher and linguist named Ferdinand de Saussure (1857–1913), who said that language should be regarded as a structure, independent of the things that it refers to.

This line of thinking led to some controversial ideas, not the least of which was that the individual is essentially a complex of meanings woven together out of language. We don't simply speak language, language speaks itself through us. For Saussure and his followers, language is like a big rug, and they pulled it out from under the time-honored concept of the rational individual.

Saussure's approach led to a whole new way of thinking about meaning. He said it isn't individuals who give language its meaning, but rather it's the way words relate to one another. These words already have meaning before people speak them, and this meaning doesn't simply depend on what the words refer to.

Saussure's approach made it so that linguists could look at language and only language without getting bogged down in other things, like the way language relates to the world or to the mind. His approach turned out to be useful in other areas too, including anthropology, political science, literary criticism, and psychoanalysis.

Most notably, by saying that meaning makes up its own system that doesn't depend on anything outside of it, Saussure got the anthropologist Claude Levi-Strauss to look at culture in a similar way. In addition, he inspired the psychoanalyst Jacques Lacan to look at the unconscious as something structured, much as Saussure said language is structured.

You Can't Beat the System

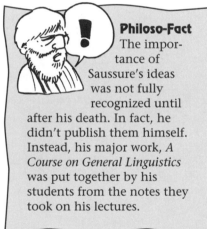

Philoso-Fact
The importance of Saussure's ideas was not fully recognized until after his death. In fact, he didn't publish them himself. Instead, his major work, *A Course on General Linguistics* was put together by his students from the notes they took on his lectures.

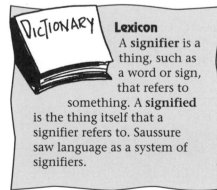

Lexicon
A **signifier** is a thing, such as a word or sign, that refers to something. A **signified** is the thing itself that a signifier refers to. Saussure saw language as a system of signifiers.

Saussure's approach to linguistics was revolutionary because it saw language as a system. He said the parts of the system of language are important, not because of the way they refer to things outside the system, but because of the way they relate to other things within the system.

"Cat" Might as Well Be "Phthaloogazop"

Saussure said that meaning has to do with two separate sets of things, which he called *signifieds* and *signifiers*. A signified is something referred to by language, and a signifier is the thing that refers to it. For example, the word, "tree" is a signifier, and the actual tree is a signified. Language is made up of signifiers but not signifieds, which aren't actually part of the system.

According to Saussure, the relationship between signifieds and signifiers is arbitrary, depending entirely on convention. In other words, there is nothing special in a particular word that makes it mean the thing it stands for. There is nothing in the word "banana," for example, that connects it to the piece of fruit we call by that name except convention, the fact that people agree to call it "banana." We might just as easily have agreed to call it something else entirely, like "golugulo," "slurd," or "fidgewonk."

Seeing signifieds and signifiers as connected in an arbitrary way completely changed the study of linguistics. It no longer made as much sense to talk about the historical development of words and their meanings, or about the origins of words. According to Saussure, looking at how words change over time doesn't tell us anything about how language works.

Saussure said the sound of a word is meaningful only because it is different from the sounds of other words. Differences between the way words sound depends on their *phonemes*. A phoneme is a sound that's part of a word that may have no meaning in itself, but that is significantly different from other sounds.

For example, the words "belch" and "belt" are different because they end with different phonemes, the ch-sound and the t-sound. It is this difference between the two words that make them meaningful. Words get their meaning largely as a result of the way they relate to other words, not from the way they relate to the things they represent.

This applies not only to the spelling and sound of words, but to their significance too. The word "boy," for example, gets its meaning not simply because of all the actual boys it refers to, but because of the way its meaning differs from other words like it, such as man, girl, and puppy. The word "boy" is meaningful in relation to all the words for things that a boy isn't.

This view of words made for a new way of thinking about how meaning happens when people talk, and also about the influence of cause and effect on the way words change through time. Cause and effect, said Saussure, doesn't have much to do with how language works. Instead, change just gets incorporated into the system.

Wisdom at Work
Use Saussure's insight that the relationship between signifiers and signifieds is arbitrary as an excuse to make up new words. Call your boss a furplescroot and tell him that it means "exemplary leader."

Lexicon
A **phoneme** is a consonant or a vowel sound that is recognizably different from other sounds used to make words. It is the smallest unit of meaningful sound in language.

History Is Now

What's important about language for Saussure is not how it began or how it changes over time, but how its parts relate to one another. Saussure used two concepts to refer to this distinction. He called the view of language as it develops through time a *diachronic* view, and the view of language as an inter-related system a *synchronic* view.

Saussure said that synchronic relationships incorporate diachronic change. In other words, if words

Lexicon
A **diachronic** view of language considers language as it develops through time. A **synchronic** view of language looks at it as a system that exists all at the same time.

209

change, the system adjusts without losing its structure. This structure can thus be studied without considering the history of words.

Language on Parole

Saussure made another important distinction between individual acts of speaking and the system of language as a whole. The system he called *langue*, the French word for language. Individual acts of speech he called *parole*, the French word for speech. Saussure said that parole makes sense only in relation to langue. And without langue there can be no parole.

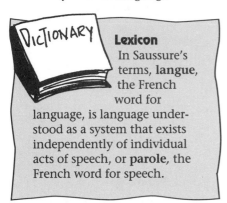

Lexicon
In Saussure's terms, **langue**, the French word for language, is language understood as a system that exists independently of individual acts of speech, or **parole**, the French word for speech.

This means that meaning is not simply a matter of the individual choice of the person who's talking. It depends on, and is limited and directed by, the way the system works as a whole. What's more, a person who is speaking is likely to be unaware of the ways the system of language makes his or her words meaningful. That meaning, then, isn't simply that person's meaning, but is part of the way the system works.

Them's Fightin' Words

Saussure's contention that meaning is structured and therefore doesn't stem from individual choice but from the system of language itself was, and remains, controversial. It undermines the existentialist notion that people are responsible for making their own meaning (see Chapter 22). And it is contrary to the empirical way of looking at things. Rather than separating language into isolated events and studying them as distinct entities, Saussure's structuralism looks at how things relate to one another.

Others who followed Saussure took his thinking even further, saying that the very notion of who you are is determined by the way you are defined by language. If you want to understand who you are, don't look at yourself in isolation from others, or at what you say about yourself in isolation from the rest of language. Instead, think about how you fit in with everyone else and how your ideas and beliefs depend on a whole larger system of thinking, which requires the use of language.

Culture Is All Talk

One of the first thinkers to recognize the importance of Saussure's ideas was the structural anthropologist, Claude Levi-Strauss (b.1908). Levi-Strauss applied Saussure's view of language to culture, saying we should understand culture as a structure that works just like language.

In other words, culture organizes things into patterns that make up a logical structure. The meaning of, say, baseball is best understood in connection with other things that resemble it, like softball, cricket, tennis, ping-pong, football, volleyball, and so on.

> **Reality Check**
>
> Critics of Levi-Strauss have pointed out that his conclusions are suspect because they are based on studies of non-industrial cultures—mostly isolated Indian tribes of Brazil. The picture gets more complicated when you look at modern culture, which isn't so neatly structured.

Meaning Gets Organized

Saussure says that you don't necessarily understand how your language works even as you use it. And Levi-Strauss says that you don't necessarily understand how your culture is structured, even though you belong to it and do things according to its logic.

This suggests that people's thinking is the product of their culture, and not the other way around. Culture, for Levi-Strauss, is a big system of meanings that influences the ways people behave within it. Language is only one of the ways in which people operate within cultural meaning. There are other ways too, such as through food and kinship patterns.

Kin to Language

Levi-Strauss went to Brazil and studied tribal cultures that had complicated rules for who you could marry and who you couldn't, depending on your kinship and your social position. He said that kinship systems among these tribes are organized just like phonemic systems in language.

Each rule, looked at in isolation, doesn't seem to mean anything, but it makes sense as part of a whole system. Levi-Strauss identified other patterns that are analogous to phonemes, such as the differences in the way people understand food. Food may be raw, partly cooked, cooked, or burnt. In addition, it may still be alive or it may be rotten.

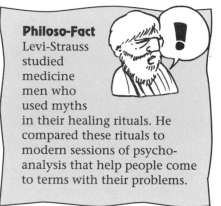

Philoso-Fact
Levi-Strauss studied medicine men who used myths in their healing rituals. He compared these rituals to modern sessions of psycho-analysis that help people come to terms with their problems.

Levi-Strauss called these different ways of understanding food *gustemes*. They're analogous to phonemes in language. Similarly, in studying myths he identified a number of different *mythemes*, statements that made sense only in relation to other statements.

Levi-Strauss said myths allow cultures to deal intellectually with problems like death, illness, and conflicts between people. It's easier to accept such hardships if they fit into logical structures traced out in the myths because people can then see their hardships as a natural part of the whole structure.

There's a Mind in Here Somewhere

Levi-Strauss' ideas attracted a considerable amount of criticism as well as support. His critics accused him of ignoring history and facts, and of idealizing non-industrialized cultures. His supporters said he found important evidence about how meaning works in human society that reveals clues about the mind itself.

There are many different systems of meaning that come together to make up culture. According to Levi-Strauss, the melding of these different systems reflects the collective human mind. Levi-Strauss' collective mind is not based on instinctual drives, as is Freud's, but rather simply on its own structure. Like Marx, Levi-Strauss recognized that people's behavior is culturally determined without their knowing it, but unlike Marx, he did not hold economic forces responsible. Rather, it is the logical structure itself that determines behavior.

Modern Views of Meaning

➤ **Marx** Meaning is shaped ideologically through the relations of production. You may be unconscious of the way the meanings you accept justify these relations of production.

➤ **Freud** Meaning may be conscious or unconscious. Unconscious meaning develops when desires are repressed. These desires may return in the form of dreams or psychotic symptoms.

➤ **Logical Positivism** Meaning must be able to be proven through observation.

➤ **Existentialism** Meaning is consciously (intentionally) decided by the individual who must choose without objective reasons.

➤ **Structuralism** Meaning is built into the system, such as the system of language. The meaning of an idea depends on its logical relationship to the other ideas in the system.

Psyching Yourself Out

Saussure's work was taken even further by the French psychoanalyst, Jacques Lacan (1901–1981). Lacan was a follower of both Freud and Saussure, and he brought their ideas together to develop his own theory of how people get their sense of themselves.

Lacan said, "The unconscious is structured like language." There is a logic to the way the different aspects of the unconscious are related to one another and to conscious thinking. The unconscious, according to Lacan, is analogous to Saussure's concept of langue, while the conscious is analogous to parole.

This means that just as langue is more important than parole in the sense that it is the source of meaning that makes speaking possible, the unconscious, for Lacan, is more important than the conscious, which is only partial and can even be misleading.

In fact, Lacan objected to other psychoanalysts who used Freud's ideas as a way of saying "we need to protect our egos from our unconscious desires." The "ego" is Freud's word for the conscious self. Lacan said the more we build up our egos, the more we deny our unconscious, which is always in conflict with our conscious selves.

Philoso-Fact
For 10 years, Lacan gave weekly seminars to teach people psychoanalysis. But his teaching became so controversial that he was censured by the International Psycho-Analytical Association.

Your Ego Is Your Enemy

Say you have a sense of yourself as a good worker. It is good for your ego to think of yourself this way. According to Lacan, though, your conscious ego and your unconscious desires structure themselves in opposition to each other, so that your desire to see yourself as a good worker is a reaction against the unconscious desire to goof off.

This desire will express itself in ways that you refuse to recognize, because recognizing it would challenge your sense of who you are—a good worker. For example, maybe you will feel really sleepy during the day and not be able to sleep at night. Of course, as a good worker, you don't have time to sleep during the day and, what's more, your ego is too big to consider that your unconscious may be playing tricks on you.

So, you get your doctor to give you drugs to keep you awake during the day, and more drugs that will put you to sleep at night. That way you can continue to live up to your idea of who you are in spite of your unconscious desire to be different.

Lacan says this kind of situation is not simply a matter of fixing the individual so he or she can be more "normal," but of realizing that the whole idea of normality is part of the problem. We can't outsmart our unconscious because it is part of a whole structure of meaning that is logically opposed to whatever egos we may build up for ourselves. Quite simply, our unconscious is bigger than we are.

Philoso-Fact
Lacan was opposed to the idea of psychoanalysis as a way of "curing" people who are "sick." Instead, he saw psychoanalysis as being more like teaching. Through such teaching people could learn to heal themselves.

Mirror, Mirror

One of Lacan's most important ideas is his explanation of how the ego develops in relation to the unconscious. This happens in early childhood, said Lacan, during what he called the *mirror stage*. The mirror stage is the time when we first "see" ourselves. His term for the self is the *subject*. The subject is the self as it is determined and understood through language.

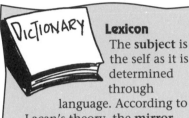

Lexicon
The **subject** is the self as it is determined through language. According to Lacan's theory, the **mirror stage** is a crucial moment in the formation of the subject.

The chain of signification is both the conscious and unconscious language that defines our selves.

What we see is a helpless little twerp who can't take care of him- or herself and who needs Mom to keep from getting squashed by all the big, strong grown-ups out there. Of course, this isn't what we want to see. We want to see someone who is well on the way to becoming a big, strong grown-up in his or her own right.

What we want to see is also the person we think Mom wants to see in us, since we want Mom to keep on taking care of us. At this moment, the mirror stage, we repress our awareness of our own weakness and identify ourselves with what we think Mom wants us to be. It is now that we also become trapped in the system of meaning Lacan calls *the chain of signification*.

The chain of signification is language, both conscious and unconscious, and, according to Lacan, it makes us who we are. We become what it tells us we are in order to protect ourselves—in order to cover up our helplessness. The problem is, we have to make sacrifices in order to make ourselves believe we really are who we want to think we are. We have to deny the desires that interfere with our egos.

Rattling the Chains

Once we become "ourselves" by becoming trapped in the chain of signification, we can't get out. The best we can do is move around in our chains as freely as they will let us.

Fortunately, the structure of language and the unconscious are not rigid, but slip around enough so that unconscious meanings emerge all over the place.

Philoso-Fact
As Lacan points out, Freud noticed a similarity between dreams and word games. This is evidence for Lacan's belief that the unconscious is structured like language.

Lacan saw the slipperiness of meaning as a positive thing and tried to show how there can be flexible meanings in his work, both as a psychoanalyst and as a writer. In psychoanalyzing people, he would play with their minds by doing things like refusing to hold to a schedule and refusing to be seen as an authority.

Lacan's writings are playful too. They are full of puns, puzzles, and riddles that make it hard to figure out what he's saying, but also show that meaning can always turn out to be more than what you might think at first.

A Formula for Excess Meaning

For example, Lacan plays around with Saussure's distinction between the signifier and the signified, a distinction that Lacan regarded as too rigid.

This formula shows the separation of signifier and signified. Lacan shows, however, that signified and signifier are not always separate things. For example, metaphors—things that represent other things—often turn signifieds into signifiers. Lacan shows this with his formula for metaphor:

$$f\left(\frac{S'}{S}\right)S \cong S(+)s$$

This formula shows that two signifiers (S and S') that have the same meaning are equal or approximate to a signifier plus a signified (S+s). The plus sign, says Lacan, represents "crossing the bar" that separates the signified and the signifier in the first part of the equation. In this way, the plus sign is both a mathematical sign and an emblem for how signifiers and signifieds aren't absolutely separate.

At the same time, Lacan is making fun of the logical positivists who use symbolic logic to represent how meaning works. Lacan says they do this by taking meaning out of the statements they analyze and substituting mathematical formulas for them. In contrast, he reads meaning back into his formulas, interpreting numbers, letters, and signs as images with meanings in order to show that you can't impose limits on meaning. Meaning pops up all over the place.

In addition to interpreting the plus sign as the signifier "crossing over" into the signified, he says the – sign represents rainwater and seawater being separated when God created Earth. What's more, he tells a story about how the "S" representing the signifier also represents someone's elbow resting on a ventilator outside a public bathroom, trying to figure out just what the words "Ladies" and "Gentlemen" are supposed to represent!

The Least You Need to Know

➤ Ferdinand de Saussure founded structural linguistics, which sees language as a system.

➤ Claude Levi-Strauss applied structuralism to culture and said that culture works like language.

➤ Jacques Lacan applied structuralism to the unconscious and said the unconscious works like language.

Part 6
Knowledge Now

Most philosophy these days reacts drastically against the philosophical tradition developed during the Enlightenment. "Reason" is not to be trusted. The very idea of reason controls people, limits people, and sets up false expectations. Apart from the academic strain of thinking called analytic philosophy that continues to advance a rational approach, reason is "out"—and many new things are "in."

But these new ways of looking at the world today don't add up to a single, bigger and better view. Instead, there are lots of small, independent perspectives jostling against one another for power and attention.

Philosophy now is largely about reacting to this age of "unreason." Some philosophy responds by wallowing in it, by showing how knowledge doesn't point anywhere beyond itself. Some philosophy reacts by trying to get more power and attention for people who have been left out of consideration by previous philosophies, namely women and minority cultures.

And then there is some philosophy that insists there really is a big picture and we are making progress in figuring out what it is. We can have global solutions to problems that humanity has struggled with since the beginning of time—but "reason" is not the answer.

Chapter 24

Pomo Sapience

In This Chapter

➤ Post-modernism

➤ Foucault's view of knowledge as harmful

➤ The "other"

➤ Derrida's view of language as misleading

➤ Rorty's defense of bourgeois liberalism

There are a number of different notions of what "pomo" (short for post-modern) philosophy is, as well as many different attitudes toward it. In fact, any one description of post-modernism (including this one!) is going to present a limited perspective that can be refuted, denied, added on to, reinterpreted, and even misinterpreted on purpose.

And this is just the way post-modern philosophers want it, because one of the keys of post-modern philosophy is that you can never get the complete picture. In fact, there's no such thing as the complete picture. The picture, however big it may be, will always be missing something. A post-modernist paradox is that the very idea of completeness means that something is being left out.

At the same time, the picture always says too much. It's like cancer cells that grow out of control and finally destroy themselves—but they still don't go away. They stick around as meanings no one ever intended. They are always politically motivated, but in the end, uncontrollable.

With post-modern philosophy, you can't have it all, but you will always get too much. Then again, some post-modernists claim that there is no such thing as "post-modern philosophy"; there is only who-knows-how-many different sets of ideas whose relevance becomes increasingly fragmented and localized.

Philosophy Eats Itself

Perhaps the most influential post-modern philosopher is the Frenchman Michel Foucault (1926–1984). Foucault started out as a structuralist, looking in particular at the way "knowledge" has been structured through language. He found that structures of knowledge exert a powerful social force that labels people as normal or abnormal, good or bad.

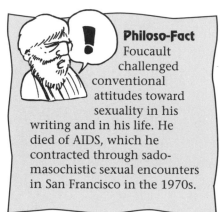

Philoso-Fact
Foucault challenged conventional attitudes toward sexuality in his writing and in his life. He died of AIDS, which he contracted through sado-masochistic sexual encounters in San Francisco in the 1970s.

Someone Who Dug Philosophy

Foucault was a historian as well as a philosopher. He described his work as "archeology" of knowledge. By analyzing old writings, he tried to "dig up" how knowledge took shape during other moments in history.

He did this by focusing on unstated assumptions of what people thought language and truth are in a variety of different fields. He found that during the Renaissance, people treated words as if they contained truth inside them, although shortly afterwards, in the 17th century, people used words, not as truth, but as signs pointing to the truth.

What You Know Can Hurt You

According to Foucault, this change in the way knowledge is structured shows that knowledge does not simply reflect the way things are, but instead forms a system that makes people think what "knowledge" says is really true.

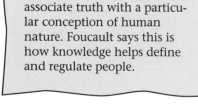

Philoso-Fact
Foucault's phrase, "will to knowledge" echoes Nietzsche's phrase, "will to power." Foucault admired Nietzsche's idea that many philosophies mistakenly associate truth with a particular conception of human nature. Foucault says this is how knowledge helps define and regulate people.

The structure of thinking does not reflect the nature of the human mind, as the structural anthropologist Claude Levi-Strauss said about the mythic beliefs of the Brazilian Indians he studied (see Chapter 23). Instead, says Foucault, thinking reflects power structures. Wherever you have knowledge, you have power exerting itself. The power of knowledge is repressive; it forces people to behave in certain ways.

Foucault focuses on the "human sciences," especially during their development in Europe: during the Renaissance and the Enlightenment. He says the human sciences, and philosophy in particular, provide ways of wielding power over others. They demonstrate a "will to knowledge," a desire to control the world, including other people, by setting up particular ideas as true.

Knowledge, says Foucault, is produced by power because power makes people accept certain ideas and reject others. Power uses knowledge to control people's thinking and behavior.

Power + Knowledge = Padded Cell

Foucault provides an example of the way knowledge exerts control over people by pointing out that the Enlightenment, a time when everyone was getting all excited about the new ideas of reason and freedom, was also the time when they invented mental institutions for locking up the "insane." Foucault suggests that mental patients were locked up not so that they could be cured, but so they could be kept out of the way and studied.

Reason and freedom were important positive values that were linked in the Enlightenment. Yet in practice, if you didn't live up to the standards of reason defined by the doctors, philosophers, and scientists, you would lose your freedom. You would be locked up, studied as a mental case, and shown off to the public as a curiosity. You might even be put to work doing jobs no "sane" person wanted to do.

Foucault argued that the ideas of freedom and reason were invented in order to exert social control over people who don't act the way they should, according to the way power is structured within society. Just as the ideas of freedom and reason provide an excuse to lock people up, those who are locked up provide reassurance to everyone else that they are free and reasonable people.

Tell Me an Other

Without the insane—who could be locked up—no one would really know what freedom and reason were, since these things only have meaning in relation to what they are not. Foucault says people always define themselves in opposition to others they regard as inferior, abnormal, and strange. Conversely, they define other groups of people in opposition to themselves. This process is called *othering*. The term othering is associated with the work of French feminist Simone de Beauvoir (see Chapter 25).

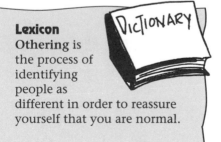

Philoso-Fact
As Foucault explains, before keeping those diagnosed as insane in mental institutions, they were put into ships that sailed around Europe. Hence, the term "ship of fools." At this time, people who were severely irrational were not thought to have a medical problem, but rather were having some sort of religious experience. The fools were more like pilgrims than patients. Putting them on ships got them out of people's hair without having to lock them up.

Lexicon
Othering is the process of identifying people as different in order to reassure yourself that you are normal.

According to Foucault, people aren't naturally different from one another; they are made different through the process of othering. Men define themselves by othering women; heterosexuals other gays and lesbians; whites other blacks; Christians other Jews; and so on.

Great Minds Think Alike

In interpreting knowledge as an expression of power rather than an expression of truth, Foucault saw the individual thinkers who are often given credit for coming up with knowledge as people who just happened to be in the right place at the right time. If you come up with an idea that changes the way everyone thinks, it's only because everyone needed that idea to think with. Someone else would have thought it up if you hadn't. In fact, others probably did.

Wisdom at Work
Use the idea that having a "great mind" is a matter of being in the right place at the right time to explain why you aren't a famous philosopher. Say you could have come up with Descartes' statement, "I think therefore I am," if you had been in his shoes.

Foucault said the "great thinkers" of the Enlightenment weren't so great. They only managed to seem great at other people's expense. In fact, according to Foucault, the idea of individual genius—of "great thinkers" who came up with "great ideas"—was invented during the Enlightenment to help make the repressive knowledge about reason and freedom be accepted more easily.

As a follower of Saussure and the other structuralists, Foucault didn't believe that ideas are simply thought up by particularly brilliant minds. Instead, they develop as part of the whole system of language. No idea can be great without a lot of other ideas keeping it in place.

Practicing What You Preach

Foucault wanted to avoid making repressive use of knowledge in his own work. He realized there was a danger of exerting power through his own knowledge—his own way of looking at the past, language, and society. In fact, Foucault's thinking actually has exerted considerable force on contemporary society.

Breaking Up the Structure

Foucault hoped that instead of one big, powerful structure dictating knowledge to everyone, there could be lots of smaller groups structuring knowledge in a variety of ways. He began to back off somewhat from his stance as a structuralist when he realized that structuralism's tendency to see things as one big whole might be contributing to the repressive power of knowledge.

Foucault regarded the study of philosophy as a repressive or liberating political act in and of itself. Good philosophy can help people recognize the ways in which their ideas influence their own actions and inhibit the actions of others.

Nowhere Man

Foucault is not the only French philosopher to become a major post-modern thinker. His fellow Frenchman, Jacques Derrida (b.1930), developed the influential interpretive activity known as *deconstruction*, the practice of taking apart a piece of writing to show how, in spite of itself, it fails to produce the consistent, reliable sense it aims at.

Meaning Turns Up Missing

Derrida emphasized the inability of language to refer to a fixed, stable meaning. Borrowing from the phenomenologist Edmund Husserl, Derrida called this inaccessible meaning *presence*. Husserl said that, apart from all the added interpretations and secondary meanings that get stuck to our perceptions and experiences, there are meanings that are specially "present" to our consciousness. Husserl wanted to recover these present meanings from all the traces of meaning that were imposed on our consciousness from outside sources.

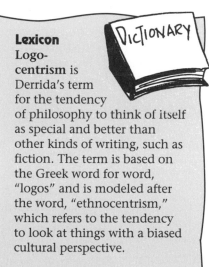

Lexicon
Deconstruction is the practice of unraveling meaning from written language to show how what's written is put together out of assumptions that can't be true. **Presence** is one of these false assumptions. It is the idea that the meaning of words is limited by the intentions of the speaker or writer.

Derrida, in contrast, says that there is no reliable distinction between present and non-present meaning. All meaning depends on language, even the meaning of our selves experienced at the level of consciousness. This meaning cannot happen without words, and words all work the same, namely by referring outside of themselves to what we can't know exists except through words.

Self-Centered Language

Derrida noticed that Western philosophy in general since Plato has been involved in a search for presence, for reliable meaning that is not simply a written trace left over when an intended meaning has dissolved into other possible meanings. He calls this tendency to believe in a special meaning that is not dependent on the workings of language *logo-centrism*. Logo-centrism is the tendency in philosophy to assume that it can refer to a self-combined meaning that is free of the problems affecting language in general.

Lexicon
Logo-centrism is Derrida's term for the tendency of philosophy to think of itself as special and better than other kinds of writing, such as fiction. The term is based on the Greek word for word, "logos" and is modeled after the word, "ethnocentrism," which refers to the tendency to look at things with a biased cultural perspective.

At the heart of logo-centrism, argued Derrida, is an attempt to separate writing and speech so that philosophy can be associated only with speech. Philosophers since Plato have regarded speech as an immediate source of meaning, and writing as a medium that is only capable of capturing mere traces of meaning. The tendencies of writing to wander off the subject, to mislead us, to change its meaning depending on who reads it and in what context, are inescapable.

Vive la Differance

Derrida invented the word "*differance*" to refer to these problems inherent in the written word. Notice Derrida's word is spelled with an "a" unlike the ordinary word, difference. This term refers to the idea that the meaning of the word depends not so much on what

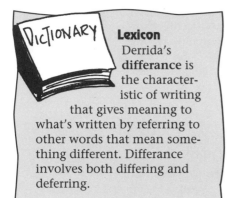

Lexicon
Derrida's **differance** is the characteristic of writing that gives meaning to what's written by referring to other words that mean something different. Differance involves both differing and deferring.

it refers to but how it relates to, and differs from, other words. This means that if you want to go on a quest for the true, complete meaning of a sentence, you have to trace all the places where the words point to other words *not* in the sentence, until the original sentence dissolves itself.

This leads to another meaning of the term "differance." In French, the words for "differ" (to be different from) and "defer" (to defer to) are spelled the same, and both concepts are suggested by "differance." Words do not simply contain meaning; they defer their ability to have meaning to other words in the language. As a result, meaning is always slipping away. The meaning of the word is different from the word itself.

Beware of Philosophy

Like Foucault, Derrida suggests that philosophy should be opposed to traditional and common sense ways of thinking. Foucault opposes traditional thinking because he sees it as politically repressive. Derrida sees it as conceptually unreliable.

Lexicon
Someone who is **bourgeois** is middle-class and conservative. Karl Marx's **proletariats** are workers who are exploited by capitalism. The bourgeoisie, on the other hand, are content under capitalism and are generally considered unsympathetic to the plight of the proletariats. A **liberal** is someone who believes in social freedom and tolerance. Liberals are criticized by radicals because their "live and let live" attitude doesn't help bring about change.

Post-Modernism Lightens Up

In sharp contrast to the negativity of these French thinkers is the more optimistic American post-modernist Richard Rorty (b.1931). Rorty's philosophy is based on pragmatism, which says that ideas are important, not because they are true, but because they are useful. He calls his philosophy "post-modernist *bourgeois liberalism*," identifying himself with some of the values that many other post-modernists had been attacking.

The Side-Show

Rorty points out that most of the social interaction that determines people's beliefs and the way they live happens independently of philosophical theorizing. He criticizes those philosophers who want to bring about social change by proposing theories that are supposed to define how society should work, once and for all. He says social relationships can't be pinned down by philosophy; instead, it is philosophy that depends on social relationships.

As far as politics is concerned, Rorty calls philosophy "just a side-show," something that intellectuals have been preoccupied with while everyone else has been trying to work their problems out in their own ways. Because philosophy has only a slight impact on political relationships, Rorty says philosophical theories of society that attempt to transform society are claiming too much for themselves.

Does Society Need Philosophy?

As a post-modern pragmatist, Rorty believes that there is no absolute truth. Instead, people's ideas about truth are produced through communicating with others. Such communication forms the basis of society, whatever ideas it may consist of. Communication doesn't need to be rooted in philosophy in order to work—in order to help people get along and make the choices they need to make.

Reality Check

Rorty's pragmatism is theoretical in the sense that it explains and justifies certain kinds of behavior. It may be that in saying we don't need theories to explain society he means we don't need *new* theories. Pragmatism has been used to bolster the idea of American commerce throughout the past century.

According to Rorty, the fact that society is not based on a "true" vision of reality does not mean it needs to be overhauled and made to conform to some philosophical plan. In fact, says Rorty, the society we have is pretty good the way it is. It is not especially coercive (it doesn't force people to do what they don't want to) and it is basically tolerant of all kinds of ideas and ways of living.

Same Concepts, Different Conclusions

Rorty agrees with much of what other post-modernist philosophers like Foucault and Derrida say about the slipperiness of language, the inability of language to refer to a reliable truth, and selfhood as based on language. This is what makes him a post-modernist. But accepting these post-modern ideas does not lead Rorty to criticize "bourgeois" values. He sees these values as a good thing insofar as they work for millions of people.

If philosophy has a role in society, says Rorty, it should be to encourage people to communicate, not to dictate the terms of discussion. Philosophers should work toward a more tolerant society without interfering in the freedom people already enjoy.

Smug or Sensible?

Rorty has been criticized for being too satisfied with society and for being unaware of the deep-seated divisions within it. What's more, according to his critics, the kind of inter-cultural communication Rorty recommends isn't always possible, since it depends on people having more in common than they actually do. For instance, not everyone is familiar with bourgeois culture and therefore comfortable with it.

The Least You Need to Know

➤ Post-modern philosophy is largely concerned with the unreliability of meaning and is hence often critical of philosophy itself.

➤ Foucault associated knowledge, including philosophical knowledge, with oppressive power.

➤ Derrida contends that meaning is never stable because it tries in vain to refer outside itself.

➤ Rorty argued that the instability of meaning should not be used to justify radical social revision.

Chapter 25

Women Get Wise

In This Chapter

➤ There's feminism, and then there's feminism

➤ French feminism

➤ Marxist and radical feminism

➤ Black feminism

➤ Queer theory

Oh, and, by the way, there are women philosophers too. It seems, though, that they've been systematically excluded from philosophical circles until only very recently. Traditionally, men have not wanted to give women credit for being able to come up with philosophical ideas. But women are getting wise. They're not only coming up with philosophical ideas of their own, they're also catching on to how the ideas and practices of male philosophers stack the deck in favor of men!

Because of deep-seated male biases in philosophy—and in most cultures in general—it isn't surprising that most of the philosophy developed by women focuses on the repression of women. The philosophy geared toward exposing, explaining, and changing this form of repression is feminism. Feminism, though, isn't just a philosophy. For many women, it's a political issue too, or even instead.

In fact, the word "feminism" includes many different ways of thinking and behaving, depending on the situation. Different feminists see different things wrong with repression and different causes and solutions for it. Although there are many disagreements within feminism, virtually all feminists agree on one key point: women everywhere have been getting a raw deal for centuries.

Woman Kinds

Not all feminism is alike. Many feminists put their emphasis on personal connections rather than abstract theories because they contend that the best way to improve women's position in general is to get them more respect. As a result, many feminists are less interested in trying to figure out an objective, timeless "truth" about reality than in challenging attitudes and ideas that hurt women and replacing these with new attitudes.

Philoso-Fact
Critics of feminism have used the fact that feminists frequently disagree among themselves as evidence that feminism can't work. At the same time, though, feminism often brings together some extremely far-flung interests for a common goal. For example, feminism has provided common ground for discussions between conservative right-to-lifers and radical Marxists.

These new attitudes can be based on all kinds of ideas: philosophical, religious, economic, cultural, personal, and political. As a result, there are many kinds of feminism.

In addition to being a philosophy, feminism has been a political movement that has had adherents throughout history. The movement really started to pick up steam in the 1960s and 1970s when a number of factors—including mass media, more women in the workforce, changing cultural values, and cheap, reliable birth control—all came together to give the movement the lift it needed to become a major social and political force.

Forms of Feminism

➤ **French feminism** and *ecriture feminine* are hard to understand because of their playful style and background in French post-structural theory.

➤ **Liberal feminism** emphasizes female "equality" with men without calling for major social or ideological change.

➤ **Marxist feminism** sees sexism as an aspect of class oppression and believes in resisting both problems together.

➤ **Radical feminism** sees the repression of women as stemming from deep-seated cultural and ideological biases that privilege men over women in virtually all things. Calls for a drastic change in attitude toward sex roles in society.

➤ **Spiritual feminism** believes that women have a special connection with divinity or with nature that can redeem and heal problems caused by male dominance.

➤ **Black feminism** cautions against the tendencies of white, middle-class feminists to ignore or trivialize racism. Focuses on racism and sexism as related problems.

➤ **Queer theory** is allied with, but not limited to, feminism. Focuses on sexual preference along with sex roles.

Imported from France

Not all feminism is philosophy. In fact, many feminists think philosophy is beside the point. Even so, philosophy has played an important role in the women's movement. This has been especially true in France.

Just as the male French philosophers Foucault, Derrida, and Lacan made a big splash with their post-structuralist thinking, a number of female French feminists have been widely influential. Among the first and most famous of the French feminists was Simone de Beauvoir (1908–1986). She made a major impact in her own country and also influenced Kate Millet, Mary Daly, and other feminists in the United States.

Philoso-Fact
During the 1970s, the women's philosophy group, *Psychoanalyse et Politique* (Psychoanalysis and Politics) played a major and controversial role in the French women's movement. They registered the initials, MLF, for Women's Liberation Movement, as a trademark for their own publishing company. Feminists not associated with *Psych et Po* took them to court over the rights to the initials. *Psych et Po* won the case.

Simone Says, "Take a Big Step Forward"

In her book *The Second Sex*, Simone de Beauvoir argued that women themselves need to overcome the social and psychological barriers to their equality with men. Drawing on existentialism and Freudian psychoanalysis, she showed how women have always been defined by male society as "the other" and how women have accepted this secondary position against their own best interests.

Simone de Beauvoir.

For de Beauvoir, existentialism provides a way for women to take control of their lives by rejecting attitudes about their secondary status. She encouraged women to work one-on-one for equality with men and to work together as a group with a common set of interests and goals.

Nature vs. Nurture

Are men and women different in the ways they think and act? Yes, said de Beauvoir. But these differences stem from social influences, not biological ones. Many, but not all, feminists agree with this view, and like de Beauvoir, they emphasize the distinction between *gender* and *sex*. Sex refers to biological characteristics; gender refers to the social roles and cultural standards associated with sex.

A Lonely Leader

As the first important philosopher of the woman's movement, de Beauvoir said things that most men didn't want to hear and most women weren't in a position to understand, since few women had the opportunity or the encouragement to study philosophy. This made her work especially difficult. Although she has been greatly admired for her knowledge of philosophy and psychology, she has also been criticized by later feminists for adopting a "male" approach—focusing on ideas that chiefly interested male intellectuals rather than finding new ways of relating to women.

Even so, she set an important example and steered feminism on a healthy course, getting it to look at philosophy from a woman's point of view. In fact, she was an active participant in the French women's movement of the '70s, working with younger women, the next generation of feminists.

Lexicon
Gender refers to attitudes and behavior about *sex* differences, not sex differences themselves, which are biological differences. Gender roles are thus the different positions society assigns the different sexes.

Philoso-Fact
De Beauvoir carried on a famous existential love relationship with fellow existentialist philosopher Jean-Paul Sartre. De Beauvoir and Sartre agreed to be lovers but rejected conventional attitudes about romance and sexuality. They were committed to each other but had separate apartments and lived independent lives.

Different, but the Same

One of the key figures of what you might call the second generation of French feminists is Julia Kristeva (b.1941). Kristeva believes, like de Beauvoir, that gender distinctions are socially *constructed*, that there is no essential, or innate, difference between the ways men and women think. But she also argues that the experience of motherhood has deep significance in shaping women's understanding of themselves and their reality.

According to Kristeva, part of the problem with philosophy as practiced by men is that it tends to emphasize the separateness of people from one another and from the world. Motherhood and pregnancy, she says, helps women see that they are not separate, that they can be so closely connected to another person that they actually share the same body.

Off the Mommy Track

Some feminists oppose Kristeva's thinking about the motherhood experience. They contend that associating women with motherhood stigmatizes them; it pigeonholes them into a particular role in society, rather than helping them to choose their own role. In fact, some feminists recommend that women choose not to be mothers so that they're able to play a more active part in society.

Labor of Love

Kristeva defends her particular ideas about feminism in a creative fashion that links the importance of writing with the importance of motherhood. As with most French feminists, Kristeva's thinking comes out not only in what she says, but in the ways she says it. In this she resembles other French post-structuralists, including Jacques Lacan, and Jacques Derrida. She wants to work past the limitations put on writing by male ideals of "reason," so her writing frequently works in unusual ways.

One example is her essay, "Stabat Mater," which means "the mother stood" and refers to a hymn about the Virgin Mary standing at the foot of the cross where Jesus was crucified. The essay attempts to defend motherhood against a feminist accusation that having children is just another thing men expect women to do. At the same time, the essay associates writing itself with the process of giving birth. She emphasizes this link by referring to Jesus as "the word made flesh," and by interrupting passages with bits of poetic passages that remind one of labor contractions!

Writing the Wrongs

Kristeva's approach to writing philosophy was part of a movement in France known as *ecriture feminine,* or "female writing." This movement is based on the belief that women

> **Lexicon**
> **Social con-structedness** refers to the degree that ideas about reality—including attitudes about differences between men and women—actually depend on social attitudes rather than on biological or physical facts. Gender, say many feminists, is socially constructed.

> **Philoso-Fact**
> Kristeva is a licensed psycho-analyst as well as a teacher and mother.

think and write in ways different from men. It proposes that women should either reject traditional male approaches to writing—or use male writing styles in new ways.

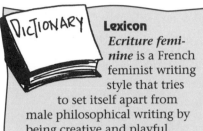

Lexicon

Ecriture feminine is a French feminist writing style that tries to set itself apart from male philosophical writing by being creative and playful, sometimes making fun of the ideas of male philosophers. **Penis envy** is a very questionable Freudian idea that has been used to discredit women's thinking and behavior.

Helene Cixous (b.1937) is another French feminist who practiced *ecriture feminine*. Cixous' work illustrates how women can turn the tables on men by taking psychological ideas developed by men to make women seem less intelligent and use them in new ways to suggest women are actually more intelligent than men.

One male concept used against women, for example, is Freud's notion of *penis envy*. Freud said that women go around wishing that they had penises like men and this desire sometimes make them think and do strange things. Cixous responds to this by suggesting that women are able to write in special ways that men can't because, unlike men, they don't have a deep-seated psychological fear of being castrated. According to Cixous, not having a penis is a good thing; it makes it easier for women to be more creative and intelligent.

Class Acts

French feminism has been influential in the United States, even though American feminists sometimes object to certain features of it, including its theoretical difficulty and the fact that it is often playful and ironic. They say that because French feminism is hard to understand, it reaches fewer people and makes sexism seem like an academic, rather than a political, problem.

In the United States, a number of radical feminists borrowed from Marxism to support their claim that women are an oppressed class in their own right, independently of the economic class distinctions that separate people. While the Marxist feminists tended to believe that sexual and economic repression need to be dealt with together as part of the same problem, the radical feminists looked at sexism as more widespread, deep-seated, and harmful than class prejudice. Both strains of feminism emphasize the importance of moving beyond merely philosophizing about these issues. It's time, they say, to take action to change things.

Politics Makes Strange Bedfellows

One of these radical feminists is Kate Millet (b.1934), whose book *Sexual Politics* calls for the recognition of women as an oppressed class of people. Millet identified a variety of related ways in which women are discriminated against legally, economically, sexually, and personally. In particular, she shows how ideas about sexuality often have political significance, affecting the status of women.

Millet's theories about discrimination against women are only one aspect of her feminist work and are intended to encourage women not simply to think about their lives in new ways, but to work to change them as well.

In addition to developing a theoretical perspective on sexism, Millet was also a leading figure in the movement for women's rights. She helped found the National Organization for Women, which continues to provide a political mouthpiece for women's issues in the U.S. In addition, she has been actively working for women's rights abroad. In fact, she was kicked out of Iran by the government there for her efforts to improve women's standing in Iranian culture.

Philoso-Fact
Millet was a leading figure in American feminism at a time when feminism started dividing into two camps. One group, made up of lesbian women, contended that women could only achieve their goals by separating themselves from men altogether. The other group, which included heterosexual women, argued that women needed to work things out with men. Millet helped keep these groups together by announcing her bisexuality.

God Gets a Sex Change

Another leading radical feminist is the theologian, Mary Daly (b.1928). Her book *The Church and the Second Sex* caused a big commotion in both Catholic and academic circles because it talks about institutionalized women-hating throughout the history of the Catholic Church.

Daly's book got her fired as a professor of theology at Boston College, but she was rehired after numerous student protests and a court case. Since then, Daly has continued to approach theology from a radical feminist perspective, promoting the rejection of the *patriarchal* aspect of Christianity.

Lexicon
Patriarchy is the system of thinking and acting that sees fatherhood as a special source of power and authority.

Patriarchy is a way of thinking that regards men—particularly fathers—as special authorities. Daly is especially opposed to the idea of God as a father, since this idea skews religion in favor of men. If God is a "father," then men are more godly than women. Daly rejects this idea and, following Nietzsche, says we need to "transvaluate" religious ideas about women.

Hooks into Race and Sex

Another important philosopher and theologian in the women's movement is Bell Hooks (b.1952). Like many black feminists, Hooks argues that white, middle-class feminists ignore or avoid the problem of racism in their opposition to sexism. This is not only wrong, it has also worked against black women.

233

When white feminists say, "the oppression of women is similar to the oppression of blacks," they are forgetting that many women *are* black. Black women, says Hooks, suffer from both kinds of oppression, so the analogy between the two doesn't make sense.

Hooks sees sexism, racism, and class prejudice as stemming from the same source, namely the desire to exert power over others. She says that everyone feels this desire. The trick is to be aware of it and to learn to express it in positive ways.

One positive expression of desire, according to Hooks, is religion. She sees religion as an important source of power that has been especially useful to black people.

Philoso-Fact

Butler has attracted a lot of attention, including a fanzine devoted to her called *Judy*, which has made wild speculations about her personal life and includes many jokes about her philosophy. One article in this 'zine fantasized about Butler (who is not opposed to pornography) refereeing a mud-wrestling contest between two famous anti-pornography activists, Andrea Dworkin and Catherine MacKinnon. Butler was not amused.

Butler Did It

One of the most influential feminist thinkers of today is Judith Butler. Butler helped develop "queer theory," a way of philosophizing about gender roles and sexual preference.

Butler talks about sexuality as something that is determined by what she calls "regimes" of knowledge. These regimes are ideas that exert power over people, including the power of getting people to be attracted to members of one sex or the other. These regimes, she says, are socially constructed. As a result, neither heterosexuality nor homosexuality is any more "natural" than the other.

Even though our sexual preferences may feel as though they are biologically determined, they actually form in response to social influences. This doesn't mean that we can simply choose our sexuality; the regimes of knowledge choose for us. Our sexual preferences are revealed to us as we interact with society.

The Least You Need to Know

➤ Simone de Beauvoir was a trailblazing French feminist who drew on existentialism and tried to theorize the oppression of women.

➤ French feminist writing tends to be more theoretical and playful than American feminist literature.

➤ Feminists debate whether the intellectual and emotional differences between women and men are essential (innate) or constructed (learned).

➤ Feminism may be associated with other political ideas including class and race consciousness.

Chapter 26

The Shift Is On

In This Chapter

➤ The New Age view of human history

➤ New Age and the brain

➤ New Age and the new physics

➤ New Age ecology

➤ New Age politics

➤ New Age business

Today's academic philosophers have pretty much rejected metaphysics; for them it's beyond the scope of serious philosophy. But that doesn't mean that it's dead. Quite the contrary!

Popular philosophy these days takes up anything that's metaphysical, mystical, mysterious, or unusual. Called New Age, it rejects most traditional Western thinking and embraces just about everything else.

New Age thinking became incredibly popular in the '80s, and is still going strong today. In fact, it has been so influential that it's more than a philosophy—it's a culture, and, for many, a way of life that includes New Age art, music, dress, food, fitness, and health care.

New Age isn't the brainchild of any single thinker. All kinds of people have been looking for new meaning for their lives and a new sense of connection with the cosmos. In fact, many New Agers hope their thinking will trigger a global shift in human consciousness. Everyone, they say, is going to catch the New Age bug in the near future, and the result will be a happier, more harmonious planet.

Shifty Characters

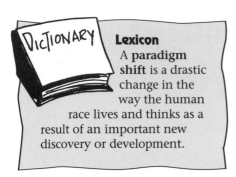

Lexicon
A **paradigm shift** is a drastic change in the way the human race lives and thinks as a result of an important new discovery or development.

New Age philosophy got its name from the belief that we are indeed at the threshold of a New Age. New Agers contend that the world is going through a *paradigm shift*, a time when accepted ways of thinking and acting change drastically, as a result of new discoveries.

For example, the invention of writing and of agriculture triggered paradigm shifts that led to whole new ways of living. According to New Agers, we're going through another paradigm shift because of new discoveries in physics and in the capabilities of the human mind.

How the Other Half Thinks

One of the spearheads of the New Age is writer Marilyn Ferguson, whose book *The Aquarian Conspiracy* helped define the New Age and fostered its growth. Ferguson draws on research on how the brain works to support the idea that each individual is chock full of untapped mental potential.

She spent years collecting research and first-hand claims that suggest people only use a small portion of their brains. As evidence for how limited traditional ideas about the mind are, Ferguson describes accounts of unusual psychological events, including out-of-body experiences and prophetic dreams. These events indicate that there's more to the human mind than previously thought.

Ferguson and other New Agers believe that through practices like meditation and yoga, and with the help of things like crystals and pyramids, which they say have occult properties, we can learn to use more of our brain power and have positive psychic experiences.

Specifically, we need to use more of our "right brain," and less of our "left brain," say New Agers. The right half of the brain is responsible for things like the emotions, intuitions, and creativity, while the left side does the reasoning, judging, and analyzing. By learning to rely more heavily on our right brains, we will become more in tune with the rest of reality. If we don't, we'll remain under the influence of our left brain, with its critical, analytical powers that limit our ability to truly experience life, and, to put it bluntly, bum us out.

> **Reality Check**
>
> Many experts on brain physiology say that both halves of the brain are involved in virtually all mental activity. So the New Agers may be getting a little carried away when they say that we can all learn to use our brains in a radically different way just by switching which half we think with.

According to many New Agers, most of what is wrong with today's world stems from the limitations imposed on us by left-brain thinking. This thinking has cut us off from an awareness of our higher selves and of our connection with one another and with the natural world, including our own bodies. Mind-body oneness is one way of improving your consciousness, say New Agers. This can be achieved through massage, meditation, yoga, aroma therapy, and other techniques.

Make Yourself a Better World

Many New Agers believe that we don't need to rely on the judgmental side of our brain, which only limits our possibilities for awareness and creativity. This judgmental side gives us a certain way of thinking about reality that keeps us back, setting limits on the possibilities. In contrast, the creative right side of the brain tells us that reality is what you make it. If you don't like your life, all you need is to be more creative in order to live up to your potential.

If we all get in touch with our creative powers, the world will become a better place. All things are possible, but they have to begin inside each individual person. Paradoxically, it's up to the individual to learn to recognize his or her connection with other people and to the cosmos.

> **Philoso-Fact**
> Actress and best-selling New Age author Shirley MacLaine claims to be God. She has also made millions writing about her mystic experiences and popularizing New Age beliefs.

In fact, some New Agers believe that we all have the power to transform the world. They say that we're actually gods, possessing mysterious powers that we don't realize we have. We can be in control and make the world the way we want it to be when we learn to develop our mental powers.

A One-derful World

New Agers say people have the power to transform the world because they are spiritually connected with it. While everyone needs to develop their sense of connection for themselves, New Agers understand this connection in two ways:

First, there's a basic similarity, or oneness, underlying all mystic beliefs. All religious and metaphysical thinking, in other words, points in basically the same direction. Spirituality, no matter what label we give it, is something we all share.

Second, the discovery by nuclear physicists that matter and energy are related suggests that everything that exists has—and is made of—energy. This can be interpreted to mean that we're all united to the cosmos.

Both of these cosmic connections are described by New Age philosopher Fritjof Capra in his book *The Tao of Physics*.

Einstein-Fu

Capra draws on strains of Eastern mysticism, which include Taoism, Buddhism, and Hinduism, to explain that we all have a mystic connection with reality. We can discover this connection through meditation, yoga, the *I Ching*, and other ways of developing our powers of intuition.

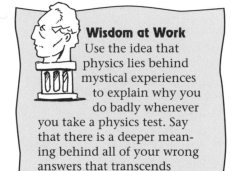

Wisdom at Work
Use the idea that physics lies behind mystical experiences to explain why you do badly whenever you take a physics test. Say that there is a deeper meaning behind all of your wrong answers that transcends human understanding!

Capra also draws on recent developments in nuclear physics, including the theory of relativity and quantum mechanics, to show that matter and energy are not separate things as physicists once believed; matter can be converted to energy and vice versa. In other words, it's all the same thing.

Einstein illustrated this in his famous formula, $E = MC^2$. E stands for energy, M stands for mass (or the quantity of matter), and C stands for the speed of light. Since matter and energy are interchangeable, says Capra, everything that exists, including people, is made up of energy in one state or another.

The fact that everything is made of energy explains mystical experiences. With the right state of mind, we can experience our connectedness by "seeing" how our energy feeds into all the energy that makes up reality.

The Metaphysical Kitchen Sink

In addition to drawing on Eastern mysticism, New Agers have come up with all kinds of ways for increasing creativity and for developing higher consciousness. Many of these methods are borrowed from other cultures and philosophies, including pagan beliefs, astrology, numerology, witchcraft, and Native American rituals. According to New Agers, any of these may be good ways of developing individual potential and mystic connections because they are all based on the idea of the spiritual oneness of human consciousness.

Not only do we have spiritual connections with one another, say the New Agers, we also have spiritual connections with people who are no longer living. Many New Agers have adopted the Hindu belief in reincarnation—that when we die, we come back again in a new life. New Agers add to this belief by saying that if you are psychically in tune, or if you have the right spiritual guidance, you can get in touch with your past lives.

All Fads Lead to Oneness

Here's a list of some popular New Age practices intended to promote spiritual awareness:

➤ **Astrology**   Your life is in tune with the stars. Learn who you are and what your potential is by having your birthchart read.

➤ **Numerology**   The numbers of your date of birth and your name have magic and mystical properties.

➤ **Tarot**   Fortune telling cards from the Middle Ages in Europe will help you plan your next move.

➤ **I Ching**   Chinese "Book of Changes"—flipping coins or shuffling yarrow stalks will help you get your yin and yang in gear.

➤ **Yoga**   Exercises for the body, mind, and spirit from the wisdom of India.

➤ **Meditation**   Get a mantra and feel the inner peace.

➤ **Massage**   If it feels this good, it must be good for you; plus, your chakras will open like lotus blossoms.

➤ **Shamanism**   Wisdom derived from Native American medicine men.

➤ **Paganism**   Especially popular among eco-feminists who are into goddess-worship and witchcraft.

➤ **Pyramids**   They generate power fields that make you more aware; they also keep your bread fresh.

➤ **Crystals**   Rocks with the right molecular shapes harmonize with your body structure to give you that energetic edge.

➤ **Aroma therapy**   You are what you smell.

➤ **Psychotechnology**   Bio-feedback machines and isolation tanks give you a high-tech mental tune-up.

➤ **Channeling**   Get the latest word from the spirit of an ancient Egyptian warrior or an entity from the ninth dimension.

Got Change for a One?

New Agers stress that developing individual consciousness can lead to political and environmental awareness, which in turn will lead to global change.

Keep the Spirit Clean

Ecology is of major importance to the New Age movement, both for practical and for spiritual reasons. Practically speaking, a polluted environment, of course, is bad for everyone's physical health.

Philoso-Fact
New Agers in Hawaii say that Pele, a local volcano goddess, caused a volcano to blow its top when she got angry at a new law allowing the mining of geothermal energy.

Pollution is bad spiritually too, say the New Agers, since it gets in the way of our ability to experience a mystic connection with the natural world, and results from a not-very-spiritual attitude toward life. After all, it's more uplifting to experience yourself as being at one with your environment if it isn't full of garbage, refuse, oil sludge, smog, and other cancer-causing substances.

In order to bring about a more spiritual, natural environment, New Agers promote solar, water, and wind power instead of fossil fuels and nuclear power, because they're renewable sources of energy that don't pollute. They also encourage zero population growth because less people means less strain on natural resources and the environment.

Bandwagon Earth

In addition to ecological change, many New Agers want global political change as well. They see government becoming less powerful and leaving more room for individual freedom, including the freedom for women to have abortions and for everyone to have mind-altering experiences with hallucinogenic drugs.

Many New Agers object to laws against so-called "victimless crimes." A victimless crime such as drug use or nude sunbathing is an illegal act that doesn't hurt anyone, except possibly the person committing it. Government should abolish laws against these acts because they believe that the main purpose of such laws is to regulate society. Government, argue the New Agers, should leave room for the individual consciousness to expand in its own way.

Although New Age political ideas tend to be liberal rather than conservative, many New Agers see themselves as neither. Instead, they want a drastic change in the way politics work. They want decentralized power so that more people can participate in government at the community level. At the same time, they want global unity. In other words, they want political as well as spiritual oneness without having to follow a lot of rules. Everyone should get along and no one should be in charge.

In order to promote global harmony, New Agers have helped to put on events, including "Hands Across America," in 1986, in which thousands of people formed human chains by holding hands all over the country. Another New Age-backed event, also in 1986, was "World Healing Day," when people from a number of countries agreed on a certain time

to be peaceful. According to New Agers, these exercises in national and global coopera-
tion reflect the developing spiritual consciousness of humanity.

Cash Consciousness

While New Agers are interested in global change, they focus on individual potential. They
understand this potential in terms of over-all happiness, spirituality, and economic
success. In fact, one of the distinguishing features of the New Age is its unique blend of
mysticism and pragmatism that often results in a spiritualized approach to making
money.

Lifting Your Spiritual Bootstraps

The link with spirituality and money is evident in lots
of New Age "self-help" books that combine techniques for psychological and spiritual well-being with
techniques for financial success. According to New
Age thinking, your spiritual health and your financial
health are closely related.

As a result, the idea that "reality is what you make it"
often turns into "your economic reality is what you
make it." Having new experiences and expanding
your consciousness goes along with taking risks and
trying new ideas as an entrepreneur. In fact, while
getting psychic advice about spiritual matters and love
relationships, New Agers sometimes turn to psychic
financial advisers for tips on how to invest their
money.

New Age thinking has also had a big impact on
business management. Companies hire New Age
advisers to train managers and to promote positive,
effective relationships among employees. Spirituality
and the idea of oneness are used to help workers
cooperate and be creative in solving problems and in
reaching a goal as a group. Many New Age business
practices reflect disenchantment with the dog-eat-
dog world of corporate capitalism.

No Business Like Know Business

Of course, one of the main ways the New Age promotes business is by selling itself. The idea of a
universal oneness revealed through a variety of mystic

Philoso-Fact
Although
New Age
thinking
draws heavily
on almost
every sort of spiritual idea, a
notable exception is
ascetism—the idea that you
become more spiritually aware
by denying yourself material
comforts. Strangely, few New
Agers go in for self-denial!

Philoso-Fact
Some recent
books on New
Age manage-
ment include
The Corporate Mystic by Gay
Hendricks (1996), *The Stirring of
the Soul in the Workplace* by
Alan Briskin (1996), *The I Ching
of Management* by William E.
Sadler (1996), and *Make It So:
Leadership Lessons from Star
Trek, the Next Generation* (1995).

practices means that there are an unlimited number of things that can lead to personal development. And most of these things are marketable: books, music, videos, artwork, and objects with spiritual properties such as crystals, perfumes, herbs, devices like massagers for reducing stress, and so-called "psychotechnology" devices that include biofeedback machines and isolation tanks.

In addition to things that can be bought and sold, New Age thinking has given a big boost to a variety of professions intended to raise individual consciousness and lead to spiritual as well as physical healing. These include alternative medical practitioners, gurus, Zen masters, channelers, psychics, psychotherapists, massage therapists, aroma therapists, astrologers, and others.

What's Ahead?

New Age has become an extremely popular philosophy. This may be because lots of people are disillusioned with traditional ways of thinking and acting. It may also be because the world seems to be getting smaller and people are looking for common ground beneath all the different ways of thinking out there.

In fact, most philosophy has something to do with dissatisfaction with old ideas and a desire for new ways of doing things. It may be that this restless search for the best philosophy will finally fail to improve on the ideas and behaviors we already have.

Then again, it may be that human beings are really getting somewhere with their thinking, forging new and better ways for people to live. We've figured out a lot about reality and ourselves. Hopefully we can make the most of what we know by living together peacefully.

The Least You Need to Know

➤ New Agers say we are in the midst of a global change in human consciousness.

➤ They say there's more going on in our brains than traditional scientists have realized.

➤ New Agers link mysticism with new developments in physics.

➤ New Agers seek global oneness and a clean planet.

➤ New Age ideas, services, and merchandise are big business.

➤ New Age reflects a search for new ways to think and live common to all philosophy.

Words for the Wise

a priori concepts   According to Kant, concepts that "come before," or presuppose experience, making it possible for us to understand things. An example is the concept of substance.

ahimsa   The Hindu and Buddhist principle of non-violence that encourages respect for all living things.

akrasia   The ancient Greek term for weakness of will that causes people to do what they know is not right.

alienation   Hegel's word for what happens when people and ideas get cut off from unified reality. Alienation takes place when thinking conflicts and doesn't get resolved. Years later, Karl Marx adapted this concept to refer to the problem of workers not having a direct stake in their own labor. Alienated labor is thus the problem of working for someone else.

allegory   The use of things in writing to represent a hidden or unstated meaning.

analytic philosophy   An approach emerging in the late 19th century that applies developments in logic to the use of language.

apocalypse   The Greek word for "revelation" has come to mean the time when the world as we know it will be destroyed.

archetypes   In Jungian psychology, patterns of images for different approaches to life.

arete   The ancient Greek term for the highest personal excellence, the integrity to do what must be done.

asceticism   The practice of denying oneself physical comforts and necessities, usually in order to get focused beyond material things. It has been practiced by many Hindus and Christians.

associationism   The view that our ideas are formed by combining sense perceptions that resemble one another or that we experience together. Hume intended this view to do for the mind what Newton did for physics.

ataraxia   The ancient Greek term for mental tranquility.

authenticity   The existentialist concept of leading your life on your own terms, refusing to accept the assumptions others make about the meaning of things.

bourgeois   Middle-class and conservative. Karl Marx contrasted the bourgeoisie to the proletariat, workers who are exploited by capitalism. The bourgeoisie, on the other hand, are content under capitalism and are generally considered unsympathetic to the plight of the laborers.

bracketing   Husserl's process of setting aside assumptions about things that stem from scientific thinking. The point is to look at things with fresh eyes.

Buddhism   Philosophy founded in India during the 5th century B.C. by Siddhartha Gautama. It stresses the transcendence of self and of desire.

capitalism   The economic practice of producing goods and selling them at a profit.

caste system   The idea that everyone is born to hold a particular position in society. It defined the social structure in India for centuries.

categorical imperative   A moral law which, according to Kant, holds true for everybody and forms the basis of our "practical reason," or moral understanding. It refers not only to how we should act, but actually enables us to behave as moral beings.

categories   A priori concepts that refer to the way the understanding makes judgments about such things as quality, quantity, and relation.

collective unconscious   In Jungian psychology, the body of symbolism and mythic images inherited from early humans that people have in their unconscious minds.

collectivism   The view that the stability of society is more important than individual rights and freedoms.

conceptualism   The view found in scholastic philosophy that universals exist as concepts in the mind.

Confucianism   Philosophy of ancient China founded by Kung fu-tzu that stresses social harmony and respect for others.

consciousness collective   According to Durkheim, the set of ideas that are shared by an entire society, making it possible for individuals to communicate and do all the things they do as members of the society.

cosmogony   The study of the origin of the world.

cosmology   The study of the nature and order of the world.

deconstruction   The practice of unraveling meaning from written language to show how it is put together out of assumptions that can't be true.

deduction   The process of determining what is true based on what is already known to be true.

deism   The belief in an unknowable God who set the world in motion at the beginning of time but has done little to interfere with nature since that time.

determinism   The idea that what happens has to happen as a result of natural laws, a divine plan, or human nature. Many deterministic ideas are incompatible with the notion of individual freedom.

dharma   In Indian philosophy, the duties we must fulfill to the gods, our families, our neighbors, and ourselves.

diachronic   A view of language, in structural linguistics, that considers language as it develops through time.

dialectic   Movement back and forth between an idea and something that idea isn't. This may involve thinking about an idea in terms of another idea or comparing and contrasting two or more ideas.

dialectics   The method of reasoning that moves back and forth between opposites.

differance   Derrida's term for the characteristic of writing that makes it have meaning by referring to other words that mean something different. Differance involves both differing and a deferring.

dogma   Any way of thinking that is accepted as true. It comes from an ancient Greek word meaning "belief."

dualism   The belief that reality can be separated into both material and spiritual components. The spiritual portion of reality makes thinking and knowledge possible.

ecriture feminine   A French feminist writing style that tries to set itself apart from male philosophical writing by being creative and playful, sometimes making fun of the ideas of male philosophers.

empiricism   The position that we can be certain of knowledge acquired by testing ideas against the evidence of the senses. Reliable knowledge, in other words, is produced by experience.

Epicureanism   Hellenistic philosophy founded by Epicurus in the 3rd century B.C. that stresses the avoidance of mental pain.

epistemology   The study of knowing. Epistemologists want to know what we mean when we say we know something.

ethics   The study of moral and social behavior. Ethical philosophers want to know what it means to be a person and how people can and should act.

Existentialism   Philosophy espoused by Kierkegaard, Heidegger, and Sartre stressing responsibility of the individual for giving meaning to reality.

feminism   Philosophy and political movement that emphasizes the systematic exclusion of women and women's best interests from male-dominated thinking and society.

feudalism   The economic structure in which the nobility owns the land that is farmed by the serfs, or peasants, who support the nobles in exchange for protection.

form   An ideal concept that, for Plato, actually exists in its own separate, ideal reality. This ideal reality influences the imperfect reality in which we live by lending it shape.

functionalism   The anthropological theory that all the various aspects of a culture serve a social purpose.

gender   Refers to ideas about sex differences, as opposed to sex differences themselves. Gender roles are thus the different positions society assigns the different sexes.

Hinduism   Indian religious thinking based on the ideas of *dharma*, or duty, and *karma*, or action.

humanism   Renaissance philosophical attitude toward human beings and human activity as an expression of divine purpose.

Hume's Law   See *natural fallacy.*

Hume's fork   The idea that facts do not exist in any necessary logical relationships and relationships do not presuppose any particular facts. Facts and relationships are joined only through association. Hume used his "fork" to criticize metaphysical notions, including causality.

hypothesis   A theoretical statement that explains things but that may be refuted or confirmed by new evidence.

idealism   The belief that ideas have existence outside of the human mind.

ideology   A system of beliefs or ideas that reinforce the values of a particular class or group of people.

individualism   The view that individual rights and freedoms should form the basis of society.

induction   Drawing general conclusions from particular evidence; if certain things are true in particular, we can induce that things of the same kind will be true in general.

infrastructure   Includes the aspects of society that have to do with economy and what Marx called "the relations of production," centered around money, labor, and material goods.

intentionality   According to Husserl, both the attitude you bring with you whenever you think about something and what it is you are thinking about. In other words, it's the relation between the thing you're thinking of and the manner in which you are thinking.

karma   In Indian philosophy, the principle of action that determines what will happen to you in the future.

langue   The French word for language. In Saussure's terms, langue is language understood as a system that exists independently of individual speech acts.

li   The Chinese word for courtesy and ceremoniousness. Confucius used the term in order to bring together the ideas of ritual and respect and apply them to daily interactions with others.

liberalism   The belief in social freedom and tolerance. Liberals are criticized by radicals because their "live-and-let-live" attitude doesn't help bring about change.

logocentrism   Derrida's term for the attempt of philosophical writing to suggest meaning that is not simply produced by writing. The term is based on the Greek word for word, "logos" and is modeled after the word "ethnocentrism," which refers to the tendency to look at things with a biased cultural perspective. In other words, logocentrism is the tendency for philosophy to think it is special and better than other kinds of writing like stories.

Machiavellianism   A term that is often used to describe ruthlessness and deception in politics. More generally, the term is used to refer to anything someone doesn't like about anything political.

macrocosm (big universe)   The world as a whole understood as a reflection of the human body.

Marxism   Philosophy based on the economic and political thinking of Karl Marx that says ideology, or the way people think, depends on the relations of production, or the way people make and use things.

materialism   The belief that existence is entirely physical and that thinking and knowing are effects produced by the physical process of sensation in the mind.

metaphysics   A branch of philosophy that studies the make-up, working, and organization of reality in general. Metaphysics is also used more specifically to refer to whatever aspects of reality there may be that cannot be observed and measured, such as God and virtue.

microcosm (little universe)   The individual human being understood as an image of the world as a whole.

mirror stage   In Lacanian psychology, a crucial moment in the formation of the subject's awareness of himself as a person.

moksa   In Indian philosophy, the release from suffering, a Hindi word for the Buddhist concept of nirvana.

monads   According to Leibniz's philosophy, simple substances that cannot be broken down any further. They do not take up space and can perceive reality.

monism   The belief that the natural world is all connected into a single whole.

monotheism   The belief in a single all-powerful God. Judaism, Christianity, and Islam are all generally considered monotheistic religions, even though they sometimes recognize additional divine or powerful beings, such as the Christian trinity, Christian and Islamic saints, and, in all three religions, the devil.

mysticism   The idea that we can have direct experience of God. This may come in the form of dreams and visions, or may come through meditation or artistic creativity.

naturalistic fallacy   The mistaken idea that we can say how things ought to be, based on a knowledge of how things are. It is also known as "Hume's law."

Neoplatonism   Medieval philosophy combining Plato and religious thinking.

New Age   Contemporary philosophy that stresses higher spiritual consciousness on a global level.

nirvana   The Buddhist term for release from suffering. It is equivalent to the Hindi concept of moksa.

nominalism   The view found in scholastic philosophy that universals exist only as names.

noumenal world   The world as it actually is. Although we cannot know the noumena, we know it's there, based on the way we understand the phenomenal world.

objectivity   The idea that knowledge does not reflect personal concerns, but is true for everybody.

Oedipus complex   In Freudian psychology, the problem young boys experience when they feel in competition with their father for their mother's love. This complex sometimes persists in later life.

ontology   The study of being, or existence. Ontologists want to know what we mean when we say something exists.

othering   The process of identifying people as different from the norm in order to reassure yourself that you are normal.

pantheism   The belief that God is all things. This means that people and Nature are aspects of God and have divine power in and of themselves.

paradigm shift   A drastic change in the way the human race lives and thinks as a result of an important new discovery or development.

paradox   A statement that includes two ideas that seem to contradict one another.

parole   The French word for speech. Saussure used the term to refer to individual speech acts made possible by *langue*, or language.

patriarchy   The system of thinking and acting that sees fatherhood as a special source of power and authority.

penis envy   A very questionable Freudian idea that women are jealous of men. It has been used to discredit women's thinking and behavior.

phenomenal world   The world as it appears to our senses.

phenomenology   Philosophy founded by Edmund Husserl that says that "intentionality," or attitude, always goes along with consciousness.

philosophes   The philosophers of the French Enlightenment. They believed that philosophy was an important means of bringing about progress.

phoneme   In linguistics, a consonant or a vowel sound that is recognizably different from other sounds used to make words. It is the smallest unit of meaningful sound in language.

physis   The ancient Greek word for the natural world.

pleasure principle   In Freudian psychology, the idea that all people from birth pursue pleasurable experience in the form of physical and emotional gratification.

pluralism   The belief that the world is made up of lots of separate, independent things.

Pragmatism   Philosophy founded by C.S. Peirce and William James that says the meaning of anything depends on its practical effects.

predestination   The Calvinist belief that God has determined ahead of time whether you will go to heaven or to hell.

premise   An assertion that leads deductively to a conclusion.

propositions   In analytic philosophy, statements in the form of language or math that may be asserted, whether or not they are asserted and whether or not they are true.

Protestant work ethic   According to Weber's sociology, the tendency among Protestants to work hard and lead thrifty lives. This work ethic contributed to the development of capitalism.

quantifier   In analytic philosophy, a concept that indicates amount. A universal quantifier indicates all of the objects of the kind referred to. An existential quantifier indicates at least one of all the objects.

rationalism   The epistemological position that we can have knowledge without experience.

realism   The belief that universals, or ideas about reality, exist in reality outside the mind.

reality principle   In Freudian psychology, the idea that our desires are often frustrated by our circumstances.

reduction   In Husserl's philosophy, the act of identifying your own intentionality or attitude in the way you see things after you have bracketed out the intentionality of science.

249

reference   In analytic philosophy, what a proposition has to do with the objects that it represents.

relativism   The idea that good and bad are not universally true, but may be different in different societies. In other words, good and bad may be understood relative to the way society works.

repression   In Freudian psychology, the subconscious inability to face unacceptable wishes.

Scholasticism   Medieval philosophy based on Aristotle's logic. It became notorious for focusing on irrelevant questions, but eventually led toward a more scientific world view.

signified   In structural linguistics, an actual thing referred to by a word, or signifier.

signifier   In structural linguistics, a thing, such as a word or sign, that refers to something. Saussure saw language as a system of signifiers.

skepticism   The idea that something someone thinks is true may in fact not be true. It comes from an ancient Greek word meaning "seeking."

social constructedness   Refers to the degree that ideas about reality—including ideas about differences between men and women— actually depend on social attitudes, rather than on biological or physical facts.

social facts   According to Durkheim, things and events that pertain to social existence. As such, they don't need to be explained in terms of non-social influences.

Stoicism   Hellenistic philosophy founded by Zeno in the 3rd century B.C. stressing emotional detachment from the workings of fate.

structuralism   The linguistic and anthropological theory that different aspects of thinking, language, and culture are related to one another in a logical pattern.

subject   According to post-structuralist theory, the self as it is structured through language.

subjectivity   The idea that knowledge stems from personal characteristics and situations.

substance   A philosophical term for what exists that can be used in different ways. Some philosophers use it to mean material stuff, others use it to refer to material and spiritual stuff.

superstructure   According to Marxism, those aspects of society that express beliefs, including religion and the arts.

syllogism   A logical statement that presents a conclusion that is deduced from two related premises.

synchronic   A view of language, in structural linguistics, that looks at language as a system that exists all at the same time.

Tao   A Chinese word meaning "way" or "path."

Taoism   A form of mystic Chinese philosophy.

teleology   The study of the purpose of things. It stems from the ancient Greek word, *telos*, meaning end or completion. Teleology has been discredited by modern scientists.

transcendence   Beyond experience. The idealists believed we can have a transcendent understanding of a unified reality.

unconscious   In Freudian psychology, the aspect of the mind that contains wishes and desires that are not consciously recognized.

universals   Attributes such as shape and color that may be shared by any number of particular things.

utilitarianism   A philosophy of moral behavior that says, "If your actions help more people than they hurt, they are good. If they hurt more people than they help, they are bad."

Vedas   Ancient texts on which most Indian philosophy is based.

vitalism   The belief that everything that makes up reality is alive and capable of thinking.

wu-wei   A Taoist principle that means receptivity. It also implies acceptance and spontaneity.

yin and yang   Complementary Taoist principles. Yin is the female aspect and yang is the male.

yoga   A form of mental and physical discipline that many Hindus believe can help lead to moksa.

Further Reading: More Food for Thought

Chandler, Russell. *Understanding the New Age*. Dallas: Word Publishing, 1988.

Collinson, Diane. *Fifty Major Philosophers: A Reference Guide*. London: Routledge, 1987.

Cover, J.A. and Mark Kulstad, eds. *Central Themes in Early Modern Philosophy*. Indianapolis: Hackett Publishing, 1990.

Creel, Herrlee Glessner. *Chinese Thought*. Chicago: University of Chicago Press, 1969.

Ferm, Virgilius T.A., ed. *A History of Philosophical Systems*. Essay Index Reprint Series. Freeport, New York: Books for Libraries Press, 1950.

Grenz, Stanley J. *A Primer on Postmodernism*. Grand Rapids, Michigan: Eerdmans, 1996.

Holland, Nancy J. *Is Women's Philosophy Possible?* Savage, Maryland: Rowman and Littlefield, 1990.

Kearney, Richard. *Modern Movements in European Philosophy*. Dover, New Hampshire: Manchester University Press, 1986.

McLeish, Kenneth, ed. *Key Ideas in Human Thought*. New York: Facts on File, 1993.

Munitz, Milton K. *Contemporary Analytic Philosophy*. New York: MacMillan, 1981.

Porter, Roy. *The Enlightenment*. London: MacMillan, 1990.

Raju, P.T. *The Philosophical Traditions of India*. Pittsburgh: University of Pittsburgh Press, 1971.

Scruton, Roger. *A Short History of Modern Philosophy: from Descartes to Wittgenstein*. New York: Routledge, 1995.

Sharples, R.W. *Stoics, Epicureans, and Skeptics: An Introduction to Hellenistic Philosophy*. New York: Routledge, 1996.

Solomon, Robert C. and Kathleen M. Higgins. *A Short History of Philosophy*. New York: Oxford University Press, 1996.

Trumble, Robert C. Jr. *Ancient Greek Philosophy: Its Development and Relevance to Our Time*. Aldershot, England and Brookfield, USA: Avebury, 1994.

Wipple, John F. and Allan B. Wolter, eds. *Medieval Philosophy: From St. Augustine to Nicholas of Cusa*. New York: Free Press, 1969.

Index

A

a priori concepts (Kant), 164, 243
Academy, The (Plato), 47
acquired and innate characteristics (Leibniz), 139
addressing ideas through logic
  deductions, 18-19
  hypothesis checks, 19-20
  inductions, 19
aesthetic stage of personal development (Kierkegaard), 176-177
afterlife
  Christianity, 107
  Islam, 107
  Judaism, 107
ahimsa, 243
  and karma, 98-99
akrasia (Plato), 52, 243
Alfred North Whitehead, 45
alienation (Hegel), 167, 243
Allah (Islam), 111
allegories, 77-78, 243
An Essay Concerning the Human Understanding (Locke), 146-147
analytic philosophy, 243
  logical positivism, 191
  pragmatism, 191
  principle of verification, 192
  versus continental philosophy, 192-193
anamnesis
  ideal reality, remembering, 51
  immortal souls (Plato), 51
Anaximander, cosmology, 37
Anaximenes, cosmology, 37
ancient Greece
  ataraxia, avoidance of life's pains, 68-69

cosmogony, 36
cosmology, 36
ontology
  Parmenides, 38
  Pythagoras, 38
philosophic schools
  The Academy, 71
  The Garden, 71
  The Lyceum, 71
  The Stoa Poikile, 71
sophists, 38-39
anthropology (Durkheim)
  functionalism, 189-190
  structuralism, 189-190
antidisestablishmentarianism, 6
antithesis (Hegel), 166-167
apocalypse, 109, 243
Aquinas, St. Thomas
  individualism, 29
  ontology, 14
"archeology of knowledge" (Foucault), 220
archetypes, 243
  collective unconscious (Jung), 187
arete, 243
arguments, logic, using
  deductions, 18-19
  hypothesis checks, 19-20
  inductions, 19
Aristotle
  books, 21
  categories of things
    action, 61-62
    kind, 61-62
    location, 61-62
    quality, 61-62
    quantity, 61-62
    reception, 61-62
    relation, 61-62
    time, 61-62

cause types
  efficient, 60
  final, 60
  formal, 60
  material, 60
change as natural event, 57
golden mean, 62-63
influence in Middle Ages, 63-64
influence on Islam, 82-83
interrelated purposes, 58-59
key components of thinking
  logic, 55-56
  purpose, 55-56
legacy, 63-64
moderation in life, 62-63
naturalness of change, 57
ontology, 14
physical reality
  essence, 56-57
  substance, 56-57
reaction of 17th century empiricists, 62
souls
  and death, 59
  no immortality, 59
  non-afterlife, 59
  purpose of, 59
syllogisms, 18
teleology, 60
thinking as purposeful part of life, 58-59
versus Darwin, changes in natural world, 58
asceticism, 100-101, 243
associationism, 244
  examples, 152
  Hume, 152
  sense impressions, 152
assumptions (Husserl), 201
ataraxia, 244
  avoidance of life's pains, 68-69
  skepticism proponents, 72-73

"atomistic philosophy" (Epicureans), 71
atoms, random nature of (Epicureans), 69-70
Augustine of Hippo
   free will, 81-82
   reason for evil, 81
   struggles with skepticism, 80
   view of God, 80
   view of limited mysticism, 80
authentic existences (Heidigger), 204
authenticity, 244
avoiding passions in our minds (Descartes), 129

B

Baruch Spinoza
   conception of substance, 135-136
   interference with passions, 138
   limited free will, 137
   pantheism, 136
   pre-determination in life, 137
   question of afterlife, 136
   substance attributes
      extension, 136
      thought, 136
   substance modes, 137
   views on eternity, 138
"beaux esprits", 155
behavior, vice and virtue (Hume), 153-154
benefits of philosophy, 4-5
Berkeley (George)
   existence of ideas, 151
   God and souls, 151
   no material existence, 151
   perception, 151
   souls to perceive, 151
Bertrand Russell, Russell's Paradox, 193-194
Bible, 106
   allegorical readings, 77-78
   Philo (Jewish philosopher), view of, 77
bibliographic resources, 253-254
black feminism, 228-229
   Hooks, 233-234
   importance of religion to power, 233-234
   racism, 233-234
   sexism, 233-234
Boethius, scholaticism, absurdity of logic rules, 82

bourgeois, 244
bracketing, 201, 244
brain
   left thinking, 236-237
   right thinking, 236-237
Bretano and intentionality, 200-201
Buddha
   asceticism, 100-101
   formal definition, 100-101
   ideas stem from Buddhism, 100-101
   rejection of caste system, 100-101
Buddhism, 244
   applying to other religions, 102
   Eightfold Path, 101-102
   prevalent global regions, 102
   state of transcedence, 98
business, New Age influence, 241
Butler
   queer theory, 234
   sexuality, nature versus society, 234

C

Calvinism and pre-destination, 188
capitalism, 244
   versus feudalism, 149
Capra
   interchangeability of matter and energy, 238
   New Age thinking, 238
caste system, 244
   brahmins, 99
   kshatriyas, 99
   sudras, 99
   vaisyas, 99
categorical imperative, 244
Cavendish (Margaret)
   basis for ideas, 141
   concept of substance, 135-136
   contradictory philosophical writings, 142
   drew from empiricism and rationalism, 141
   forceable thoughts, 142
   imaginative writing, 143-144
   substances
      only matter, 142
      results of disagreements, 142
   thought conflicts, 143
chain of signification (Lacan), 214
Charles Sanders Pierce, pragmatism, 197-198

China, Confucius's views
   end of inherited family rule, 90-91
   ideas on good government, 90-91
   obedience as two-way street, 91
Christianity
   atonement of human sin, 110
   Book of Revelation, 110
   human destiny, 109
   interpretation of Bible's Old Testament, 111
   Jesus Christ, 110
   monotheism, 105
   neoplatonism, 76
   personal salvation, 110
   philosophers in Middle Ages, 12
class oppression and feminism, 232-233
class warfare and feminism, 232
collective unconscious (Jung), 187, 244
collectivism, 244
   vs. individualism, 27
communism
   alternative to capitalism, 175
   as generally failed experiment, 175
   insignificance of money, 175
   Marx, 175
conceptualism, 244
   universals (Peter Abelard), 84-85
conflicting thoughts (Cavendish), 143
Confucius, 26, 244
   changing traditions, 92
   concern with governmental corruption, 90
   end of sacrifices to the dead, 92
   end of inherited family rule, 90-91
   ethics
      collectivism, 26-27
      guidelines, establishing, 26
   government, obedience as two-way street, 91
   idea of good government, 90-91
   li principle, 91
      applying to everyday life, 92-93
      applying to the living, 91
   obedience
      to leaders, 91
      to the people, 91
   respect towards fellow man, 92
   role of conventions, 92
   social harmony, 26
   versus Taoism, 93

conscious and unconscious
     thinking (Lacan), 212-213
collective consciousness, 244
     social facts, 189
     sum of its culture, 189
continental philosophy
     origins, 191
     versus analytic philosophy,
          192-193
cosmogony, 36, 244
cosmology, 244
     Anaximander, 37
     Anaximenes, 37
     Heraclitus, 37
     origins in ancient Greece, 36
     Parmendies, 38
     Pathagoras, 37-38
     responses, 36-38
courage (Plato), 48-49
culture (Durkheim), 189

D

Daly
     opposition to patriarchal
          Catholicism, 233
     transvaluation of religious
          roles, 233
Darwin (Charles)
     evolutionary changes, 58
     versus Aristotle, changes in
          natural world, 58
de Beauvoir
     gender versus sex, 230
     The Second Sex, 229-230
De Tocqueville, Alexis, on
     individualism, 27-28
debates on existence of God, 11-12
deconstruction (Derrida), 223, 245
deduction, 245
defining the ideal world, 48-49
deism, 245
     Voltaire, 158
Derrida (Jacques), 10
     deconstruction, 223
     logocentrism, 223-224
     non-present meaning, 223
     present meaning, 223
Descartes (Rene)
     body versus mind, 128-129
     brain dissections, 128-129
     dualism, 128-129
     ethics, 31
     individual behavior, 129
     opponent of Thomas
          Hobbes, 129

passions, 129
popularity, 129
pursuit of natural investiga-
     tions, 128
science expertise, 128
scientific philosopher, 128
societal atomosphere, 16
spiritual mind, 128-129
study of natural world, 128
determinism, 245
     historical, 172
     mechanical, 172
dharma, 99, 245
diachronic view of language
     (Saussure), 209-210, 245
dialectic, 20-23, 245
     empiricists' view, 21
     Hegel's view, 22-23
     Marx's view, 23
     rationalists' view, 21
dialectic dialogue, 43
dialectic process (Hegel), 166-167
dialogues (Plato)
     form, 47
     performances, 47
divine rights of kings, 148-149
dogma, 245
dogmatic thinking and skepticism,
     72-73
double standards (relativism),
     39-40
dreams and the unconscious
     mind, 184
dualism, 13, 245
     body versus mind, 128-129
     Descartes, Rene, 13-14
     versus materialism, 13
dualist, 13
Durkheim (Emile)
     anthropology
          functionalism, 189-190
          structuralism, 189-190
     conciousness collective, 189
     father of anthropology, 184

E

Eastern philosophy
     collectivism, 27
     Confucianism, 89
     New Age, 238-239
     Taoism, 89
     versus Western philosophy, 89
Eckhart, Meister, 11
ecological politics in New Age
     philosophy, 240

ecriture feminine (female
     writing), 245
     Cixous, 231-232
     Kristeva, 231-232
efficient cause (Aristotle), 60
Eightfold Path (Buddhism),
     101-102
emanation theory (Plotinus), 79
empiricism, 6, 14, 245
     Bacon, Francis, 17
     ethics, 31
     famous British philosophers,
          146
     reaction against Aristotle, 62
     view of dialectic, 21
*Encyclopedia of Science, Art, and
     Trade*, 159
Enlightenment
     *Encyclopedia of Science, Art, and
          Trade*, 159
     famed philosophers, 156
     French Revolution, 155
     philosophical disagreements
          among thinkers of the time,
          158-159
     relations of government to its
          people, 158-159
Epicureans
     avoidance of life's pains, 68-69
     avoidance of marriage and
          politics, 70-71
     origins, 68
     personal freedom, 70
     pleasures
          mental, 68
          sensual, 68
     primary goals, 68-69
     pursuit of tranquility, 70-71
     sometimes referred to as
          "atomistic philosophy", 71
     The Garden School, 70-71
     versus stoicists, 68-69
     view of gods, 69
     world is atomic creation, 69-70
epistemology, 6, 245
     logic, 17-20
          deductions, 18-19
          dialetic, 20-23
          hypothesis checks, 19-20
          induction, 19
     Middle Ages, 22
          empiricism, 17
          rationalism, 16
     responses
          empiricism, 17
          idealism, 22-23
          ideology, 23
          rationalism, 16

Erasmus
    dissertation on truth, 120
    In Praise of Folly, 120
    on church authorities, 120
    on split of Martin Luther from
        Catholic Church, 120
    personal approach to religion,
        120
"erudites", 155
escaping suffering through
    Eightfold Path (Buddhism),
    101-102
essays, originated by de Montaigne,
    122
essence (Aristotle), 56-57
eternal recurrence (Nietzsche), 179
eternity view (Spinoza), 138
ethical stage of personal develop-
    ment (Kierkegaard), 176-177
ethics (study of personal actions), 6
    ancient Greece
        double standards, 39-40
        relativism, 39
    Confucius
        collectivism, 26-27
        guidelines, establishing, 26
    De Tocqueville on collec-
        tivism, 27
    Descartes, 31
    empiricists, 31
    existentialists, 31
    Foucault, 31
    individualism (Aquinas,
        St. Thomas), 29
    Kant, Immanuel, 31
    Kierkegaard, Soren, 31
    Marx, Karl, 31
    naturalistic fallacy, 154
    Plato, 29
    post-structuralists, 31
    rationalists, 31
    responses
        collectivism, 26-27
        individualism, 27-31
evil
    and free will (Augustine of
        Hippo), 81-82
    and God, 108
evolutionary changes (Darwin), 58
existence of God
    Middle Ages
        debates, 11-12
        proving, 12
    Protagoras, 39
existentialism, 6, 246
    also known as phenomenology,
    199-200

authentic existences
    (Heidigger), 204
da-sein (Heidigger), 202-203
ethics, 31
fictional heroes, 205
Kierkegaard, 177
origins, 202-203
experience, combining with
    reason, 22
expressing repressed desires
    via dreams, 185
    via jokes, 185
    via obsessions, 185

F

fairness and the social order, 40-41
faith and reason, 76
falsifability of hypotheses, 20
fate
    main tenet of stoicism, 67
    stoicism versus Epicurean-
        ism, 70
feminism, 246
    based on multiple ideas, 228
    class oppression (Millet),
        232-233
    class warfare, 232
    opposition to patriarchal
        Catholicism (Daly), 233
    origins, 228
    penis envy, 231-232
    philosophy debate, 229
    queer theory (Butler), 234
    types
        black, 228-229
        French, 228-229
        liberal, 228-229
        Marxist, 228-229
        queer, 228-229
        radical, 228-229
        spiritual, 228-229
Ferguson (Marilyn)
    The Aquarian Conspiracy, 236
    right and left brain thinking,
        236-237
feudalism, 246
    versus capitalism, 149
    violation of natural rights, 149
Filmer, Robert and divine rights of
    kings, 148-149
final cause (Aristotle), 60
forceable thoughts (Cavendish),
    142
formal cause (Aristotle), 60
forms (Plato), 47

Foucault
    "archeology of knowledge", 220
    ethics, 31
    knowledge
        interpreting, 222
        repressive use of, 222
    knowledge is power, 220-221
    on mental patients, 221
    othering process, 221-222
    post-modern philosopher, 220
Francis Bacon, 60
    campaign against misinforma-
        tion, 127
    clear definition of words, 127
    criticism of Aristotle and other
        scholastic philosophy, 126
    idolizing false beliefs
        Idols of the Cave, 126-127
        Idols of the Marketplace,
            126-127
        Idols of the Theater, 126-127
        Idols of the Tribe, 126-127
    importance of being right, 126
    investigation of the natural
        world, 126
    knowledge, pursuit of, 126
    search for the truth, 127
free will
    Augustine of Hippo, 81-82
    resistence to evil, 108
freedom (Mill), 173
Frege (Gottlob)
    advocacy of logic, 193-194
    class, 193-194
    propositions
        reference, 194-195
        sense, 194-195
    Russell's Paradox, 193-194
    sets, 193-194
    symbolic logic, 195
French feminism, 228-229
French Revolution (Enlighten-
    ment), 155
Freud (Sigmund)
    father of psychology, 184
    Oedipus complex, 186
    opposition by Carl Jung, 187
    penis envy, 231-232
    pleasure principle, 185
    psychoanalysis, 186
    reality principle, 185
    repressed desires, 185
    unconscious mind, 184
        sexuality, 185
        storehouse of repressed
            desires, 185
functionalism (Durkheim),
    189-190, 246

G

gender, 246
versus sex (de Beauvoir), 230
"general will" (Rousseau), 160
generalizations, making inductions, 19
German idealists
famous philosophers of the
time, 162
reaction against British
empiricists, 161-162
"transcendental idealism", 161
God
afterlife rewards/punishment,
107
and existence of evil, 108
and war crusades, 106
Augustine of Hippo, view of
limited mysticism, 80
breaking his laws, 107
Calvin pre-destination, 188
Christianity (The Bible),
106-107
commiting sins, 107
describing in words, Philo
(Jewish philosopher), 77
existence
debates (Middle Ages), 11-12
knowledge, 13-14
Protagoras, 39
free will (Augustine of Hippo),
81-82
holy wars, 106
human destiny, 109
Islam (The Koran), 106-107
Judaism (The Old Testament),
106-107
logical proofs (St. Thomas
Aquinas), 83
Messiah, 109
monotheism, 105
ontological proof (St. Anselm of
Canterbury), 83
Protestant work ethic, 188
punishment, 107
sins, 107
golden mean
Aristotle, 62-63
avoidance of extremes, 62-63
Gottfried Wilhelm Leibniz, concept
of substance, 135-136
governments
and natural inequality, 52
decentralization (New Age),
240-241
Locke's proposed idea, 148

Greece, early philosophers
Anaximander, 37
Anaximenes, 37
cosmology, 36-37
Heraclitus, 37
Parmendies, 38
Protagoras, 39-40
Pythagoras, 37-38
Thales, 36-37

H

Hebrew Bible, view of Philo (Jewish
philosopher), 77
Hegel (Georg Wilhelm Friedrich),
22-23
alienation, 167
antithesis, 166-167
critics of writing, 168
dialectic process, 166-167
follower of Kant, 166-167
self-recognition, 167-168
synthesis, 166-167
thesis, 166-167
young followers called
"Hegelians", 168
Heidigger on existentialism
authentic existences, 204
da-sein, 202-203
origins, 202-203
Heraclitus, cosmology, 37
Hermes Trismegistus
beliefs, 78-79
contemporary of Philo, 78-79
discovery of writings, 78-79
father of Hermetic philosophy,
78-79
higher pleasures versus lower
pleasures, (Mill), 173
Hinduism, 246
dharma, 99
Pythagoras, 38
role in independence from
Britain, 103
sense of duty, 99
state of transcedence, 98
historical determinism, 172
Hobbes
advocate of strong ruler, 130
disdain for spiritual enthusiasts,
130
mind is machine, 131
natural propensity for people to
fight, 131
nature, "nasty, brutish, and
short", 131

no spirit of the mind, 130
obedience to strong rulers, 131
opponent of Descartes, 129
physical mind, 130-131
preservation of order, 130
spiritual mind is merely
physical senses, 131
The Leviathan, 130
holy wars in name of God, 106
Hooks on black feminism, 233-234
human behavior and sophist
philosophy, 41-42
human beings
macrocosm, 118
microcosm, 118
Parmendies' views, 38
Protagoras' views, 40
Pythagoras' views, 38
humanism, 246
defined, 115-116
"learned ignorance", 116-117
Hume (David)
associationism, 152
decision making, 153-154
"Hume's Fork", facts versus
reason, 152-153
making judgments, 153-154
vice and virtue, 153-154
"Hume's Fork"
facts versus reason, 152-153,
246
naturalistic fallacy, 154
Husserl (Edmund)
basis for thinking, 200-201
bracketing assumptions, 201
idea of life-world, 202
phenomenology
and Bretano's intentionality,
201
origins, 200
reality and experience, 200
use of modern art, 201-202
reduction process, 201
hypothesis, 246

I

I Ching (Book of Changes)
how to read, 96
interpreting, 96
yin and yang, 96
Ibn Rushd (Islamic philosopher),
82-83
Ibn Sina (Islamic philosopher),
82-83
ideal reality, remembering, 51

ideal world (Plato)
    intuitive reality, 48-49
    logical, defining, 48-49
    visible reality, 49
idealism, 6, 246
    Kant, Immanuel, 22
    universals (Peter Abelard), 84-85
ideas
    defined (Plato), 47
    dialetics, 20-23
    forms (Plato), 47
    logic, 17-20
        deductions, 18-19
        hypothesis checks, 19-20
        inductions, 19
    versus ideology, 49
ideology versus ideas, 49, 246
Idols of the Cave (Francis Bacon), 126-127
Idols of the Marketplace (Francis Bacon), 126-127
Idols of the Theater (Francis Bacon), 126-127
Idols of the Tribe (Francis Bacon), 126-127
imaginative writing (Cavendish), 143-144
immortal souls (Plato), 51
implied governments (Locke), 150
In Praise of Folly (Erasmus), 120
India
    caste system
        brahmins, 99
        karma, 98-99
        kshatriyas, 99
        sudras, 99
        vaisyas, 99
    history of domination by foreign powers, 103
    independence from Britain, 103
    Mohandas Gandhi, 103
individual development (Nietzsche), 177-178
individualism, 246
    influential factors, 28
        economics, 30
        religion, 28-29
        science, 30
    pros/cons, 27-28
    versus collectivism, 27
induction process (Plato), 48-49, 246
infinite minds (Leibniz), 139
infinity (Nicholas of Cusa), 117-118
infrastructure, 246
innate and acquired characteristics (Leibniz), 139

intentionality (Bretano), 200-201, 246
interpreting *I Ching (Book of Changes)*, 96
intuitive reality, *Parable of the Cave* (Plato), 49-50
Islam
    Allah, 111
    human destiny, 109
    Ibn Rushd, 82-83
    Ibn Sina, 82-83
    importance of religious justice, 112
    influence of Aristotle, 82-83
    monotheism, 105
    Muhammad, the prophet, 111
    origins, 111
    punishment for the disobedient, 112
    splintering sects, 112
    "The Five Pillars of Islam", 111-112
isms, 5
    antidisestablishmentarianism, 6
    collectivism (Confucius), 26-27
    dualism (Descartes), 13
    empiricism, 6, 14
    existentialism, 6
    Hegel, George Fredreich, 22-23
    idealism, 6, 22-23
    ideology, 23
    ididividualism (De Tocqueville)
        pros/cons, 27-28
        religion's influence, 28-29
        science's influence, 30
    Marx, Karl, 23
    materialism, 6
    mysticism, 6
    naturalism, 6
    pragmatism, 6
    rationalism, 6, 14
    relativism, 39
    scholasticism, 6
    skepticism, 6
    sophism, 6
    stoicism, 6
    Taoism, 6
    vitalism (Spinoza), 13

J

Jacques Louis David, 42
James, William, pragmatism, 197-198
Judaism
    coming of the Messiah, 109
    hardships of people, 109-110

history, 109-110
human destiny, 109
interpretation of Bible's Old Testament, 111
monotheism, 105
neoplatonism, 76
rituals, 109
wrath of God's punishment, 109-110
Jung (Carl)
    collective unconcious, 187
    opposition to Freud's psychoanalysis theories, 187

K

Kant (Immanual)
    a priori concepts, 164
    categories of understanding, 163-164
    defining reality, 163
    ethics, 31
    metaphysics, 163
    noumena, 163
    objective basis for moral ideas, 165
    objects organized by the mind, 163-164
    phenomena, 163
    practical reason, 165
    pure reason, 165
karma, 98, 247
    and ahimsa, 98-99
    and reincarnation, 98-99
    Indian caste system, 98-99
    practicing, 100
    pros and cons, 100
Kierkegaard (Soren)
    ethics, 31
    existentialism, 177
    importance of meaningful existences, 176
    objections to Hegel, 176
    personal commitment to religion, 177
    stages of personal development
        aesthetic, 176-177
        ethical, 176-177
        religious, 176-177
kingships, Hobbes' advocacy, 131
kinship systems (Levi-Strauss), 211-212
knowledge
    criticism of Aristotlean philosophers (Bacon), 126
    Foucault, interpreting, 220-222

investigation of the natural
world (Bacon), 126
Middle Age (Spinoza), 13-14
repressive use of (Foncault), 222
Koran, 106
"The Five Pillars of Islam",
111-112
Kristeva
experience of motherhood,
230-231
opposition to her motherhood
theories, 231
socially constructed gender
distinctions, 230-231
Stabat Mater essay about
motherhood, 231

L

Lacan
conscious and unconscious
thinking, 212-213
ego development
chain of signification, 214
mirror stage, 214
ego-building, 212-213
excess meanings, 215
language
diachronic view (Saussure),
209-210
"differance" (Derrida), 224
langue (Saussure), 210
logocentrism, 223-224
parole (Saussure), 210
structuralism, 207-208
synchronic view (Saussure),
209-210
systematic approach (Saussure),
208
langue, 247
Lao-tzu (Taoism)
natural order versus social
order, 94
origins, 94
"learned ignorance" (humanism),
116-117
Leibniz
infinite minds, 139
innate and acquired characteristics, 139
mathematical ideas, 139-140
monads, 138
multiple worlds, 139-140
principles of
identity of indiscerna-
bles, 140

non-contradiction, 140
predication, 140
sufficient reason, 140
the best world, 140
reality-based logic, 140-141
substance, 135-136
Levi-Strauss
collective mind, 212
culture and structural patterns,
210-211
kinship systems, 211-212
myths, 211-212
study of tribal cultures, 211-212
lexicons, 5
li principle, 247
applying to everyday life, 92-93
defined, 91
liberal feminism, 228-229
liberalism, 247
life
acceptance of fate (stoicism), 67
eternal recurrence (Nietzsche),
179
golden mean, avoidance of
extremes, 62-63
pre-determined nature of
(Leibniz), 139
stoicism versus Epicureanism, 70
life-world (Husserl), 202
Locke (John)
*An Essay Concerning the Human
Understanding*, 146-147
argument against the divine
right of kings, 148
capitalist thoughts, 149
concept of natural rights, 149
empiricism, 146-147
existence of God, 148
governments
based on reason and natural
rights, 148-149
official or implied, 150
importance of experience in
knowledge, 146-147
influence on Thomas Jefferson,
150
knowledge
experiences, 147
observations, 147
no innate ideas, 146-147
opposed by Leibniz, 147-148
popularity of writings, 147-148
purpose of government, 150
social compacts, 150
tabula rasa (blank slate), 147

logic
epistemological probems,
solving, 17
induction process (Plato), 48-49
philosophical discussions, 17-20
deductions, 18-19
hypothesis checks, 19-20
inductions, 19
relationship with mathematics
(Frege), 193-194
logic chopping (scholaticism), 83
logical atoms (Wittgenstein), 196
logical ideal world, 48-49
logocentrism (Derrida), 223-224,
247
lower pleasures versus higher
pleasures (Mill), 173

M

Machiavelli, 247
involvement in Italian
politics, 121
maximizing power, 121-122
pursuit of power, 121-122
redefinition of virtue, 121-122
The Prince, 121-122
macrocosm, 118, 247
managing businesses through New
Age thinking, 241
Martin Luther (Protestantism), 119
Marx (Karl)
alienated labor, 175
beliefs and economies, 188
believed capitalism doomed to
failure, 175
communist form of govern-
ment, 175
definition of freedom, 175
infrastructure and super-
structure, 188
proponent of economic and
political freedom, 174
versus Rousseau, 160
"worker's paradise", 175
Marxist feminism, 228-229
material cause (Aristotle), 60
material world
interfering with connection to
God, 76-77
words to describe God, 77
materialism, 6, 247
versus dualism, 13
mathematics
importance to Plato, 11
relationship with logic (Frege),
193-194

mechanical determinism, 172
metaphysics, 11, 247
microcosm, 118, 247
Middle Ages
    allegories, 77-78
    Bacon, Francis, empiricism, 17
    Christian philosophers, 12
    concept of knowledge
        (Spinoza), 13-14
    Descartes, rationalism, 16
    epistemology
        empiricism, 17
        idealism, 22
        rationalism, 16
    Hegel, idealism, 22-23
    importance of written word, 78
    Kant, idealism, 22
    ontonology
        dualism, 13
        vitalism, 13
    religious debates on existence of
        God, 11-12
Mill (John Stuart)
    justice and happiness, 173
    objects to determinism, 172-173
    pleasures, higher versus lower,
        173
    relationship between freedom
        and happiness, 173
    rights for women, 174
    The Subjugation of Women, 174
    utilitarianism, 172-173
millenium, 109
Millet (Kate)
    feminism, class oppression,
        232-233
    National Organization of
        Women (NOW), 232-233
minds
    associationism, sense impres-
        sions, 152
    passions (Descartes), 129
mirror stage (Lacan), 214, 247
modern science
    rise of, 125
    seeds of doubt, skepticism, 73
modern-day politicians and sophist
    philosophy, 41-42
modes (substances), Spinoza, 137
Mohandas Gandhi, 103
    non-violence philosophy, 103
    principle of ahimsa, 103
    social activism, 103
moksa, 98, 247
monads (Leibniz), 138, 247
monism, 248

monoists
    Anaximander, 37
    Anaximenes, 37
    Heraclitus, 37
    Pythagoras, 37-38
monotheism, 105, 248
    and war crusades, 106
    books, 106-107
    elimination of mortal kings,
        106
    theory of human equality, 106
Montaigne
    flexibility towards others, 122
    originator of essays, 122
    skeptical approach to life, 122
Montesquieu (Baron)
    admiration for English form of
        government, 157
    government in moderation, 157
    opposition to kings, 157
    reason and societal laws,
        156-157
    relativism, 156-157
    "separation of powers", 157
morality (Kant)
    objective basis, 165
    practical reason, 165
    see also ethics
mysticism, 6, 248
    Augustine of Hippo
        neoplatonism, 79-80
        view of limited mysticism,
            80
    elements, 79-80
myth-makers versus philoso-
    phers, 10
mythology, 9-10

N

"nasty, brutish, and short"
    (nature), 131
natural inequality (Plato), 52
natural rights (Locke)
    freedom of choice, 149
    live without injury from
        others, 149
    ownership of property, 149
naturalism, 6
naturalistic fallacy (Hume's Law),
    154, 248
neoplatonism
    allegorical readings of Bible,
        77-78
    defined, 76
    divine inspiration from Greek
        philosophy, 78

faith and reason, 76
    importance of written word, 78
    mysticism, 79-80
Neoplatonism, 116, 248
New Age, 248
    Capra, 238
    Eastern mystic influences,
        238-239
    ecological politics, 240
    individual freedom
        abortions, 240-241
        decentralization of govern-
            ment, 240-241
        drugs, 240-241
        victimless crimes, 240-241
    influence on corporate capital-
        ism, 241
    interchangeability of matter
        and energy, 238
    mental powers development,
        237
    merchandising, 241-242
    origins, 235-236
    paradigm shift, 236
    professions, 241-242
    rise, 235-236
    spiritual connections
        energy, 237-238
        oneness, 237-238
    The Aquarian Conspiracy, 236
Nicholas of Cusa
    concept of infinity, 117-118
    humanity as work of art,
        117-118
    "learned ignorance", 116-117
    personal responsibility, 117-118
Nietzsche (Friedrich)
    absence of good and evil,
        178-179
    eternal recurrence, 179
    superman versus "the herd",
        178-179
    transvaluation, 178
    ubermensche (superman),
        177-178
nirvana, 98, 248
nominalism, 248
    universals (Peter Abelard), 84-85
non-present meaning (Derrida),
    223
noumena versus phenomena
    (Kant), 163
noumenal world, 248

O

objectivity, 248
Ockham's Razor (William of Ockham), 85
Oedipus complex (Freud), 186, 248
official governments (Locke), 150
"oneness of God", Philo (Jewish philosopher), 76-77
only matter (Cavendish), 142
ontological proof
    Aquinas, St. Thomas, 14
    of God (St. Anselm of Canterbury), 83
ontology, 248
    ancient Greece
        Parmenides, 38
        Pythagoras, 38
    Aristotle, 14
    dualism versus materialism, 13-14
    knowledge/ontology, 14
    metaphysics, 11
    mythology, 9-10
    Plato, 14
    Pythagoras, 38
    Spinoza, 13
    technological developments, effect of, 10-11
ontonology
    dualism, 13
    vitalism, 13
othering process (Foucault), 221-222, 248
othology (Thales), 10

P

pantheism, 136, 248
Parable of the Cave, likely interpretations (Plato), 49-50
paradigm shift, 236, 248
paradox, 248
Paramendies, 38
parole, 248
passions in minds (Descartes), 129
Pathagoras, 37-38
patriarchy, 248
penis envy, 231-232, 249
personal life, stoicism versus Epicureanism, 70
Peter Abelard, universals, 84-85
phenomena versus noumena (Kant), 163

phenomenology, 249
    also known as existentialism, 199-200
    and Bretano's intentionality, 201
    anti-social criticisms, 202
    reality and experience (Husserl), 200
    use of modern art (Husserl), 201-202
Philo (Jewish philosopher)
    allegorical readings of Bible, 77-78
    explanation of Bible as series of metaphors, 77
    faith and reason, 76
    God, describing in words, 77
    idea of oneness of God in all things, 76-77
    Platonic ideas, 77
philosophers versus mythmakers, 10
philosophy, Eastern versus Western, 89
phonemes (Saussure), 209, 249
physical world
    and mathematics, 132-133
    light and color composition, 133
physis, 249
Pierce, Charles Sanders, pragmatism, 197-198
Plato, 4, 6, 14
    admiration of Egyptians, 46-47
    akrasia, 52
    anamnesis, 51
    arete, 52
    as rationalist, 48
    classes of people
        rulers, 52-53
        soldiers, 52-53
        tradespeople, 52-53
    death of Socrates, 46-47
    dialogues, 47
        form, 47
        number, 47
    disillusionment with politics, 46-47
    dissatisfaction with democracy and tyranny, 53
    follower of Socrates, 42-43
    governmental form, maximum stability, 53
    human charcteristics
        appetite, 53
        courage, 53
        wisdom, 53

ideal world
    class society, 52-53
    defining, 48
ideas
    defined, 47
    notion of, 47
immortal souls, 51
importance of mathematics, 11
induction process, 48-49
influence of Socrates, 46-47
natural inequality, 52
neoplatonism, 76
notion of ideas, 47
on idea of courage, 48-49
Parable of the Cave, 49-50
philosophers as kings, 49
philosophy as part of government, 46-47
pursuit of ideal world, 48
The Academy, 47
true sciences, 51
visible reality, 49
Plato's Republic, 49-50
pleasure principle (Freud), 185, 249
pleasures in life (Epicureans), 68
Plotinus, emanation theory, 79
pluralism, 249
Popper, Karl, 20
post-modernist bourgeois liberalism, 224
post-structuralists, 31
power and knowledge (Foucault), 220-221
practical reason (Kant)
    categorical imperatives, 165
    imperatives, 165
    versus pure reason, 165
practicing karma, pros and cons, 100
pragmatism, 6, 197-198, 249
pre-destination (Calvinism), 188
pre-determination (Spinoza), 137
pre-Socratic philosophers, 37
    Anaximander, 37
    Anaximenes, 37
    Heraclitus, 37
    Parmendies, 38
    Pathagoras, 37-38
    Protagoras, 39
predestination, 249
premises, 19, 249
present meaning (Derrida), 223
principle of verification, analytic philosophy, 192
principles of non-contradiction (Leibniz), 140
principles of predication (Leibniz), 140

principles of sufficient reason
(Leibniz), 140
principles of the best world
(Leibniz), 140
principles of the identity of
indiscernables (Leibniz), 140
propositions, 249
reference (Frege), 194-195
sense (Frege), 194-195
symbolic logic, 195
Protagoras
ethics, 39
versus Thrasymachus, 40-41
Protestant work ethic, 188, 249
psychoanalysis (Freud), 186
pure reason versus practical reason
(Kant), 165
purpose, naturalness of change, 57
purpose of philosophy, 4
Pyrrho of Ellis, skepticism, 72

Q - R

quantifier, 249
queer feminism, 228-229
queer theory (Butler), 234
radical feminism, 228-229
random changes (Darwin), 58
rationalism, 6, 14-16, 249
rationalists
ethics, 31
view of dialectic, 21
realism, 249
universals (Peter Abelard), 84-85
reality principle (Freud), 185, 249
reality-based logic (Spinoza and
Leibniz), 140-141
reduction process (Husserl),
201, 249
reference, 250
reference resources, 253-254
reincarnation
and karma, 98-99
Pythagoras' view, 38
relativism, 39, 250
Montesquieu, 156-157
relativists and ethics
double standards, 39-40
sophists, 39
religion
Kierkegaard's philosophy, 177
neoplatonism, 76
Western philosophy versus
Eastern philosophy, 89

religious debates, existence of God,
11-12
religious stage of personal development (Kierkegaard), 176-177
remembering ideal reality, 51
Renaissance
classical writings, 119-120
humanistic thinking, 116
important thinkers
de Montaigne, 119-120
Erasmus, 119-120
Machiavelli, 119-120
neoplatonists, 116
rebirth of Hellenistic philosophies, 119-120
revolution
arts, 118-119
engineering, 118-119
medicine, 118-119
science, 118-119
theology, 118-119
rise of humanist philosophy,
115-116
shift from religious to scientific
view of world, 115-116
repressed desires, expressing, 185
repressive knowledge (Foucault),
222, 250
responsibility and free will
(Augustine of Hippo), 81-82
Rodin, Auguste, 4
Rorty
instability of meaning, 225-226
no absolute truths, 225
post-modernist bourgeois
liberalism, 224
pragmatism, 225
society works despite philosophers, 225
Rousseau
civilization and emotions,
159-160
invention of vice and
virtue, 160
laws created with regared to
"general will", 160
"noble savages", 159-160
similarity to Marx's concept of
ideology, 160
society and corruption, 159-160
state of nature in humanity,
160
value of emotions, 159
versus Marx, 160
Russell's Paradox, 193-194

S

Sartre (Jean-Paul)
absurdity of reality, 204
atheism, 205-206
conscious of being, 205
defining one's self, 205-206
lack of purpose in lives, 205
life choices, 205-206
Saussure
language
diachronic view, 209-210
langue, 210
parole, 210
signifieds, 208-209
signifiers, 208-209
synchronic view, 209-210
systematic approach, 208
phonemes, 209
structuralism, 207-208
scapegoating, 108
scholasticism, 6, 250
absurdity of logic rules
(Boethius), 82
criticisms, 83
logic chopping, 83
Schopenhauer (Arthur)
Eastern influences, 169-170
importance of will, 168-169
relationship between will and
knowledge, 169
suffering of the will, 169-170
ubiquitous nature of will,
168-169
will, transcending, 169-170
science
above political wrangling, 132
and political disagreements, 132
as way to work out disagreements, 132
etiquette, 132
formerly reserved for aristocracy, 132
individualism, influence on, 30
rise of, 125
scientific methods and skepticism, 73
seeds of doubt, formed basis for
modern scientific methods, 73
self-recognition (Hegel), 167-168
"separation of powers"
(Montesquieu), 157
sexuality
developmental stages
(Freud), 185
Oedipus complex (Freud), 186

queer theory, 234
    versus gender (de Beauvoir), 230
signifieds (Saussure), 208-209, 250
signifiers (Saussure), 208-209, 250
Sir Isaac Newton
    applied mathematics to study of
        nature, 132-133
    developed calculus, 132-133
    gravity, 132-133
    law of physics, 132-133
    light and color composition,
        133
skepticism, 6, 250
    defined, 72
    degrees, 72
    examples, 72
    formed basis for modern
        scientific methods, 73
    imaginary world, 72
    oppostition to dogmatic
        thinking, 72-73
    origins, 72
    primary beliefs, 72-73
    proponents of ataraxia, 72-73
    Pyrrho of Ellis, 72
    untrusting of senses, 72
social constructedness, 250
social facts, 250
social order and justice, 40-41
societal atmosphere (Descartes), 16
societal harmony, 26
Socrates, 4
    death of, 42-43
    dialectics, 20-23
    legacy, 43
    opponent of democracy, 43
    opponent of sophistic thinking,
        42-43
    Plato as student, 42-43
    politics as an art, 43
Socratic method, 20
    purpose, 43
    questioning, 43
    results, 43
    rooted in Greek dialectic
        dialogue, 43
sophism, 6
sophists, 38-39
    individual behavior, 41-42
    modern-day politicians, 41-42
    social order and justice, 40-41
    Thrasymachus, 40-41
souls (Aristotle)
    and death, 59
    and mortality, 59

Spinoza (Baruch)
    dualism, 13
    reality-based logic, 140-141
    substance, 135-136
spiritual connections (New Age)
    energy, 237-238
    oneness, 237-238
spiritual feminism, 228-229
St. Anselm of Canterbury, ontologi-
    cal proof, 83
St. Thomas Aquinas, logical proofs
    of God, 83
stoicism, 6, 250
    accceptance of pain in life, 66
    and Taoism, 94-95
        view of fate, 94-95
    defined, 66
    example of attitude, 66
    famous philosophers
        Epictetus, 66
        Marcus Aurelius, 66
        Seneca, 66
    importance of fate in life, 67
    influence on Roman law, 67
    life is governed by destiny, 70
    opinions on individuals, 67
    origins, 66
    versus Epicureans, 68-69
structuralism, 207-208, 250
    Durkheim 189-190
subjectivity, 250
substances, 250
    defined, 135
    modes (Spinoza), 137
    reality components, 56-57
    results of disagreements
        (Cavendish), 142
suffering
    escaping, Eightfold Path
        (Buddhism), 101-102
    moksa (Hinduism), 98
    nirvana (Buddhism), 98
sun-centered universe, 16
superman versus "the herd"
    (Nietzsche), 177-179
superstructure, 250
syllogisms (Aristotle), 18, 250
symbolic logic
    Frege, 195
    propositions, 195
synchronic view (Saussure),
    209-210, 250
synthesis (Hegel), 166-167

T

tabula rasa (blank slate), 147
Taoism, 6, 251
    acceptance of death, 95
    and stoicism, 94-95
        view of fate, 94-95
    I Ching (Book of Changes), yin
        and yang, 96
    life in constant state of flux, 95
    love of nature, 94-95
    natural order versus social
        order, 94
    origins, 94
    paradoxes, 95
    principle of opposites, 95
    social detachment, 94
    the path or the way, 93
    versus Confucianism, 93
    wu-wei principle, 94-95
    yin and yang, 95-96
        classifications, 95-96
        harmonious change, 95-96
        shape, 95-96
teaching with Socratic method, 20
technological developments, effect
    of (ontology), 10-11
telelogy (Aristotle), 60, 251
Thales
    cosmology, 36-37
    othology, 10
The Academy (Plato), 47
The Aquarian Conspiracy, 236
"The Five Pillars of Islam", 111-112
The Garden School (Epicureans),
    70-71
"the herd"
    mentality of (Nietzsche),
        178-179
    versus superman (Nietzsche),
        178-179
The Prince (Machiavelli), 121-122
The Second Sex (de Beauvoir),
    229-230
The Thinker (statue), 4
thesis (Hegel), 166-167
things, categories (Aristotle)
        kind, 61-62
        location, 61-62
        quality, 61-62
        quantity, 61-62
        reception, 61-62
        relation, 61-62
        time, 61-62
Thomas Hobbes, opponent of
    Descartes, 129

thought conflicts (Cavendish), 143
Thrasymachus
    prominent sophist, 40-41
    social order and justice, 40-41
    versus Protagoras, 40-41
transcendence, 251
"transcendental idealism", German
    idealists, 161
transcending will (Schopenhauer),
    169-170
transforming world with mental
    powers (New Age), 237
transvaluation (Nietzsche), 178
true sciences (Plato)
    arithmetic, 51
    astronomy, 51
    geometry, 51
    music, 51

U - V

ubermensche (superman),
    Nietzsche, 177-178
unconscious, defined, 251
unconscious desires versus
    conscious ego (Lacan), 213
unconscious mind and dreams
    (Freud), 184
universals (Abelard), 251
    conceptualism, 84-85
    idealism, 84-85
    nominalism, 84-85
    realism, 84-85
universe
    pilosophers' views on, 16
    Pythagoras' view, 37-38
utilitarianism (Mill), 172-173, 251

Vedas, 99, 251
views of philosophy
    epistemology
        empiricism, 17
        idealism, 22-23

idealogy, 23
    rationalism, 16
ethics
    collectivism, 26-27
    individualism, 27-31
ontology
    dualism, 13
    Parmenides, 38-42
    Pythagoras, 38
    vitalisms, 13
vitalism (Spinoza), 13-14, 251
vitalist, 13
Voltaire
    advocated freedom of religion,
        157-158
    criticism of atheism, 157-158
    criticism of practices of Catholic
        Church, 158
    deism, 158
    empiral philosophy, 157
    escape from France, 157
    philosophical skepticism, 158
    religious intolerance, 157-158

W

Weber (Max)
    beliefs and economies, 188
    father of sociology, 184
    link between rise of capitalism
        and Protestant religions, 188
Western philosophy
    individualism, 27-28
        capitalism's influence, 30
        factors influencing, 28
        pros/cons, 27-28
        religion's influence, 28-29
        science's influence, 30
    versus Eastern philosophy, 89
Whitehead, Alfred North, 45
will (Schopenhauer)

suffering, 169-170
    transcending, 169-170
    uncontrollable nature of, 169
William James, pragmatism,
    197-198
William of Ockham
    nominalist approach to
        universals, 85
    Ockham's Razor, 85
Wittgenstein (Ludwig)
    early teachings, 195
    language
        and communication, 197
        between at least two people,
            196-197
        meaning, 196-197
        ownership of, 196-197
        use of, 196
    logical atoms, 196
    "Vienna Circle", 195
women's rights (Mill), 174
world created by random atoms
    (Epicureans), 69-70
wu-wei principle (Taoism), 94-95,
    251

X - Y - Z

yin and yang (Taoism), 251
    classifications, 95-96
    harmonious change, 95-96
    I Ching (Book of Changes), 96
    shape, 95-96
yoga and transcedence, 98, 251

Zeno, origins of stoicism, 66